WAKE UP AND SELL THE COFFEE!

THE STORY OF COFFEE NATION AND HOW TO START, BUILD AND SELL A HIGH-GROWTH BUSINESS

BY MARTYN DAWES

HARRIMAN HOUSE LTD

3A Penns Road
Petersfield
Hampshire
GU32 2EW
GREAT BRITAIN

Tel: +44 (0)1730 233870
Email: enquiries@harriman-house.com
Website: www.harriman-house.com

First published in Great Britain in 2013

ISBN: 9780857192509

British Library Cataloguing in Publication Data
A CIP catalogue record for this book can be obtained from the British Library.

Hh   Harriman House

EBOOK EDITION

As a buyer of the print edition of *Wake Up and Sell the Coffee* you can now download the eBook edition free of charge to read on an eBook reader, your smartphone or your computer. Simply go to:

http://ebooks.harriman-house.com/coffee

or point your smartphone at the QRC below.

You can then register and download your free eBook.

Follow us on Twitter – **@harrimanhouse** – for the latest on new titles and special offers.

www.harriman-house.com

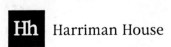 Harriman House

CONTENTS

ACKNOWLEDGEMENTS

I would like to thank everyone who helped Coffee Nation on its way from the very early days through to the sale of the company in 2008 and beyond.

To our customer organisations – Welcome Break, ChevronTexaco, Tesco, Moto, Somerfield, Esso, Sainsbury & Malthurst Pace – thank you for choosing Coffee Nation and becoming our long-term partners.

To our suppliers – thank you for your unflinching support and loyalty over many years – I know we were demanding and a little difficult at times.

To the millions of loyal Coffee Nation customers across the UK – a huge thank you for trying our coffee and then coming back so many times. Thank you for telling us when we got it right and an even bigger thank you to those of you that told us when we got it wrong.

And finally, to our team, without whom my vision would have remained just that. It was through the combined enthusiasm, energy, talent, dedication, long hours and sheer determination of you all that we built something to be proud of. We shared many highs and a few lows along the way. Thank you to you all.

The early team (1997-1999):
Lou Saydrouten, Amani Standring, Helena Walbrook

The Coffee Nation team (2000-2008):
Aaron Potton, Andy Oliver, Annabelle Ward, Cath Everitt, Charlotte Taylor, Chris Miller, Chrissie Drewitt, Dan Aston, Darren Record, Delvene Bee, Dominic Taylor, Don Shirley, Emma Howard, Fran Ball, Gary Sawyers, Ieuan Andrews, James Repper, Kate Watts, Keith Waite, Kristofer Gibson, Mel Taylor, Sean Bowles, Nikki Starling, Peter Lynn,

Paul Dempsey, Richard Evans, Roy Richards, Sami Williams, Sarah Kelly, Sarah Perry, Shane Moates, Simon Hawking, Stephen Hughes, Sue Stallwood, Tessa Johnson, Tim Cox, Toby Earl, Tom Stazicker

The Coffee Nation Board:
Derek Harris, Martin Harris, Scott Martin, Neil Wallace, Vivien Hale, Carl Jackson, Simon Vardigans

...and to my wife Trudi – who was my first inspiration, is my rock and partner, I will always love you.

ABOUT THE AUTHOR

MARTYN DAWES IS a successful entrepreneur. He founded his first business, MDA (Martyn Dawes Associates) in the recession of 1991. That business continues to trade successfully to this day under two brands, Coachmatch and Dawes Ryan Consulting..

His idea for Coffee Nation came from a combination of seeing how popular takeaway coffee was in convenience stores in New York and reading about the business model of a photocopier company. Four years later, after proving the concept, he raised £4m in development capital from a London-based private equity firm.

Coffee Nation grew fast and secured long-term contracts with major retailers including Tesco, Sainsbury, Esso, Moto, Welcome Break and Somerfield.

In 2008 the company was sold for £23m, returning investors four times their money and was finally sold to Whitbread/Costa in 2011 for almost £60m.

Martyn and Coffee Nation have won numerous awards, including:

- *Sunday Times*/Virgin Atlantic Fast Track Awards 2006: Winner of the Innovation Award

- Ernst & Young Entrepreneur of the Year 2005, South Region, Consumer Products & Services

- Coffee Nation featured in *Real Business* Hot 100 Index of the Top 100 Fastest Growing Privately Owned Companies in the UK, 2005 and 2006

- *Sunday Times*/Virgin Atlantic Index of the Top 100 Fastest Growing Privately Owned Companies in the UK, December 2005, ranked no. 13

- Sage Business Awards 2003, Best Business Leader (to 25 employees category)
- Orange Small is Beautiful Award 2003; Best Demonstration of Entrepreneurial Passion

INTRODUCTION

WHEN I STARTED my business Coffee Nation in late 1996 I believed I had found a good opportunity. I also thought I knew something about business, as by then I had been running and growing my own consulting firm for almost five years. I set out a growth path in my business plan which I thought realistic.

I was soon to discover that this path was going to be a whole lot tougher than I had bargained for. My previous business experience counted for very little – the modest ambitions for growth I had set out meant that the entire venture was not worth the effort required and the idea that I thought so simple proved to be anything but.

I persevered but had to make drastic changes along the way. The business plan was soon out of the window and I was experimenting constantly with limited funds – and hence time – in which to find the answer. It was nothing like I expected and to be honest, for much of this period, it wasn't a lot of fun either. I had to change and I learnt much about myself along the way.

For as long as I could hold on I was determined to never ever give up. It was truly at the eleventh hour – as I was thinking I would have to call it a day – that some light emerged at the end of the tunnel. From there events moved quickly and ten years later Coffee Nation had become a known and loved brand up and down the UK. By now that little business I started has probably served over 100m cups of coffee.

So why have I written this book? Many friends and colleagues with whom I shared the journey of building Coffee Nation encouraged me to tell the story. Contrary to what you might expect, it's not intended to be an *anyone can do it* inspirational guide to starting your own business written by a successful entrepreneur. Although if my words do inspire you to start your own venture then that's great.

What really encouraged me to write *Wake Up and Sell the Coffee* is the need to help more entrepreneurs not just start a business but to survive and grow. I noticed that so much of what is written and talked about relates to start-ups, not what comes later. The journey beyond survival and on towards growth gets little coverage.

Looking at the figures, out of almost 250,000 businesses that started in 1998 only roughly one-third survived to 2008. The odds are not great, but if you can start from the right place then your chances of success may be greater. Merely encouraging more start-ups is not enough. We need more of these businesses to survive and go on to become high-growth companies. We need *quantity* and *quality*.

It is high-quality businesses that survive long enough to become high growth ones, evidenced by the fact that 70% of high-growth companies are at least five years old. Most businesses start small and stay small - they lack the ambition, potential or both to grow beyond this. Only 1.5% of start-ups reach 20 employees. High-growth companies represent only 6% of all UK companies employing ten or more people.[1]

High growth is not about vanity. These businesses are proven to be more resilient through recession and account for a disproportionate share of job creation. In the period 2007 to 2010 the number of UK businesses growing at over 20% per year remained broadly similar to that in the periods 2002 to 2005 and 2005 to 2008. In these periods, insolvency rates for high-growth firms were approximately 2.5% compared with 4% for non-high growth businesses.[2] It is the tiny number of UK firms experiencing high growth (around 12,000 businesses, or just 6% of those employing more than ten people) that account for more than half the growth in jobs. Between 2005 and 2008 the average high growth UK company almost tripled their headcount.[3] High-growth firms attract and retain the best talent and advance society.

[1] 'Measuring Business Growth, High growth firms and their contribution to employment in the UK', NESTA (October 2009).

[2] 'Vital Growth: The Importance of High Growth Business to the recovery', NESTA (March 2011).

[3] 'Measuring Business Growth, High growth firms and their contribution to employment in the UK', NESTA (October 2009).

There has never been a better time to start your own business in Britain. I would like to encourage more entrepreneurs to think and dream big and then look for an idea that could be one of those high-growth businesses, rather than settling for starting something less ambitious and with less potential.

I hope *Wake Up and Sell the Coffee* can play some part in helping more British start-ups start well, survive and get on the right track to becoming successful mid-market growth companies with annual sales of £10m or more and heading on to £100m and beyond. We need more of these, a lot more, if Britain is to maintain its position as one of the world's strongest economies in the coming years.

I do not deny the role of luck and opportunism, but I think we can do much to enhance the prospects of success. Through telling my own growth story, sharing the lessons I learnt and setting out how to start with the end in mind to design a high-growth business, I hope *Wake Up and Sell the Coffee* can help more of Britain's entrepreneurs dream big and achieve big.

Martyn Dawes
November 2013

MY EARLY LIFE

BEGINNINGS

MY CHILDHOOD WAS unremarkable – I was born in Coventry and grew up in the small town of Nuneaton in Warwickshire. What did mark me out as different was being an adopted child. Whilst I came from a very loving home, there was an imbalance somewhere; I felt I had something to prove. I think my drive was a result of not knowing where I came from.

At school I was above average but not amazing. I studied really hard to get seven O levels and then left sixth-form college after only 12 months to join Sterling Metals as a management trainee, a foundry making components for automotive and aerospace industries where my father also worked. All my friends were off to university but I knew I was going in the right direction – it didn't feel like a big risk.

EARLY CAREER

I progressed quickly at Sterling, but in 1990 I left when I was headhunted by Massey Ferguson the agricultural tractor manufacturer. I had a great time with this company but came to realise life in a big company was not for me. By the summer of 1991 I had met my future wife Trudi via Dateline and declared my intention to move in with her in London and start my own business.

I registered for a one-week training programme with the British Standards Institute on auditing management systems of companies and in August of that year I left Nuneaton, moved in with Trudi in her flat in Crystal Palace and started my business. I was providing quality assurance and training consultancy to small businesses, mostly within manufacturing. The word entrepreneur meant nothing to me at that time, but unbeknown to me I was on my way.

MY FIRST BUSINESS – MARTYN DAWES ASSOCIATES

There are a number of things I notice from my early entrepreneurial endeavours. Firstly, I was not looking for a gap in the market to fill. Instead, I was applying what I knew from my professional career to date. This was enough to get me started. I also began to recognise that very often your environment plays a big part in the success you achieve.

Two such factors laid the foundations for me to start my own business. My career in quality assurance and the training I had undertaken (paid for by myself) gave me the credentials to help businesses introduce quality management systems to the ISO9000 standard, which at the time more and more companies were being required to implement by their customers.

The second factor was my girlfriend. Crucially, she supported my ambitions 100% and encouraged me to think bigger than I knew. She had just met me and was happy to be the main source of income whilst I got my business off the ground.

My business was called (somewhat unimaginatively) Martyn Dawes Associates (MDA). I had no idea who the associates were, but somehow it gave the impression that it was more than just me operating out of the back bedroom in Trudi's south London flat. I was successfully winning clients from day one. I noticed I loved the thrill of identifying the opportunity and winning the business.

When Trudi joined me as a business partner we started winning clients such as The Burton Group and delivering consultancy support to help companies achieve the Investors in People standard. We really started to motor and landed clients such as *USA Today*, Selfridges and Sandvik.

MDA gave me a terrific grounding in business basics. We were very successful, but after about four years I started to ask myself whether what I wanted to achieve with the business was realistic. I was determined to scale up and build a larger firm and longer-term client base to grow the firm to the next level. Driving the momentum of a growth business is essential – a sense of pace and urgency is critical – but this behaviour has to go with the right sort of business.

I realised that as a professional services firm we were forever trying to create products or services that could be delivered repeatedly in order to create some degree of predictable fee income – but it became clear that it was almost impossible to build this kind of business in a planned and measured way. Worse still, MDA (by now renamed Dawes Ryan Consulting, DRC) was an adjunct to its clients. If they grew so did we, if they contracted it was likely our fee income would shrink too.

DRC was a great business I could be proud of but I realised I craved building a company that could really grow and trying to drive DRC forward at breakneck speed was not the answer. I would have to look elsewhere.

My realisation was that I wanted to build a business with a product and that wasn't so reliant on a small number of high-value clients, something that wasn't all about a fee for a day's work. It was time to set my sights higher and look for a high-growth business opportunity.

LEARNING POINTS

- When you know it's right, jump. Don't hesitate or over analyse.

- Be prepared to stand up for what you believe in and don't follow the crowd; if you need to fit in with friends and colleagues you're probably not an entrepreneur.

- Think bigger than you know and set goals that are almost beyond you – they won't always come off but when they do the confidence boost will propel you forward to the next goal.

- Pushing forward is vital but all businesses can only grow at a certain rate; learn what is the optimum pace of expansion for your business and sector.

1996 – MY BIG IDEA

IN THE SPRING of 1996 I worked three days a week on DRC clients and the rest of the week looking for a business idea. To be honest I probably looked for any excuse to pad the three days out a bit, the dark side of the week loomed up and I often had a sinking feeling about what I would do with my time in those other two days. DRC was my comfort blanket.

I decided I needed to physically separate myself from my old business so I rented a little office in Wardour Street in London's Soho. This was a buzzing neighbourhood and it felt fresh and exciting to go there, even if I hadn't a clue what I was going to do when I arrived at the office. The next step was to find the business idea.

TRM PHOTOCOPIERS

At the time I subscribed to a magazine called *Business Age*. It was part entrepreneur, part management. During the summer I read a small article about an American photocopier business called TRM, listed on the NASDAQ stock market. It had 30,000 photocopiers located in small retailers across America and the UK, and it was now expanding into France.

What caught my eye about the article was the way this business operated. It bought used photocopiers, refurbished them and then located them in newsagents and drugstores completely free of charge to the retailer. TRM supplied all the consumables and maintained the machines. A rep would visit each store and take a reading from the machines to see how many copies had been made. The revenue (we're talking 4p a page here) was then split between the shopkeeper and TRM. The more the photocopier was used the greater the percentage of takings kept by the retailer.

It was a simple revenue-share model and somehow it attracted me. It occurred to me as being a win-win model – the retailer would benefit by offering an additional service to their customers and apart from keeping it switched on and full of paper they didn't have to worry about anything else. The shopkeeper didn't have the financial outlay for the machine or even the toner and ink cartridges; they were supplied by TRM.

What I also liked was the idea that these machines were working away generating revenue day in, day out. I wondered if I could find another product that would fit this model and then take it to Britain's small shopkeepers.

A RESEARCH MISSION TO THE US

Whatever business idea I did eventually land on, I was going to need to be able to fund its birth. Trudi and I talked this through and agreed that I take £50K from DRC to fund my new venture.

At around the same time, I attended a business start-up conference and exhibition and talked to the accountancy firm Baker Tilly, who had a stand there. I explained to one of their corporate finance partners that I had £100k – a small lie, but it sounded better than £50K – to invest in a new business. They were interested in working with start-up businesses, so now I had money, a business model and an advisory firm keen to work with me.

I just had to find the product. I asked myself where would be a great place to look for new ideas and before I knew it I was booking a ticket to New York. It occurred to me that great ideas often come out of the US and they inevitably find their way across the Atlantic.

I had never been to New York and here I was off to find an idea for a new business to start in London. I suppose this kind of thing is part of what makes being an entrepreneur such fun; it is an adventure that unfolds day by day and if you relish this you will relish entrepreneurship.

When in New York, each day I would head into town on the subway and pick a different area to explore. My tendency was to look at retail businesses, who sold direct to customers. From what I saw, three opportunities stood out:

1. A small retail outlet called Custard Beach. It sold tubs of frozen yoghurt for customers to eat in or take away.
2. A restaurant and cinema called The Screening Room. This was basically a large, casual restaurant with various cinema screens incorporated into it.
3. Filter coffee being sold in convenience stores (c-stores), like 7-Eleven. I remember seeing all types – suited business people, office workers, delivery drivers, builders, New York cabbies – buying cups of coffee to take away in Styrofoam cups for a dollar a go.

All of these appealed to me. Custard Beach was fun and the product tasted great. People were clearly buying and loving it; it could be a real success rolled out across London. But I had a nagging doubt – the British weather.

The Screening Room was just opening and I could see the concept working in the UK, particularly London. However, combining food and cinema seemed a big task and it was also reliant on the right kind of property.

This left the coffee in convenience stores. What appealed was the sheer volume of filter coffee in plain cups that was flying out of the door of these no frills convenience chains. There was no real estate, no staff and I was aware that coffee bars such as the Seattle Coffee Company had started opening in London. Maybe there was a new trend emerging for coffee drinking in Britain?

I was in New York for a week and then decided to visit the largest shopping mall in America – the Mall of America in Minneapolis – in the hope that I might see an exciting idea there. After a long day walking this enormous mall, one night I found myself flicking through the yellow pages in my hotel room. I reached 'coffee making equipment' and decided to call one of the companies listed. They were very helpful and I arranged to meet them the following morning at my hotel.

When I went downstairs to the lobby I was met by a representative of the company who took me out to the car park, where there was a very, very large *A-team*-type transit van branded in the company's logo and colours. He slid the side door open and a fully kitted out coffee equipment showroom emerged, complete with leather swivel chairs and the most enormous coffee machine. He gave me the full demonstration and I sampled the coffee, which was amazing.

Three things occurred to me; the machine was huge, could I really see this in a newsagent? Also it was not a machine that a customer could use themselves. Finally, it was expensive, or at least I thought so, and I'd need to sell a lot of coffee to make this work. If this idea was to be the one I ran with I'd need a much smaller, lower-cost machine that was really easy for people to use.

MY MIND TURNS TO COFFEE

I returned home thinking that coffee sold in takeaway cups was my idea and there were a number of positive trends I quickly picked up on:

- Coffee and sandwich shops were expanding in the UK. Aroma and Seattle Coffee Company were making waves and Coffee Republic opened its first store in 1996.

- One of these chains already had some concessions in Waterstones bookshops, so this gave me confidence in the idea of coffee being sold in locations other than standard cafes.

- I discovered that fresh coffee was one of the most important elements of the American c-store product range.

I started to list the potential locations where takeaway hot drinks could be sold. I began with CTNs (confectioners, tobacconist, newsagents) and quickly decided that post offices, small grocery stores, opticians, doctor's surgeries, chemists, tube stations and fashion stores could all be possible locations. If even a small fraction of these worked I'd be looking at thousands of locations.

Then I started to research the equipment and supply side of the model. I found a number of small table top beverage dispensers that were made in the UK, meaning it would be easy to deal with the manufacturers. These were also, I thought, a good price at less than £1000. They used instant coffee granules and powdered milk whisked together with water to produce a cappuccino-style drink.

I researched ingredient and consumable supply and met suppliers. I could produce a coffee for 4p and a cup, lid, sugar and stirrer were another 4.5p. Recognising that I wasn't competing against coffee bars

– this was a convenience product, not an indulgence – I set the drink price in my mind at 6op. Many of my friends would recall me asking them around that time: "Would you buy a coffee from a newsagent and what would you pay?" Simple market research indeed.

I envisaged the coffee dispenser sitting atop a small fabricated unit that would incorporate cups, lids and other consumables, and a bin for discarded sugar tubes and stirrers. I took some design cues from coffee bars. I remember newspaper articles from that time talking about this US import of drink-thru' lids which were becoming popular in coffee bars, so I decided to use them as well.

One of the obvious ingredient suppliers for me to speak to was Nestlé, owners of the brand Nescafé. I figured that if I could use the world's leading brand of instant coffee in the machine this would bring immediate credibility.

It turned out that Nestlé too recognised the development of a food-on-the-move culture in the UK and had an eye on the takeaway coffee market. I was soon meeting them in their head office tower in Croydon, South London. My revenue share business model appealed as they could see that by me owning the equipment and splitting the revenue with the retailer it opened up literally thousands of locations.

They were excited at the prospects of the Nescafé brand being able to penetrate this new market channel and quickly agreed to pay for point of sale material and in-store signage for each location. They also agreed to pay for each machine to be Nescafé branded. This was a real coup for me; all this marketing support at zero cost. I also negotiated great rates for the coffee prices. Nestlé had other brands in petrol station forecourts in central London and we went on a tour of those together. I figured I could learn a lot from these guys.

Despite my comfort with my own business model of selling instant coffee in small shops, I do recall thinking that perhaps Nestlé were being naive in not recognising the growth of roast and ground coffee, which was fuelling the growth of the new breed of coffee bars. This didn't cause me much concern, however, as I felt people would not be prepared to pay the price for ground coffee in a corner shop or petrol forecourt.

EARLY BUSINESS PLANNING

My planning continued. I met with the National Federation of Retail Newsagents and the Association of Convenience Stores. All saw the need for my business and welcomed anything that helped the small retailer. I lined up Dynorod (a franchise-based, nationwide plumbing company) to install mains water into each location. They provided me with detailed costs and I decided that I would pass this on as a set-up cost to the retailer. This was all they would pay up front.

The coffee machines would require maintenance. This was simple and would take less than an hour a week, so I decided that the staff in the shop could and should do this. An early – and accurate – realisation was that getting the retailer to play their part in the enterprise, i.e. by cleaning the machines, would be critical to success. For technical maintenance of the machines I met with a company called Neopost who maintained franking machines and were keen to diversify.

I thought long and hard about undertaking formal market research and had a number of proposals for face-to-face street interviews with consumers outside of newsagents and other potential locations. With my limited funds though, to blow £5k on a market study seemed like a big chunk to spend. I also questioned what market research could really tell me. My concern was that until the product was there, available to buy, all consumers could tell me was what they *might* do. This was not factual research.

So I abandoned this plan and instead spent a fraction of £5000 with a company called Verdict Research, asking them to look at each channel to market (e.g. CTNs, dry cleaners, doctor's surgeries, estate agent's offices, etc.). How many locations did they see per channel and what was the best way to target them?

With the thinking really taking shape I started to put together a business plan and worked out that each machine needed to sell a minimum of 100 cups per week. A typical newsagent was open for around 80 hours per week so 100 cups sold would mean 1.25 per hour. Surely this was realistic?

My plan dictated 190 machines installed across 1997. On that basis the business would turn profitable by the end of the year and with 500 machines by the end of 1998 it would achieve sales of around £1.5m and make 7% net profit.

What to name the business didn't seem that important, particularly as we were using Nescafé as the public face and brand to the consumer. But a name was needed. A few mates congregated in our front room for the purposes of a brainstorming session. Trudi agreed to do supper, I supplied a few bottles of wine and we were off. Someone came up with West 1 Coffee (this sounded too much like a courier company) and Power Coffee (for bodybuilders?). Trudi's leftfield response was Climax Coffee; after a few bottles of wine we loved this. In reality though... coffee that makes you orgasm? Not sure about that one.

I reminded those assembled that this was really about making coffee-to-go part of everyday life across the nation. I'm not sure who finally suggested Coffee Nation but it stuck and epitomised what we were about. Within weeks I had a logo to boot; a cheerful coffee pot going around the world in a smart blue and yellow colour scheme.

KNOCKING ON DOORS

The only reliable way to secure locations quickly was to get out on the street and literally knock on doors. I bought a cheap A4 presentation folder and knocked up some simple sales pages.

I practised my sales pitch – "High quality drinks at affordable prices for your customers" – and worked out what share of the revenues the shop could keep depending on how many drinks they sold. The more they sold the more they kept. There was a digital drinks counter in the machine so once a month I would visit, take a reading and then invoice them for my share of the sales.

In South London I started walking in off the street and asking to speak with store owners. There were lots of responses such as "Not interested", "It won't work" or "I have no space", but after several weeks I had a small list of independent stores who were willing to try it out. I had prepared a checklist to assess their suitability. Did they sell morning goods? Did they have a lottery terminal to bring in footfall?

I figured that for all the No's, the Yes's would come, but I do remember days of getting absolutely nowhere. Many of these small shops were not modern retail to say the least and I did think that many of them lacked the motivation to develop their offer to be more attractive to the consumer. One winter's day in particular stands out – it was so cold, it started to snow and I thought to myself that there must be an easier way to make money.

Despite this – and several of the stores who at first said yes then backing out – as 1996 drew to a close I had the first machines installed and trading. I scribbled in my notebook "We are a retailer not a vending machine operator."

PROFESSIONAL BUSINESS SUPPORT

So I had live sites, a business plan I had researched thoroughly and I had also met with my bank to talk about asset finance for the machines. The Baker Tilly business card was still sitting on my desk and it was time to call them. A meeting was arranged with a lady called Christine Corner.

I thought about what I wanted from the meeting. Feedback on the business plan, how they could help me secure finance of the right type, how they can support me now, through growth and to a stock market float (AIM was all the rage at the time) and how they could help me think and act big were all on my mind.

My calculations showed I needed about £150K at the time so a Small Firms Loans (SFL) combined with my own funds and perhaps a bank overdraft would be sufficient. Christine agreed to write to me with a proposal. This was to be for one year, for a fixed fee and would include support in helping me develop the business plan and line up funding. She agreed to a three month payment holiday, though she wanted the fee to increase as the business became successful. I wasted no time in signing them up. I felt they were genuinely interested in seeing my fledgling business succeed.

SPAR

As well as targeting individual retailers, I also approached larger convenience store chains Spar and Alldays. I had read an article in *The Grocer* quoting the retail director of Spar:

> "Coffee and food to go represent a huge opportunity for UK independents. Cappuccino machines offer a real profit opportunity that require little maintenance. Wawa sells over 2600 cups per day per store and refer to it as liquid gold."

If ever I needed proof that I was on to something this was it! Wawa was a US convenience store chain and it appeared Spar had spotted the same opportunity I had. They were clearly open to the idea of selling takeaway coffee from their stores.

Within days I had penned a letter to Spar setting out how Coffee Nation was the only company set up to provide a bespoke coffee service exclusively for the c-store market. I didn't have to wait long for an answer. They called me and on 23 December I was in their offices. Spar, by volume of locations, was actually the largest retailer in the world. There were no nerves though – I couldn't wait to get in there.

I diligently talked through the Coffee Nation offer and how Spar could basically outsource coffee to us. I painted a picture of how we would make coffee-to-go from the local c-store an everyday part of life for the British public by emphasising quality, speed, value for money and the complementary nature of coffee to other products. By the end of the afternoon he had agreed that we should map out a programme of trials in various stores across the UK and if successful Spar would start rolling-out Coffee Nation across their estate.

Those breakthrough moments are extraordinary in the life of the entrepreneur and are like stepping stones across a pond. I was so excited when I left the Spar offices in Harrow and drove back into London.

On the way out of town to the meeting I had noticed a car dealer called Sparks on the A40 near Shepherd's Bush, they had a beautiful Aston Martin Virage in the window. On the way home I couldn't resist popping in and soon I was sitting behind the wheel. The car was not for now, but it made my dream real. I was sure I was going in the right direction.

LEARNING POINTS

- Recognise that winning ideas often come in different forms – for me it was the business model that came first, not the product or customer need.

- Look for evidence that your idea is low risk and that elements of it are already proven. Coffee bars were becoming trendy in the UK and takeaway coffee was sold in enormous volumes in US c-stores.

- Beware of tie ups with other parties at an early stage. They complicate the business and can go wrong. The other guys' priorities can also change and deals between tiny businesses and global corporations are very unlikely to be on an equitable basis.

- Watch for secondary priorities that are noble causes but utterly pointless and simply serve to distract from what actually generates the revenue. Helping small retailers fight back against supermarkets was all well and good but how did that help me?

- Get the best possible advice early on when risks are at their highest. If accountants and advisers want big fees up front, they don't get you or your business. Find ones that do and offer them loyalty in the long term in lieu of fees today – if they demonstrate commitment to you.

- Market research can be dangerous if you are trying to discover what people *might* do in the future.

- Passion kills fear. They cannot co-exist. An entrepreneur that knows their idea from every angle and knows deep down they are really on to something can skip into that first sales pitch.

- Be able to tell the story of your business in one sentence. Does it light people up or do you get a sarcastic "Oh, that's interesting," in response? In 1996 I was able to say I was going to make coffee-to-go an everyday part of life for the British public even before I had one machine live.

1997 – ONE STEP FORWARD, TWO STEPS BACK

IF I WAS excited at the way 1996 had ended, by the end of 1997 I was able to look back and see 1996 as my time of beginner's luck. With any endeavour requiring serious commitment, there will often be an initial flush of success, but almost without fail the true test comes after. I found this out the hard way in 1997.

LETTERS FROM SPAR, ALLDAYS AND NESTLÉ

At the start of the year I had two sites trading, both small independent stores, one in South London and the other in Wandsworth. Results were hardly spectacular, with sales of 40 to 50 cups per week. I realised that I needed to be in more professional retail environments and the meeting just before Christmas with Spar could not have come sooner. I was keen to get what we had discussed formalised on paper.

By March I had a letter of commitment from Spar to working "in partnership over a trial period to bring the best coffee offer to the consumer." The plan involved me undertaking assessments of a list of potential locations in order to identify a minimum of ten trial sites. If all went well we expected to be reviewing the trials in the autumn and planning a 100 store roll-out.

Spar was excited to bring convenience coffee to the British marketplace and they sent me their internal scoping document. It was highly complimentary to my little company. They had met with four other businesses and selected Coffee Nation for a number of reasons: knowledge of the independent sector; willingness to work with Spar to develop the offer; and vision and skill in looking to develop the concept.

With an initial list of 30 Spar stores from which to work – all keen to sell coffee – I clocked up the miles visiting them around the UK. I was armed with data on store size, weekly footfall and sales turnover, and I felt I was going about this in a professional manner.

I had also been introduced to the Alldays convenience store group. I thought I would start at the top so I wrote a letter to the CEO, feeling that as I was the managing director of Coffee Nation I could talk to the MD of any other business.

By mid-February I had met with the Alldays CEO and new business development director. They wrote to me setting out their goal of hot drinks becoming "a valuable high margin revenue generator featured as a standard offer across our estate. We have both seen coffee approaching 10% of store turnover in the US and this remains the target we must aim for." They also agreed to work with me exclusively on the trials.

Alldays had an estate of 700 stores and Spar some 2500. The potential seemed almost limitless and I had commitments in writing from both these groups. Alldays agreed to pilot 20 machines in grab'n'go locations. This was bloody exciting!

I was keen to get something on paper with Nestlé too. They wrote to me describing Coffee Nation as innovative and entrepreneurial. They set out how consumers were starting to embrace quality food solutions available out of home and how "Coffee Nation offers the retailer an ideal way of exploiting this trend."

I relocated the business away from my tiny office in Soho and for about the same price I rented a two room office in a managed workspace building called Leroy House in Islington, North London.

QUEST FOR FUNDING

Baker Tilly were delighted with the progress I was making and they (Christine specifically) became a trusted friend on the journey. They suggested I set up a factoring facility as I was going to be invoicing small retail businesses (Spar and Alldays were the names over the door but they were essentially independents offering broadly the same offer under an umbrella brand).

Factoring would mean I would get up to 90% of the value of an invoice paid to me within seven days. The factor also provided a full credit management facility to collect payment from each location. Their fee was a reasonable £6k in year one, which seemed a small price for the peace of mind it would bring.

My £50k that I had invested into the business was only going to go so far and with a commitment of 30 trial locations and each machine costing around £1000, not to mention the cost of the cabinet the machine would sit on that would house the cups and lids, I was going to require additional funds.

The first port of call was to meet a bank and my accountant arranged a meeting with RBS with a view to securing a Small Firms Loan for £100k. This, perhaps alongside an overdraft facility and the factoring arrangement, was considered sufficient to reach 200 stores trading in year one.

A letter from RBS landed on my desk on 11 March. It stated they could not take the proposal forward given "the unproven nature of the product." They appreciated the progress I had made with Spar and Alldays, but wanted to see "firm orders in place from retailers before finance could be granted." They also wanted to see my funding committed to establishing "a small number of machines producing realistic sales and profits and this micro market would give further credence to the assumptions in my business plan."

Of course this was a blow, although Baker Tilly weren't surprised. Nonetheless, I had to listen to RBS' feedback, understand it and work out what to do to address these issues. I took every positive word as an indication I was on to something exciting. Given I had been able to secure exclusive pilots with two retailers representing over 3000 locations in the UK, I was confident it would only be a matter of time before we could be back at the bank doing the deal. That confidence was to be sorely tested many times in the coming months.

Fortunately, I was able to set up a business bank account with Barclays in Soho Square and secured a £30k overdraft with the help of an introduction from my accountants.

I spent time thinking about the structure of the business and decided I needed an operations manager to work alongside me. He or she would lead the day-to-day management of the business, overseeing each installation and working with each site to maximise sales. They would likely come from a fast moving retail background.

I decided to appoint a recruitment firm and do the job properly. I appointed Berkeley Scott Selection who were specialists in retail and food business recruitment. We ran a full page advertisement in *The Grocer* in March 1997. I went with their suggestion for the header "Magic Beans? Seriously! Coffee Nation has a bold objective; to make cappuccino an everyday drink in the UK by offering self-serve dispensers in the out of home marketplace."

By late spring I had found my man. He had been an area operations manager with Holland & Barrett, the health food retailer. He was sharp, highly articulate and had a great track record. He also stood out as wanting to make a conscious decision to join an early-stage business. We negotiated a package and he joined me. His name was Lou. He would be on £30k with a bonus and company car. I was now starting to spend real money and was ultimately responsible for someone else's livelihood.

Baker Tilly was setting me up with various business angel groups and wealthy individuals who invested in early-stage businesses. I met with Beer & Partners, a leading source of business angel investment in the UK for growing small businesses. I came close and several angels were interested, but I wasn't able to close a deal.

I started to realise that one could spend a great deal of time with potential investors, many of whom very rarely invested in anything. Even if they did go on to invest, they may not be right for me and my business. Personal chemistry would be critical unless they were completely out of sight after investing. It seemed to make more sense to have someone on board who could add real value.

TRIALS BEGIN AT SPAR AND ALLDAYS

By mid-year we had launched our first stores with Spar in Cardiff and with Alldays in Faversham, Kent. The Faversham site was opposite a railway station and Spar in Cardiff was a busy city centre convenience store with a good hot food to-go business.

By August we had nine sites trading, seven with Spar and two with Alldays. We had very few bright lights in an otherwise dull landscape of sales results. We were seeing anything from 20 to 100 or so sales per machine per week. One Spar store in the West Midlands had hit 174 in a single week and our second Alldays had reached 344 cups. These figures weren't being sustained though so Lou and I were desperately trying to identify what made these stores different. Both had strong food to-go sales of sandwiches and pastries and both were large city centre stores.

I believed we were on to something. Even at 100 cups of coffee sold each week that meant on average someone was buying a drink every hour given typical store trading hours. We embarked on all forms of promotional activity. This included free coffee for the first week of trading for all customers, loyalty cards, a free Kit Kat (another Nestlé product) with each coffee, and a bundle offer of a coffee and a newspaper. We proactively targeted the local area with flyers to tell residents they could now buy coffee to go in their local store. We targeted offices, taxi ranks, railway staff at Faversham and even schools in the area.

No one was being forced to buy a drink, people were choosing to. But after 13 weeks of trading we were only selling 420 cups per week from nine stores, so not even 50 cups per week on average. It was true that most of our openings had been during a warm summer but this was an excuse, really.

There was a dawning realisation that pushing harder and finding that elusive breakthrough promotional activity to catapult sales forward just wasn't the answer. I knew I needed pull not push but I didn't know what I meant by that, it was almost just a feeling.

It seemed that whatever we did we couldn't really move the needle. The CEO of Alldays had recently restated their commitment to having coffee in all of their stores to complement their in-store concessions of Dunkin' Donuts, Domino's Pizza, Movie Nights video rental, dry cleaning services and Post Office counters. I was staring down the barrel of a potential 700 site business with this customer alone, but I might as well have been trying to fly to Mars.

I worked hard to manage my relationships with Spar and Alldays, being sure to stand my ground. I knew the machines needed to be in high-visibility locations in each store and next to other snacking food offers. I had to decline some good sites as there simply wasn't the right in-store location available without a costly re-jig of the store layout.

For the first time, cash was now starting to worry me. I had started with effectively £80k (my £50k investment and the £30k Barclays overdraft) but this was shrinking on a monthly basis. I had bought machines, cabinets, stocks of cups and other consumables. I also had rent to pay each month, Lou's salary, travel costs and so on. What we'd got was promising but it wasn't convincing.

In the search for more money we pitched to new potential investors with another business plan. A couple of friends came close to tipping money in, one of whom was Alistair from Dawes Ryan Consulting, but close was as far as he got.

Then Spar wrote me a nice letter:

> "It seems that Americans have a strong coffee culture. Currently of course the UK is very much different, however we do see that the UK market will establish itself in the same way if the right offer is in place. Much of the opposition is due to the state of mind of the customer and availability of convenience coffee. Spar, with the help of Coffee Nation, hope to be the people who change this perception."

They went on:

> "Spar have chosen Coffee Nation because they have the best package for our stores. Also the backup and support far exceeds any competitors. At this stage we are both on a very steep learning curve, but by the time the market is ready to take off we will be the most experienced partnership in the market."

Another compelling factor in our favour was our revenue share model. If Spar went elsewhere they would have to buy or rent the machines and pay this cost regardless of whether they sold a single cup of coffee.

All of this pointed to our business model being able to retain major retailers' interest, which was great, but that wasn't what investors were putting their money into. We had to sell more coffee for this to be an attractive proposition to the retailer and neither I nor Spar had any idea when the market would be ready to take off.

By August 1997 my latest business plan showed I needed to raise £250k. This would take us to 400 locations after two years. We were still selling drinks at 59p. Pret A Manger had introduced coffee at 69p and that was real espresso coffee with fresh milk, so I couldn't easily put the price up.

My issue was one line in my Executive Summary, which read:

> "Two of the stores have traded ahead of expectation and one has traded within expectation."

Out of nine live sites I had six non-starters. The business plan was really a combination of asking people to see the potential and get the vision of what *should* happen based on the US experience and what UK retailers and food companies *hoped* would happen, combined with some unconvincing results from a pilot operation. It was a Hope Plan, not a Business Plan.

At this time, Alldays wanted me to commit to a full package of in-store promotional activity and materials. This included a full eight-week promotional cycle, external store signage, wobblers, ceiling-mounted signage, coffee cup mobiles on sandwich chillers, sales counter banners, swing signs on the pavement outside, plus caps, badges and balloons on launch day.

Some of this I put in place, but I had realised that all of this was simply noise. Chances were if none of it was there, the sales would be just the same. They had to understand I was a small company with big aspirations, but also a small purse that was being depleted by the day. If my "No" to more costly marketing activity meant I lost Alldays as a customer, so be it. I had to stay alive and I knew more of the same was not going to generate different results.

INSIGHT FROM VENTURE CAPITAL FIRM

I continued working hard to raise money and met with 3i (the leading international venture capital firm). My presentation to them sold hard on me and my background, the Coffee Nation vision, research, customer and supplier relationships, and current status. Trouble was, it was light on results.

The outcome of the meeting was predictable. They wanted to stay in contact but identified a lack of hard evidence in the form of compelling sales results from our pilot sites as a reason not to arrange a follow up meeting. They were also highly wary of our relationship with Nestlé.

I had also met with Venture Capital Report (VCR), based in Oxford. Interestingly, Coffee Republic, a start-up coffee bar chain had just months before been featured in the same report. VCR wrote up a four-page piece on my business, presenting various profit and loss scenarios. The base case was 100 stores doing 100 cups per week. At this level the business would break even, but at present out of my nine stores not one of them was averaging more than 100 cups per week.

I was pinning my hopes on my business being "a new concept at the very early stage of sales." The problem was that I couldn't be in enough stores quick enough for the concept to become part of everyday life; for that I'd need £millions.

I was offering 45% of the company in return for £250k investment. There were no takers. My enthusiasm remained undiminished as I strongly believed the concept would come good eventually. I still had almost 2500 people buying my coffee every month – but these numbers just weren't enough.

Life away from Coffee Nation had also taken an unexpected twist in the road; my wife and I had separated in the summer. Trudi and I simply grew apart; we still loved each other but I was 29 and she was 37. I think we both realised we probably wanted different things at that time in our lives. We remained close and I saw her and my little girl Maia (who was born in 1995) at least twice every week. I moved into a house share in west London and maintained a small income from the consultancy.

The year drew to a close. It was certainly not how I had expected it to be 12 months earlier. The strengths and weaknesses table in the VCR article was chillingly accurate:

Strengths	Weaknesses
1. Pilot sites in operation	1. Poor initial sales
2. Based on successful model	2. Weak balance sheet
3. Two large retailers and Nestlé involved	3. Widely spaced sites around the UK

What a difference a year makes!

LEARNING POINTS

- If you are launching a consumer business, regardless of relationships or agreements with distribution partners, if you don't win with the consumer you will fail.

- 3i was right about Nestlé. It added little of real value, wasn't a real contract and merely diverted some existing marketing spend my way on a signage package and a small discount on coffee. This could have been withdrawn overnight. The Coffee Nation name would never be worth anything whilst I was selling Nescafé coffee.

- I created my cash issue. I didn't need a 30-store trial programme and certainly not all over the UK. Trials should have been close to home.

- I tried to raise money for an unproven business. I was lucky to have failed in the fundraising at that time.

- I was busy managing trials, writing and rewriting my business plan and chasing investors. All of this appeared sensible but it did not give me the answer of why I was not selling more coffee. Learn to recognise the busy fool syndrome; it's a common ailment amongst start-ups.

- If a product doesn't sell (or in sufficient volumes to become profitable) it's usually because not enough people want to buy it regardless of how much promotional activity is put behind it.

- I was right to hold on to the fact that some people were buying – it gave me hope and energy to keep at it. Thank God I did. Many people give up just before victory is theirs. My mantra was I would never, ever give up.

- Sell in at the highest level – if you get a meeting with the CEO you'll actually be talking to someone who can make decisions.

- My agreements with Spar and Alldays were warm, feel-good letters but not trial agreements with clear success criteria signed by both parties.

- It was right – eventually – to call a halt to the expensive promotional plan with Alldays. Many small (and even bigger) companies go bust trying to please their customers. Tell the truth and chances are they'll stick with you.

1998 – BREAKTHROUGH YEAR

AS 1998 BEGAN I was focused on three things:

1. How do I sell more?
2. How do I raise money?
3. How do I stem the cash burn?

At the same time, I stayed close to my creditors. Where I couldn't pay in full I agreed minimal regular payments and talked them through the position I was in with the business. In most cases people were understanding, wanted to see me succeed and asked how they could help.

Honesty normally brings out the best in people and creditors are no different. Nonetheless, I was in dire straits. I had expanded my estate of machines to 19 locations but was only generating £3000 per month in sales. I had to find the answer fast or it was game over.

EUREKA MOMENT

One of the business angels I had met recently had asked me a question and for some reason this had popped back into my mind: "How much time are you really spending on the business against just servicing something going nowhere?"

He was right; all I was doing was servicing a nationwide network of underperforming machines and had almost no time left to find that breakthrough I so badly needed.

I realised I needed to be out there at each site connecting with customers, including those buying and those that weren't. Everything else was of little importance. I decided to go on a tour of our locations with no particular agenda. My spirits lifted a little.

One of the machines I visited was in a Spar convenience store on a petrol forecourt near to the Merry Hill shopping centre in the West Midlands. The location should have been a winner, but we weren't even managing to sell 100 cups per week.

While I was at the store, someone approached me. He said he thought it was a great idea and explained he was a manager at a recently opened car showroom just the other side of the roundabout and often came into the shop for a sandwich. Then came the "But…" and in his next statement lay my eureka moment. He had bought a coffee, but only once. He said:

> "Why should I buy a cup of instant coffee for 59p when I can put the kettle on in the office? If you want me to buy a coffee in here it's got to be an amazing product – it has to really wow me."

In that single sentence I suddenly saw the answer to my issues. My mistake was to think that because I was selling in convenience stores the customer wouldn't expect real, freshly ground coffee made from beans and fresh milk as they would in a coffee bar. Clearly they would. *That was the opportunity – to put a coffee bar product into convenience stores.*

My other mistake had been to look at the cost of espresso machines and decide I couldn't possibly justify that expense. It was now so obvious. How could I have missed this? Giving people a Nescafé drink called *cappuccino* with whisked up powdered milk and thinking that would work because it was a c-store had been my error.

A low price won't guarantee sales – if you wow people with the product, then sales will rocket. You then have the makings of a proper business. The next dawning realisation was that this was the *pull* I had been thinking about, as opposed to trying to *push* more with signage and promotions. The product itself had to be the champion, the hero, the attraction.

This realisation was the answer to my prayers. All it had taken was for me to get out and spend time listening to what people told me. I had been so close and now I had the answer.

THE PRODUCT MUST BE THE HERO

Everything fell into place in my mind very quickly. I had been trying to build this new concept with a grocery brand of coffee because the machines were low cost. But the growth of coffee was all in roast and ground. I'd been backing the wrong horse.

Within days I had shared my insight with my accountants and my bank manager. The latter was sceptical – I think he'd heard it all before, but did sign off my facility for another three months.

There was no time to lose. I approached several espresso machine companies in the UK and found a small Swiss-built machine that appeared robust, did a good job of steaming and foaming fresh milk, and was easy to clean. This was a different game altogether though; it was a £4000 piece of kit.

I realised that the coffee itself had to be the focal point. We needed to create an in-store destination. We worked with a product and brand design company to create a concession unit that would house the espresso machine (and a small hot chocolate dispenser). The Nescafé name was gone and the Coffee Nation logo sat proudly at the top, beneath which it said "Fresh ground Coffee". I decided that a price rise of 10p, to 69p, was in order.

I approached one of the UK's largest coffee roasters to work with me on the product. I chose a 100% Arabica blend of beans from Brazil, Nicaragua and Kenya that would give a great espresso but also work well with milk for cappuccinos. We'd now be able to talk about where our product came from – it wasn't just somebody else's grocery brand anymore.

For both the espresso machine and coffee bean supply I couldn't offer any guarantee of volumes or business growth. The truth was I couldn't even pay them. The machine distributor agreed to lend me four machines and the roaster – as they were quite entrepreneurial – said they were happy to develop the blend up front without any minimum volume commitment. They could genuinely see that there might just be something in this and I was brimming with energy and wanted to move fast.

It's often down to the persuasiveness of the entrepreneur in the early days and I was true to my word. Ten years later we were still buying our coffee from the same company. They continued to give us great service and pricing, and worked with us on product development. We went from my first order of 12kg of beans in 1998 to hundreds of tons a year a decade later.

The concession prototype came together and I had Coffee Nation branded cups produced. Now I had the makings of a brand, all because I had got the product right.

CREATING A DESTINATION

I engaged with Alldays and Spar once more and sent them a glossy presentation under the heading of 'The country's first true self-service gourmet coffee concession'. I set out the journey we had been on to develop coffee in their stores and what I had learnt.

I explained how there just weren't enough reasons to buy what we had been selling. Table-top instant coffee machines were commonplace in offices. We needed to create an experience, some degree of theatre and a destination. People were going to plan to visit a store for a Coffee Nation coffee in the future. They bought my vision and we identified four stores between the two companies from which the instant machines would be removed and replaced with the new offer.

The first was our original location in Faversham. My in-store unit had a back-lit menu panel to tell people what types of coffee drink were available. I had some menu cards produced for customers to take away and designed some branded loyalty cards. We trained the staff on-site how to clean the machine and look after the fresh milk.

The gamble paid off. Almost from day one we were outselling the old Nescafé offer, even though the price was 10p more per cup. Within weeks we were averaging 160 cups per week per machine against 85 per week with Nescafé. No promotions, no free doughnut offer, just great coffee and sales volumes were up 90%.

Of course, I couldn't do all of this and spend nothing. My overdraft had now exceeded its limit and I could see a disaster looming. I finally had my proof but I was out of cash.

SEARCH FOR NEW FUNDING

I met with various espresso machine distributors and coffee companies and some of these suggested they could invest in the company in return for preferential terms on their equipment. Of course, they were starting to see there really could be a new market channel here. Convenience retailing was fast growing and I offered a new route to machine and coffee sales.

Various offers came in and I spent considerable time trying to close these deals. On many occasions since I have thanked God that none of them came off. They all came with conditions. I'd be tied into a single brand of espresso machine, I'd have to use their service team to maintain the equipment, base my company out of their site, use their call centre teams and administration support, etc. It was Nestlé all over again but in a different guise and all for small amounts of money and big equity stakes (I think the worst was an offer of £30k for 30% of the business).

Another realisation that came to me was that many of these companies, whilst successful, were all selling someone else's product. They were decent businesses and great people but despite my precarious state I had something truly different and exciting. I wanted to build a high-growth consumer company that was doing something nobody else was. I'd got the formula right now – I just needed someone who believed in this.

I held my nerve and met with an old contact from my consultancy days. Martin and I met a number of times and I took him to Faversham to experience the new concept. He *got* it, we had good rapport and he saw it as the democratisation of coffee, or "coffee without the bollocks" as he put it (no newspapers, no leather armchairs, no muffins).

He agreed to invest £30k. We signed and he transferred the money at the end of the week. I still have the bank statements: -£40k went to -£10k. I had a stay of execution.

I gained an enthusiastic supporter in Martin. It was a fair deal for both parties. He is a dear friend to this day and he eventually made good money from his very bold and brave investment back in 1998. I gladly offered him a seat on the board, which he held until 2002. He helped me on many occasions.

SALES PROGRESS BUT ON BORROWED TIME

My two highest performing Spar sites were in Manchester so these were next in line for my new offer. Together with Faversham and Edinburgh that gave me my four new test sites. The cash burn resumed as I now had to buy those pricey espresso machines and have three more concession units constructed.

I was back on a steep learning curve, operating this new type of product. It was far from perfect. The concession unit was made of MDF, which wasn't terribly robust, particularly if it got wet with coffee spills. The espresso machine was a pig to clean, with fiddly parts that had to be removed. The milk was kept cold in a small separate fridge with a pipe going into the coffee machine. If the machine wasn't cleaned exactly as per schedule and that pipe flushed with cleaner then I would soon have milk solidifying at room temperature in the pipe. Not good for the product or the consumer!

The coffee machine was really designed for use in a cafe and so had steam and water pipes (for frothing milk and boiling water for tea) that I didn't need. Remarkably, dispensing simple items like stirrers and lids was a nightmare as they were fiddly and difficult to stack. Despite the challenges, I had a strong feeling that I was going in the right direction and nobody was ahead of me.

By September the four re-fitted espresso machine sites were all operating and we were selling up to 800 cups per month from each machine. This was great news, but of course the costs were now much higher. I started to increase the drink price, first to 75p and then up to 99p. I was far too timid and cautious with pricing but eventually the market did the talking for me; on the high street a cappuccino was now at £1.50 so I could afford to charge more.

There was no doubt I had the makings of a proven proposition for the consumer, but I had not quite reached true commercial viability. The cost of an installation was now £5000, versus the £1500 I had paid for each instant coffee machine.

I started to give serious consideration to the possibility that I now had the offer right but the wrong locations. Perhaps this concept really lived in much higher volume locations like busy petrol forecourts, motorway services and supermarkets?

A short summary I had prepared on the business had been sent out by Baker Tilly to a targeted collection of venture capitalists. The answers were consistent. They either thought my business was too early stage to invest in or questioned if it would be profitable enough to make a return for a VC. I was making progress but was it quick enough? Would

I raise some proper investment for this business before the patience of Barclays ran out and they called in my overdraft?

The need to conserve cash whilst I figured out how to secure investment was severe. I had to let Lou go. I could now see I had employed him way too early, when I thought that success would simply be a question of following what I had written in my business plan. I didn't need any employees – I just needed to run a small test market of my new gourmet coffee machines and find the right investor. He had been so loyal and believed in Coffee Nation and me without doubt. He took the decision well.

At about that time I reconnected with Tony, who I had met at an Institute of Directors networking event a couple of years earlier. He ran a small advisory firm, mostly focused on company turnarounds and distressed businesses and I asked his view. Simple, he said. I needed a new business plan and then had to secure some proper funding.

RETHINKING THE BUSINESS PLAN

I had strong evidence that I now had something that worked and could be scaled up to a large number of locations. Sure, there were still considerable gaps and I was far from certain I was in the right locations, but no business is perfect.

Tony introduced me to his colleague Mark and the three of us set to work. Again, I faced the issue of not being able to pay them for their help. We agreed a deal whereby for funds raised they would take a percentage of the company, depending on the amount. I really had nothing to lose. I'd be happy for them to own a small part of the business (ordinary shares, non-voting) if we raised some proper money.

The new business plan was half the size of my original document. It talked more about what I had achieved. It actually read like a plan *for* a business:

> "We are the UK's first brand of fully self-service fresh ground coffee concessions."
> "There is a large unexploited market in the UK for coffee-to-go, sold anywhere that demand can be created."
> "Each unit offers a high net margin based on premium pricing and low cost of operation. Each concession requires no dedicated staff to operate them and occupies only 1sq.m. of floor space."

There was a section on market focus and our unique selling points, broken down into consumer (e.g. fresh ground coffee, convenient in less than 30 seconds) and retailer features and benefits (e.g. additional revenue stream, minimal day-to-day servicing, no maintenance and minimal cost).

Evidence from my latest test sites that the new offer was actually bringing people into the stores as they could now get a fresh coffee to go with a pastry from the in-store bakery went into the plan.

I set out that each machine had a life of five years, although we would depreciate over three. Sales continued to climb month on month and in the preceding four weeks we had averaged over 900 cups per location.

The forecast showed we would be consistently profitable from month 18 and the gross margin was 60%. Importantly, it highlighted that the continued growth of the business could be funded from cash flow after that. If there truly were thousands of locations where a Coffee Nation concession could be located, the business would inevitably need further growth funding down the line, but this plan was written around a sensible investment for what had been achieved to date.

PRESENTING TO INVESTORS

We now needed an audience. Tony suggested I contact a business angel network in the Cambridge area called the Great Eastern Investment Forum (GEIF). I'd put in a call but hadn't heard back from them.

Meanwhile, we had a slot confirmed for me to present at a similar event run by an accountancy firm in Yorkshire. I enthusiastically prepared a presentation. Mark and I set off up north. It was the first time I had actually stood up and presented in front of a live audience armed with chequebooks.

I knew it was my big moment and I was certain I had prepared well. In ten minutes I was done and there was applause from the audience, but I knew immediately that although everything I'd said was fine it somehow hadn't hit the spot.

After the talks there was a buffet laid on, with time for networking and the opportunity for the entrepreneurs who had pitched to meet the investors. I didn't have the stomach to eat and I fumbled with a glass of wine. I had one or two enquiries but it was all a bit polite and I just felt I hadn't gained any real traction.

As I was about to leave the event someone approached me and Mark. I didn't even get his name. He said as an investment it wasn't for him but he could see we were on to a winner.

This was another one of those moments of pure serendipity; we never saw that gentleman again but what he said had a profound impact: "You've got a great business but you've got to sell yourself, make them want you, make them believe they'll lose out if they don't invest. You sounded desperate."

"Desperate, of course I'm fucking desperate," ran through my mind at a million miles an hour but I kept my mouth shut and listened to this helpful stranger.

We both thanked him and almost ran with excitement back to the car. In the space of a minute I had gone from sheer despondency to a sense of deep elation because I now understood how to present to potential investors.

It was late and we had to get back to London. I didn't waste a minute. Mark drove and I rewrote the entire presentation. I'd write a section, even a sentence or two, and read it out. I hardly slept and by the middle of the following morning had completely rewritten my presentation. Rather than now talking to each slide I had prepared an impactful speech that supported the presentation. It pressed all the buttons that investors would want to hear.

PRESENTATION AT THE GEIF

The GEIF then called and asked if I could send them my business plan. A few days later they called me again and invited me to present at the next forum, which was in May 1999. "When!?" I bellowed down the phone. "I'll be bust by then, surely you're running an event before then?" They were, the following week, but it was already full.

Something in me had changed. I had the test market sites performing well and I felt confident, really confident, for the first time. "I don't care, put me on in the coffee break, I don't care, I'll do anything," I said. I really wasn't going to take no for an answer. I wasn't rude, just confident and a little cheeky.

I didn't have long to wait for an answer. They called me back later the same day and asked if I could present to the board of GEIF the next morning in Cambridge. They asked all presenting entrepreneurs to go through this so that they could then coach them in their pitch. When they heard what I had to say they didn't want me to change anything, not a word. I could not have been happier.

The day of the big pitch arrived. I felt confident and was sure I had all the ingredients together this time. There were eight companies presenting and it was a packed auditorium of mostly business angels, but with some banks, venture capitalists and advisers.

"It's fresh, it's frothy, it's Coffee Nation coffee!"

That was my opening line. I didn't say it, I shouted it. No one was going to nod off in my presentation. If I at least got everyone's attention I'd surely increase my chances.

"You've seen the success of other coffee companies – Starbucks in the US (value $3bn) and Coffee Republic (floated on AIM this year) – Coffee Nation is set to become the next coffee revolution."

Investors (usually) look for an emerging trend, wait for signs of success and then invest. This line was a deliberate play to this. They wanted to know what had *already happened* in the peer group. This would – I hoped – provide reassurance. Then I told them, super confidently, we would be next.

"Nestlé are forecasting exponential growth in premium quality out-of-home food and beverages well into the next decade."

I wasn't buying Nestlé coffee any more but it didn't stop me from quoting their research. After all, they are one of the largest food companies in the world.

"We are creating an entirely new market category, no one else has the experience we do of developing this and it is giving us a distinct competitive advantage."

Talking about customers, I said:

"We got a quote from a customer in Manchester. 'Best coffee in Manchester – we don't go anywhere else! It's nice not to have to queue.' "

We were indeed now getting great customer feedback with some regularity. My aim was to reassure the audience that it worked for the consumer and not having to queue underpinned a benefit of this new category.

I helped them with that a little:

> "This customer called us on our freephone number to give us this feedback. When was the last time you went in to a convenience store and had such a great experience that you went home to call the company and tell them?"

This was an ace. I could almost hear people thinking "Wow, all for a 99p cup of coffee."

> "We have four concessions that have been trading for a combined 40 months so we don't need your money to test, research or prove the concept – we seek straight roll-out funding. We've already done the hard bit and we now seek investors who share our vision and want to join us on the journey."

The aim here was to reassure them that there weren't going to be endless rounds of further fundraising where these investors would get diluted.

Finally, I also projected my vision forwards and invited the audience to consider what success might look like. I explained that I was going to read out a section of a hypothetical newspaper article written about Coffee Nation. The date is July 2000:

> "Little Coffee Nation stations are popping up everywhere giving the urban customer what they want when they want it. No hassle, no queues and no need to speak to anyone. Suddenly it's hip to help yourself!"

Of course it was actually November 1998 and this article had yet to be written but it was believable. It brought everything I had talked about to a point, a singularity that they could all get their heads around.

I finished comfortably within the 12 minutes allocated. You know when you've nailed it. I knew it before I even finished. The applause was very different to that for the previous companies' presentations. It wasn't out of obligation to be polite – it was because what they'd just heard had impressed them. It had been a very long time in the coming but on that day it finally came together for me. I had learnt when and how to raise money for a young business, just in time.

As I sat down and the founder of the eighth and final company took to the stage his opening remark was, "How can I follow that?" Even the founder of another company was still selling my proposition for me.

After the presentations, investors could meet with presenting companies face to face. I was mobbed. I took names, addresses and answered questions. I wasted no time in asking directly if they wanted to invest and how much. I was offering 20% for £100k. I had to maintain the momentum.

The day was a complete success. My bank had also now set out an offer in principle of a £90k Small Firms Loan that was 75% underwritten by the government. This would be available if I was able to match that debt with an equal equity investment.

I followed up with the prospects and had £75k committed by the end of the week. Once some angels heard others had committed they were prepared to invest themselves. The balance was shored up and I soon reached the magic £100k required before the Small Firms Loan could be triggered.

A KILLER THREAT FROM LEFT FIELD

Despite having made such a leap forward I still faced some short-term serious issues. I had to manage the day job as well as bring these investors on board.

A call came in from a creative agency that I had used to design our cups and the menu panels on the concession unit. I owed them £8k and had been upfront with them that I couldn't pay it until I had secured further investment in the business. They said if they weren't paid within 48 hours, in full, they would issue a winding up order against the business. This could be a disaster. A notice would be posted in the *London Gazette* and my bank account would most likely be frozen. I attempted to speak with their MD but he wasn't having any of it.

I couldn't believe this was happening. I felt I had been so careful in managing my creditors through this difficult period. I was a whisker away from nearly £200k in funds but I was still facing the end of the road if I didn't sort this and fast. I literally sat down and wrote a list of all the friends and family I could ask to help me. Martin (who had just invested in the business) and my good friends Anthony and Heath came to the rescue. This was a reminder to never take your eye off the ball. Killer threats may come at an unexpected time and from unexpected places.

LEARNING POINTS

- Don't try to build a business before you *really* know it works – hoping it all goes according to plan before your money runs out is not smart.

- Prove the concept on a small scale. If you then need to raise funds to grow the business later on you will be seen as far lower risk and hence give away less of your equity.

- Spend time listening to people who buy your product and those that don't, especially those that don't. Focus on understanding your customers and how to unlock explosive sales growth. Little else matters at this stage.

- You can spend days chasing private investors, modelling and remodelling different scenarios. Answer their questions but there then comes a point where you have to ask "Are you going to invest?" Don't let yourself be pulled around.

- Don't try to build a business by putting costs first. Sales growth ignites new business success. You want people flocking to you and talking about your offer. Sales always have to come first. Profitability is then unlikely to be an issue.

- With the product right, be confident about your pricing. Demand continued to grow as my prices increased.

- Don't be afraid to ask for help from suppliers. Most will want to help. If you can't afford to pay going rates or can't pay at all then strike a deal. Get them excited about the prospects for your business and the opportunity this presents them. Offer your loyalty once your business is proven.

- If you fail to ignite potential investors and sell yourself, you won't raise money, regardless of how good the business is. Investors know any business is only as good as its management. My early-stage investors came on board because my vision was believable, I had evidence it worked and I presented myself well. They were attracted by my confidence.

COFFEE LIKE IT'S 1999

A CHAIRMAN JOINS

ONE OF THE business angels I met in Cambridge was a little different to the others. Whilst they all brought money, Derek offered more. He came to meet me in Islington, where he asked intelligent questions and we arranged to meet again.

Derek had an interesting background. For some years he had chaired a number of growth companies and had been successful at it. We had solid discussions about Coffee Nation and he was genuinely enthusiastic about what I had and where it could go. He also brought real experience of how to get there.

We continued to talk over a period of some weeks, doing our own due diligence on each other. His previous business had been the largest independent operator of public payphones across Europe, so there was logic to his interest in Coffee Nation. There was a similarity between Coffee Nation machines and payphones; both were remote, unmanned, revenue-generating assets. I figured he could add a lot to my business. Derek proposed that he became chairman of the company and I was happy for him to do so.

Right from the start we were absolutely clear with each other that regardless of how painful the truth, it must always be told. Complete honesty was essential. It formed the bedrock of a very successful relationship that weathered various ups and downs over the next nine years.

PUTTING DEVELOPMENT FUNDING TO USE

With £190k funding now available for proper development and a chairman in place, there were two areas I needed to focus on:

1. Get the offer right – great coffee from easy-to-use machines which were clean, reliable and attractive.

2. Get big customers that could commit to a substantial numbers of sites.

I set to work on the identity of the company first. I met with a small brand and packaging design consultancy in London who had good credentials.

We started with a new brand logo. When they showed me a picture of a cappuccino in a takeaway cup on one side with coffee beans behind and a girl and a guy on the right, I knew instantly this was the logo we should use.

It worked for me because it was more about people (*Nation*) choosing our product (*Coffee*) instead of standing in line at a coffee shop. We also came up with a strapline: "Ex**press Yourself**". This was intended to have a double meaning. Be yourself, be who you want to be and *press* yourself, i.e. self-serve coffee.

The next challenge was to find a robust espresso machine. The machine I had been using was little more than a beefed up home coffee maker. Almost three years earlier I had met a coffee machine company in Minneapolis and they had the perfect machines.

They were big pieces of kit, very sturdy and with easy-to-use touch buttons that we could configure and brand as we wanted. I could see that they would be tough enough to withstand any trading environment. They had an onboard fridge for the milk and no parts to remove for cleaning. I thought this would be much easier for store staff to look after.

I met with their UK distributor in North London and then planned a trip to visit the factory in Seattle to meet their CEO. Those few days in Seattle were the start of a long and successful collaboration for both companies.

We now had the machine we needed so the next task was to develop the *shop front*, or concession that the machine would sit in. I had learnt that the more space we could take up in a store the more chance we had of attracting customers. We settled on a fibreglass unit 1.5m wide that would be backlit to stand out in a busy store. We had regular and large cups and – just like in a coffee bar – tiny espresso cups. I didn't expect to sell much espresso but it was the signature product and a mark of authenticity.

There was an integral bin, wooden stirrers, storage inside the unit, an automatic chocolate duster for cappuccinos and even an aroma pump at floor level to pump out the smell of coffee beans into the store. It had to be easy to use for customers, easy to keep clean for staff and easy to work on for maintenance purposes. This unit had to work and look good for at least four years, which was the time period over which we elected to depreciate the installation.

GOOD MANAGEMENT DISCIPLINES

Things were now moving fast and there was a terrific momentum building. Derek thought it would be a good idea to hold an annual AGM with our business angel shareholders. We arranged for one of our new machines to be powered up in our lawyer's offices so everyone could try the coffee and see the progress we were making. The night was a great success. I did a presentation, Derek fielded questions about future fundraising and there was some food and wine laid on. Martin – my first angel investor – was there too.

Two recollections stand out from the evening: being so nervous just before my presentation I had to run to the loo to throw up – funny how now I actually had the investment I got nervous – and Derek asking Martin if he thought I could make it as a CEO. I didn't like the question but I knew it wasn't personal. I had convinced people to back me with my business but there ultimately comes a time when the start-up entrepreneur has to grow into the role of CEO. I needn't have worried; I was to lead the company for the next eight years.

By now we had set up proper monthly board meetings at Baker Tilly's offices. The board comprised Derek (chairman), myself (founder/CEO) and Martin (non-executive director), with Christine from Baker Tilly in attendance. Right from this early stage I was exposed to good management disciplines which were to prove invaluable.

I wanted to test out the new concession design and espresso machine on the public before installing it on a customer's site. We couldn't build one – as a one off it would cost too much – so instead we had a full-size mock up created out of foamex and installed it for a day in a busy shopping centre in Leicester. We used a professional retail consultancy to ask passers by what they thought it was. Most people understood that it was a self-serve coffee machine. They said they thought the design looked high-quality and virtually everyone said they would be prepared to pay more than £1 for a coffee from such a machine.

PITCHING TO RETAIL PARTNERS

All we needed now were great locations for our machines where people would have a reason to buy a coffee. No more neighbourhood stores. I compiled a long list and researched names. The sectors I thought could work were oil companies (petrol forecourts), motorway service areas, supermarkets, cinemas, bookstores, fast food outlets, DIY superstores, the London Underground, airports, music retailers and health clubs.

SUMMARISING THE COFFEE NATION IDEA

To achieve success with major retailers I needed to be in the sweet spot with my message. Part of this was getting the language right and communicating it concisely. I put together a set of notes – a presentation to myself really – on Coffee Nation.

I worked out my simple core idea:

> "Smart urban gourmet coffee stations – a way of life in 21st-century Britain."

This could then be expanded to:

- An exciting new category
- Wherever people are, 24/7
- Self-serve
- Playing to a long-term trend

In my mind I purposely downplayed talking about the coffee; I knew that as soon as people heard *coffee* I would be categorised in their mind either as a vending company or as a coffee supplier. I had to keep the dialogue focused on how we were building a new, high-growth category *that happens to sell takeaway coffee.*

I then built on what we were doing for the consumer by asking the question: "Why should you have to go to a coffee bar or cafe for a good coffee? People love coffee, not the staff that serve it."

In others areas of retail similar things were happening, with the old way of doing things being overturned. This included interactive multimedia kiosks (just appearing at that time), self-scanning in supermarkets, and food served on conveyors in YO! Sushi.

I then thought about the coffee market. The coffee bars were the vanguard of the revolution, awakening people to great coffee. Of course, there would be many high street locations for coffee bars, but I saw us as the evolution, putting gourmet coffee in tiny spaces, for example inside other retailers – only the largest of which could accommodate a full coffee bar offer. We were creating mass access – taking great coffee to the people, wherever they were in their day.

The final piece of the jigsaw was how this would work for the host location. Having come a long way in developing the concept I realised that we could never offer the highest margin to the retailer, which is what people looked at traditionally. I would set out that as creators of this new, self-serve gourmet coffee category, we would maximise the cash profits generated for the host site, not by giving them the highest margin but by actually maximising sales of coffee. Our focus was on real cash profits, not paper margins.

MAKING CALLS

I condensed all of this into a few key statements in the form of a crib sheet for making calls. The next job was to get names and phone numbers and get some appointments. I swallowed hard picking the phone up for the first time. My target was different now. I was after retail and development directors of some of the biggest names on the British retail and consumer landscape. I knew I had to get in at the top. New initiatives happen because they get senior buy-in; they can get stuck if introduced lower down as middle management usually lack the authority to take risks with new ideas.

Some days I didn't make any calls if I didn't feel in the right mindset. I had to defeat the inevitable "Thank you but we already have our coffee suppliers" and "You'll need to speak to the buyer" responses. I combated these by recognising they weren't trying to get rid of me, they just didn't understand.

I explained that we were different and were carefully choosing which retailers we wanted to work with. They hadn't seen our category before and I was certain their boss would want to talk to me. Slowly, things started to happen. I quite literally didn't take no for an answer and when I finally got through to the key person I usually found we were talking the same language: how to wow customers, bring more people through the door, keep them inside for longer and get them spending. Most were interested in hearing what I had to say and across the summer of 1999 my diary was virtually full meeting potential customers.

I met with a long list of companies including Esso, BP, Marks & Spencer, B&Q, Waitrose, Safeway, Rank Leisure (Odeon Cinemas), Warner Village Cinemas (now Vue), Holiday Inn Express, Topnotch Health Clubs, Homebase, BAA (now Heathrow Airport Holdings), Boots, Currys, Our Price and London Underground.

TEXACO AND WELCOME BREAK

One meeting was with Texaco at the end of May. As usual I had aimed high, attempting to get to the directors of the company, and although I had failed to reach them I had been referred to a manager who did have authority to make real decisions. I met her in Canary Wharf where Texaco was based. She liked the concept and explained that they already sold coffee but it was a bit of an amateurish operation and was with instant coffee anyway.

I explained that we were looking to undertake trials and if successful we were then seeking roll-out contracts. There was no commitment beyond the trial, but that was the game plan. "Great, ok, we'd love to work with you," she said. I don't think I heard this for some minutes as I continued to talk enthusiastically. She actually stopped me and said, "Er, Martyn, we're in – let's get the trial agreement from you and move forward." This was the moment all entrepreneurs love – the thrill of the big breakthrough.

Our trial agreement was signed with Texaco and we then gained a commitment from the retail director of Welcome Break Motorway Service Areas (MSA) to trial Coffee Nation. Their immediate interest was to replace a low-price Kenco offer in their petrol forecourt stores. I could see another opportunity though, which was to position Coffee Nation within the main buildings of each MSA.

My thinking was that we could be in the general retail store that sold sandwiches, cold drinks, newspapers and all manner of motoring paraphernalia. That way if customers visited the main building wanting a coffee they could get a fast solution rather than lining up in the main catering area. Welcome Break liked the idea. This was our first trial where we were not replacing another coffee offer – instead we were potentially creating new demand.

OPERATIONS DIRECTOR COMES ONBOARD

It was time to recruit the next member of the team, an operations director. One of our suppliers suggested someone they knew who could be up for a new career challenge. I knew the man they were talking about. He was running a group within Unilever called Branded Concepts Group (BCG), which I had met the year before at the Alldays store in Edinburgh. In fact, I think I had asked him if BCG wanted to invest in Coffee Nation.

I called Scott and we agreed to meet at the Design Museum in Islington. We talked about him joining the company and he pretty much said right away that he'd love to. This meeting had not been arranged through expensive headhunters or recruitment firms and there was no brief or job description written. This was all put in place later but we agreed that he would join the company on a handshake. He shared my vision of what we could achieve with Coffee Nation and was ready to make the jump from big company life. He joined as operations director on 18 October 1999 and soon we were working well together as a team. Scott would go on to make an enormous contribution to the success of the company.

Part of the value that Derek brought right from the start was an appreciation of the steps that had to be taken and in what order to achieve the goal of getting the business established on a sound footing to enable rapid growth. Appointing an operations director early on was one step in this process.

Getting great people onboard once you have enough evidence that you are on to something is essential if you are going to truly seize the opportunity. Judging the timing is critical. Lou had been far too early and he'd paid the price for this with his job. It's through the combined efforts of a passionate and aligned team that great start-ups become great businesses.

Having access to a sharp mind that had been through all of this before was so valuable. Derek was always positive in his outlook with me and was always a great sounding board. Risks are high at this stage and the lone entrepreneur is vulnerable to tackling the wrong issue at the wrong time or failing to address a potentially fatal risk.

TRIALS BEGIN AT SERVICE STATIONS

As we progressed into the autumn, plans were coming together for the launch of our trials. There was to be one machine with Texaco in Clerkenwell, London, and two with Welcome Break, one at Oxford services on the M40 motorway in the petrol forecourt shop, where we would replace two Kenco machines, and one in the retail shop at Warwick Services also on the M40.

Clerkenwell Road opened on 27 October 1999. We had been furnished with sales data from the previous Nescafé instant coffee machine that Texaco had operated at that forecourt. The results were astonishing. Within one month of launch:

- Weekly drink sales volumes were up 56% to around 500 cups per week.
- Cash sales were up by 260% to £558 per week.
- Profit for Texaco was up by 19% to £139 per week.

We had increased the selling price from 55p to £1.20. It's funny now to think of how cautious I was of increasing the drink price when few coffee drinks are available for less than double that price today. This was the power of timing in a new business; customers were ready to pay more, they just needed someone to come up with a reason for them to do so.

Scott and I virtually lived at Clerkenwell Road; I spent an entire weekend there to witness customer behaviour. It was a great site to launch with. The legendary nightclub Turnmills was virtually opposite and the store traded around the clock so it was a real baptism of fire for our operating model. We sold quite a lot of coffee in the early hours to some pretty wasted customers, but it all worked. While there, Scott and I could never resist the temptation to go up and clean the shelf of sticky stirrers and napkins! One customer even told us what she thought:

> "I walked past, thought what the bloody hell is that – I've just got to have a coffee – beautiful coffee, beautiful machine!"

Within a few weeks we had anecdotal evidence we were bringing more people into the store. I asked one customer why he hadn't gone to the very contemporary Benugo cafe at the end of the road. He replied that he can't get coffee, a newspaper and a sandwich there, but he could now at Texaco.

A few weeks after opening in Texaco we launched our two Welcome Break locations. The results were just as strong. Versus the previous Kenco offer in the Oxford Services forecourt shop we increased Welcome Break's profits by 15%, actually exceeding what they previously took in cash. At Warwick we were quickly generating some £900 per week in revenue where they hadn't even sold coffee before. We were clocking up 2400 drinks sold per week from these three machines. Given the results we didn't waste a minute in seeking to clarify the position of both retailers. We wanted a commitment to roll-out from both.

In less than eight weeks from launch Texaco wrote to us confirming they would commit to a further 15 London locations for Coffee Nation. The retail director of Welcome Break wrote: "Following successful trials we intend to roll-out to as many sites in our network as commercially viable." They believed they could identify 40 locations to start with. This gave us a combined commitment for 55 installations from two large companies.

SEEKING GROWTH FINANCE

With success from our trials and commitments to add a substantial number of sites, now was the time to write a new business plan. We didn't yet have commitment for trials with other customers, but Texaco and Welcome Break together would take us a long way. Our thinking was that we should be able to build an infrastructure that would support those 55 sites and achieve break-even. That way we wouldn't be burning our cash reserves and it would then be a case of waiting to land the next major customer to grow the business to the next level, and so on.

Of course, a business plan without any money wouldn't get us far. We were working through the cash we had raised from our angels in Cambridge at a fair pace and so now was the time we finally did need to raise substantial roll-out funding. I'd written my first business plan back in 1996 but the only one that had mattered so far was the one I used to raise the seed capital in 1998. That had got me this far. We were now going to enter an even more competitive world of companies vying for growth capital; we would need to be at the top of our game.

Corporate finance advisers were needed who could make the introductions to the appropriate sources of funding and help us develop our business plan and presentation. Derek had a good relationship with Deloitte and so introduced me to one of their partners. This was to become a long-standing relationship as they became our auditor.

We also met with Ashurst, the City law firm. We had important contracts to get right with new customers and suppliers, as well as new shareholders agreements with an incoming investor. Neither of these firms routinely worked with start-up businesses but the combination of Derek's previous business relationship with both firms, a compelling business proposition, Texaco and Welcome Break's commitments to more locations and my passion brought them onboard.

As 1999 drew to a close my priorities shifted from building a tranche of trial customers to ensuring all was working at Texaco and Welcome Break and developing a sensible business plan. Scott focused on operations with both customers. We had to deal with issues of wasted drinks and housekeeping standards. There would inevitably be teething issues with a new product like this being operated by a retailer's own staff.

In parallel with this we were on site a lot of the time, talking to customers and educating them that this wasn't great coffee from a machine or great coffee for a petrol station. It was great coffee full stop. This always proved to be one of our constant challenges – getting people to recognise that our coffee was no different to that served in a coffee bar. We had put the same equipment into a different location and made it easy for people to use.

This had been the year we had proved the product, the business and operating model all in the right locations. Next year – 2000 – would be when we'd see if we could actually start to grow a company.

Scott had the last laugh as we ended the year. He called me on Boxing Day morning when I was driving to my father's house, with Trudi and my daughter with me in the car.

He told me that our machine at Warwick had caught fire and caused major damage to Welcome Break's building. I turned white. Then he followed up with, "Only joking – Happy Christmas!"

"You bastard," I replied.

LEARNING POINTS

- Find low-cost methods of testing consumer demand. Not just once, but as your concept evolves through multiple trials.

- Invite someone who has been through the growth company experience to join you. They can add value by helping you plan what to do next. Identifying what the key milestones are and reaching them is vital. This sounds simple but it is surprisingly challenging for the first-time entrepreneur. The experienced, objective and dispassionate adviser/chairman/non-executive director can make for a powerful combination with the passionate and inexperienced entrepreneur, who is not always as objective as is necessary.

- I quickly learnt the value of monthly board meetings. It's an opportunity to down tools, stand back from the day to day and discuss progress objectively, without distraction.

- If your market is other businesses, find out who you need to speak to and then phone them or send them a well crafted letter (email) setting out the clear commercial benefit you can bring to their organisation. Finish by saying exactly when you will call them. Call them when you said you would and keep calling back until they have taken your call.

- When you get the call, have prepared what you are going to say and say it with precision and confidence. I downplayed *coffee* and focused on *new category*. No one wants to miss out on the next big thing, least of all the PA that didn't put your call through.

- Avoid buyers in big companies like the plague. Most are paid to buy at the lowest price and lack imagination. If you have something new they won't know where to put you so you might as well start with the CEO. You never know, you might just get him/her onboard then things will move fast.

- Set the agenda and drive the pace with corporate customers. We had a letter of commitment to roll-out with Texaco within eight weeks of our trial going live – because we asked for it. If you don't ask you won't get.

- Starting salary should not be the reason anyone joins a young company of high-growth potential. Tell the story to attract great people.

- Recognise the transition you will need to make from entrepreneur to CEO/entrepreneur as your business starts to grow. Learn from others who have made this change.

- Accountants and corporate finance advisers become necessary and valuable partners. Establish that yours have the resources, capability and track record to deliver what you need today and as your business grows in the future.

2000 – RAISING A MILLION

A NEW BUSINESS PLAN

THE NEW YEAR got off to a flying start. Before the end of January we had a letter from Welcome Break committing to an initial roll-out across their forecourts and they had identified 15 retail shop locations where we would fit in terms of space and economics.

We were busy preparing the business plan we would use for fundraising. Deloitte fielded a great team to help us. We also met with RBS, who were to become the company's bankers as well as a loyal and supportive partner over the coming years.

The plan started to take shape. Part of this was to have a team of Brand Guardians who would visit sites and audit housekeeping standards as well as help each site grow sales. There would be a round-the-clock call centre operating from Coffee Nation's offices (we called them Coffee Nation angels!), who would be able to take calls from sites and provide a troubleshooting service. Our machines would all be maintained by our UK machine distributor. Our trial locations continued to perform well and we set a target to pay back the cost of each machine inside 12 months, which the trial machines were achieving on a run-rate basis, more or less.

A key challenge in writing the business plan was how to predict the growth rate of the company. We had commitments for 55 installations from our launch customers, as well as agreements to trial with another group of clients, including Our Price, Blackwell Retail, Currys and Tesco. This could take us to upwards of 100 locations in year 1. The difficulty was that the plan had to be exciting enough to get the attention of professional investors, but not so ambitious that it would be seen as unrealistic.

We decided to focus on motorways and petrol forecourts as the major sectors, followed by cinemas, supermarkets, music stores, bookstores and offices. If we took all the companies we were talking to across these sectors there were some 6000 potential locations (most being petrol forecourts, motorway service stations, supermarkets and offices). We figured that to penetrate 10% of these within three years of launch seemed an ambitious but nonetheless achievable target, so the year 1 target was set at 133 and year 3 was 616 locations. Of course, until we undertook trials in some of these sectors we would have no real idea as to their commercial viability. Setting targets is a difficult line to tread for an early-stage business.

Our plan covered a five-year period to March 2005 and took us to just short of 1100 sites by that time. In a more mature business you should know what is going to happen in the year ahead and have a reasonable idea for the year after, with uncertainties increasing as you look out three years and beyond. We were shooting for four-year contracts from our launch customers so this would give us a degree of certainty, but until we landed more of these we could not be certain of the growth trajectory the business would take. We identified this issue in the 'Risks' section of our business plan.

I started talking about Coffee Nation as the 'ATM of coffee'. This was a really short statement that used an analogy with a completely different product and category to help visualise what we were about. It was helpful that ATMs are ubiquitous and that was also a useful image to convey, i.e. that soon we could be everywhere.

Our mission on page 1 of the plan was: "To establish the company as the leading European brand of self-serve gourmet coffee stations." Simple, focused and believable. This also helps people – whether that's investors, customers, suppliers or potential employees – understand quickly what you are about.

We had a powerful quote from Welcome Break that we incorporated into our plan: "If all goes according to plan we should be doing about £5m of sales on coffee at retail selling price – if you'd come in and said that two months ago we'd probably have all fallen about laughing."

Our eventual investor told me later on that our plan had nearly hit the bin because the last line of the executive summary said "Make this your first great decision of the New Millennium." I remember writing this and feeling so passionate about it but potential investors see so many opportunities that it really can be difficult to see past this froth and bullshit to an underlying sound venture. Avoid cheesy statements.

When the plan was done, Derek said to me at the time that regardless of how well I thought I knew my business now, it would take me at least another two years before I really understood it. This was good advice as no matter how much you know you will be tested many times not just in your understanding of your space but also in your ability to flex and adapt to changing circumstances.

I had set out a one-page vision for the company that I stuck on the wall in my office. This was full of bold statements including touch-screen drink selection, 1000 sites in three years, *nutraceutical* drink additives (vitamin shots in the coffee!), etc. Having a grand vision is essential but I learnt quickly that your vision must be focused. Rapid growth is usually about finding the single line of least resistance to gaining real traction and then exploiting this relentlessly. For us this meant selling as many cups of coffee from as many machines as quickly as possible. The more you narrow the focus the stronger you get. Most successful companies do one thing brilliantly and focus on that almost to the exclusion of all else.

PRIVATE EQUITY INVESTOR ROADSHOW

We started our investor roadshow early in 2000. We met or had calls with a long list of private equity investors, including 3i, Gresham, Pi Capital, Close Bros., ECI Ventures, Phildrew Ventures and Advent.

Among other things, we were questioned as to the competitive threat. Of course, it was easy to imagine that we would be easily seen off by the likes of Starbucks, who by then had acquired Seattle Coffee Company in the UK and were expanding, or a company like Kraft, who owned the Kenco brand we had displaced in the Welcome Break trials. It was critical we didn't appear defensive and we needed to answer these kinds of questions intelligently and convincingly. Shaky answers to first meeting questions could mean no second meeting and, as Derek reminded me, you'll never know the real reason they say no.

Interestingly, the retail director at Welcome Break knew Kraft well and said to me in passing that he didn't see them as a threat. Coffee Nation was a nimble start-up whereas Kraft was a global organisation who wouldn't be able to mobilise quickly to compete with us. To get this kind of statement from a customer was brilliant; he was a real ally.

The more we thought about it we also came to realise that whilst it was easy to imagine Starbucks entering our space, in reality we felt it was unlikely they would. Starbucks was a public company and to continue its growth in earnings it was going to stick to its model and roll out coffee bars around the world. That was what it knew. Why would their management divert attention to chase a niche of which they had no experience with a completely different operating model to what they had invested so much in creating?

This proved to be an accurate view of the world. We decided not to concern ourselves with potential competition until it became real. We had one job to do; gain an unassailable lead in the marketplace, secured with long-term customer contracts. That would give us room to land the next customer, then the next customer, and so on.

Eventually we believed customers would start to question the value in meeting competitors (if we had any) when Coffee Nation had a long list of contracts from prestigious customers. Derek recalled a saying from his earlier career: "No one ever got fired for choosing IBM." We had to become the IBM of self-serve gourmet coffee.

It was late February and we had seen plenty of potential funders. In fact I don't think we were turned down for a first meeting by any. We had been back for second meetings with two or three. Nonetheless, we couldn't escape the fact that we hadn't nailed a deal. Whilst we had considerable goodwill with our launch customers – we had demonstrated the commercial potential of Coffee Nation – and they were likely to stay with us until we had the funds to roll-out, I was also lining up trial agreements with other companies and these trials couldn't be launched without fresh funding.

There was a danger that we could lose momentum, not to mention run out of cash. There was an increasing tension on my time between progressing discussions with potential new customers on the one hand and, on the other, doing whatever it took to attract funding.

FEEDBACK ON OUR PROPOSAL

We did get useful feedback from one investor. They were concerned about the relative inexperience of the management team, felt the business was too early-stage for them to invest in and were also concerned that we were exposed to a single critical supplier, i.e. our machine supplier in Seattle. They also expressed a concern that we were trying to raise too much money in one go for this early stage. This feedback was useful. It gave us a steer on what might be going through the minds of not just that investor, but others too.

We were able to modify our funding requirements and in the end something nearer £4m looked sensible. If the business was performing strongly there would never be a problem in raising more money.

Management experience was a trickier question. There was not a lot we could do about who we were and Derek did add considerable gravitas in the sense of someone who'd been there and done it. Of course, he was the non-executive chairman, not a full time member of the management team. To some potential investors the experience of the team would be a problem whilst to others it wouldn't. That was just life.

Likewise, we could understand that investors might consider us too early-stage. Many preferred to invest in management buy-outs (MBOs) of already established and profitable companies where risks were far lower. Again, there was not much we could do about this. Maybe we would need to do this in two stages after all; another tranche of business angel funding to take us part way and then private equity once we were a safer, more established business? To be honest none of us relished this as we just wanted to be focused on building the company, not forever having one eye on fundraising.

One investor asked us to prepare a paper showing how we could grow the business faster. This I couldn't believe. Whilst some said we weren't investable because we lacked sufficient experience, now others were saying go faster. It really did feel like a lottery.

Nonetheless, we drafted a new document with an extended view out to seven years and we included Europe. To be honest we all thought it was a pointless exercise. We really didn't know beyond what we had committed from Welcome Break and Texaco, so how the hell could we say what would happen seven years down the line? Nonetheless if this is what it took to raise our money, so be it.

The investor called a week later to say that all but one of its management committee was in favour of investing in our business. Unfortunately, their constitution meant that one vote against and they would have to turn down what could be a great proposition. Tragically, that is what happened with us. We were all dressed up with nowhere to go.

AN APPROACH FROM BP

At this time, we were in discussions with BP about installing Coffee Nation in their petrol forecourts. Their forecourt shop offer was quite limited and they told us they were planning a major investment in this area. We had had several meetings with them and they accompanied us to our machine distributor's premises to see how the machine worked. They then made an offer which took us by complete surprise.

They did want to commit to work with us and were talking about potentially hundreds of locations up and down the UK. This couldn't be better. BP was the most prestigious customer, without doubt, in the roadside market. But there was a catch, a big one. What they were interested in was our operating system, which meant all of what we did in store and behind the scenes to make our business work. They wanted to pick this up and roll it out right across their estate. The catch was that it wouldn't be called Coffee Nation.

They effectively were asking us to provide a white label solution that they would then brand as they chose. On the plus side it was great that they could see the value in what we had created and had decided that it would be much easier to work with us rather than attempt to develop their own solution. But why not let us build our brand in their sites?

BP were hardly known for their coffee and if we rolled out with them under the Coffee Nation name our brand would be seen in more and more locations providing trust and reassurance to the consumer, assuming we consistently delivered great coffee in every site. None of this was lost on them and we got the feeling they believed what we were saying, but what they were telling us – that they would roll out with their own branding – had come from the highest levels in the company.

We had a decision to make. In the end, it wasn't a difficult one – our plan said we would be the leading brand of self-serve gourmet coffee and that was what we were committed to. If we deviated now before we were even beyond pilot stage, what hope was there for us in the future? Had we accepted this white label offer, undoubtedly we would then have been in a weaker position when negotiating with other companies. We believed it would be difficult to offer a white label solution and be committed to building our own brand in parallel. How many other companies would want to see their own name over our machines instead of the Coffee Nation name?

Looking back we were always glad we turned down this offer. We would have become a machine supply company and likely have suffered from lower margins. We would have been almost completely a business-to-business company. Why would we have cared about the consumer when the consumer wouldn't even know who we were? We never knew what happened to this project inside BP but their Wild Bean coffee shop appeared soon after.

PRIMARY CAPITAL INVESTS

One potential investor we met – Primary Capital – had raised their first fund in 1997 and was now busy investing it. They had received our business plan and Derek knew their CEO. We were invited to meet them and present our case. Their main focus was, like many others, investing in later-stage developed businesses and often for management teams to buy their companies from the owners. We didn't fit this mould but they said they would be prepared to invest in earlier-stage businesses in exceptional circumstances.

They also highlighted that they saw hundreds of business plans each year but at that stage had made just four investments. The odds were hardly in our favour. We went for it. Within a week or so we were back for a follow-up meeting. In fact, there were a number of follow-up meetings in quick succession and we had soon met the entire team of four directors. Derek, Scott and I joked that the telltale sign that things were moving our way was the good food (hot mini sausages!) that was laid out for us in the follow-up meetings.

The news we had all been hoping for finally came; they made their offer in late March. They set out in their offer letter that they were willing to invest £1m in ordinary shares and a further £2m in cumulative redeemable preference shares. A further £1m of preference shares was available on the same terms later if required.

The preference shares were interest bearing and the interest would be rolled up and paid on 31 December 2005, or on exit if at an earlier date. This was an all equity offer and meant that there was no need for any secondary debt, mezzanine finance or equipment leasing.

Their rationale was simple and this is how they explained it:

1. Very high growth of UK coffee market.

2. Our unique offering in a new market segment, complementary to branded coffee bars and giving us a significant first-mover advantage.

3. Compelling financial case for host customers as well as providing an increase in consumer service.

4. Management had demonstrated an impressive ability to grow the business from scratch and were highly committed to its success.

5. As a development capital opportunity the potential returns were seen as commensurate with the increased risk (this meant the potential returns outweighed the fact that we were an early-stage business).

Scott and I were out visiting sites on the day we got the great news. At long last we had the funds to fuel our growth. We could now formalise our agreements with Welcome Break, Texaco and our machine supplier into long-term contracts. We were on our way! Time for a cigar and out came the champagne. What a truly wonderful moment.

On that day we met one of our first employees. Scott was keen to introduce me to the guy who ran the wine shop in his village. He didn't say anything but after we left the shop I said how helpful the sales assistant behind the counter had been. He certainly knew all about wine and cigars. Scott told me he had got to know him since moving to the village and thought he'd make an excellent member of the team, utterly committed to great service and passionate about his product. I couldn't agree more and we made a note to speak to him again the moment we had completed with Primary.

It felt as if we now just had to keep the faith, hold our nerve and we would get there. This is so often the way with start-ups. It was almost four years since I had left my consultancy business to launch a new venture and only now was I really at the start line. Winston Churchill once said, "If you're going through hell, keep going" and at times the last four years had indeed felt like hell.

Our new investors wanted to move fast and of course had seen fit to avoid the threat of competitive offers. We worked through due diligence towards a completion set for late May, which in the event turned into early June after due diligence by both sides. This process involved Primary visiting all of our locations to check on our operations and taking references on those involved with Coffee Nation.

All proceeded well – it was important that we maintained the good news and pace throughout the pre-investment period. We prepared detailed updates of trading that we could send to Primary, pushed on with drafting of customer contracts and worked to finesse the detail of the first six month's installation programme. The more confidence that we could give Primary that in the first few months after their investment we would deliver what we said we would the better. Scott started talking to a property agent about new offices and worked up the contract for our machine supply. We were able to secure the factory's commitment that we would be their exclusive customer for the self-serve marketplace and aside from existing customers they would not sell to anyone attempting to compete with Coffee Nation on a similar model.

Primary worked through the due diligence. They took references on each of us and I spoke to companies they had already invested in. Of course, as a new fund they hadn't made any exits yet. We all got on well and we liked the fact they were a small team. Their aim was to see the company sold or floated within five years and our funding would come from their No.1 Fund, which had been raised in 1997. Five years felt a long way off but Derek cautioned me that this wasn't long at all, particularly starting from scratch as we effectively were.

In reality it is almost unheard of for a business to be sold successfully within five years of start-up. Almost every early-stage business over estimates its potential growth rate and we were probably no exception. It is simply impossible to know how fast a venture will grow and particularly one where a new category is created and consumer habits are being changed.

The Primary team visited all of our locations and met with Texaco and Welcome Break. One of our machines was not working when one of the Primary team visited, which of course was not what we wanted. Nonetheless, he asked the check-out staff about us, what customers thought about the product and how we responded to problems. Of course, we had briefed them all to expect a visit from a potential investor but they spoke their minds. Fortunately they said they had very few issues with the machine, customers loved the coffee, and Scott and I were good guys.

Deals always seem to take forever and then come together very quickly. We completed on 9 June 2000, with our customer and supplier contracts being signed the night before. I had started down this path back in May 1996. It had been quite a journey in every sense. We were all in great spirits.

There was a completion lunch at the Asia de Cuba restaurant at the St Martin's Lane Hotel in the West End. I still have the menu from that day. We were all there: Derek, Scott, myself, Martin, Neil (our newly appointed non-executive director from Primary who would sit on our board to oversee their investment), one of the Deloitte team and Amani (my assistant I had hired after I had raised the business angel funding).

We had a great lunch and met up with Trudi later on and drank a lot more. Before we all headed in separate directions that night Derek said to me, "Have a great weekend Martyn, you deserve it. But be ready because on Monday the hard work really starts." This stopped me in my tracks – Christ, what the hell had the last four years been?

Of course, I knew what he meant and he was absolutely right. The start-up to growth journey is the toughest game there is. Those four years of my life had been bloody hard work and I had had to dig deep into my resolve and tenacity to keep going. Now we had the funding and could not afford to waste a moment in starting to build the company.

NEW PREMISES, NEW TEAM MEMBERS

Monday morning came around all too soon. I had a meeting with Waterstones bookstores planned that day and of course felt super confident. I was soon brought down to size. Just because we had funds in the business it didn't mean the world would beat a path to our door. At that point, don't forget, we still had just four machines trading. Waterstones were interested but, as with so many of these large businesses, decisions were not taken quickly and we had to work with this and not against it.

In our business plan we had set out future management needs and the most immediate requirement was to recruit a finance director. We appointed a recruitment firm and of course we enlisted Deloitte's help in the process. Our person needed to understand life in a small, fast-growth business and recognise that they would probably have to put in place the necessary financial disciplines themselves. Not having an entire finance function around them means the FD role in a small company can be very hard work and long hours. We needed someone principled, rigorous and who operated to the highest standards.

Our successful candidate was actually known to one of the lawyers representing Primary on the deal with us. Vivien was a strong character. I thought it would be great to have a woman on the board and she said she wanted to make the move to a small business and work with it to help it grow. She also impressed me when she said we needed to run the business to young public company standards. The FD is such an important board member in any company and particularly one that is intending to grow. They are the navigator on the bridge of the ship, helping you plot a course towards your goal, but avoiding nasty icebergs and other perils along the way. Vivien's appointment completed the board at that time.

Our next step was to develop a new concession unit to replace the hand-built work of art that our trials had used. We had identified a company called Sloane Group in Wellingborough, Northamptonshire. They were a trusted designer, developer and supplier of in-store fixtures for major retailers.

Sloane did a great job and developed the messaging all the way down from brand logo and strapline to product imagery and photography and on to menu, drink descriptions, cup size options and pricing. The first units would be ready for installation by September.

Our first board meetings were held in Primary's offices but we had soon found an amazing building we could call home. We needed a new office as my tiny space in Islington was now home to myself, Scott, Vivien and Amani. We moved into a warehouse type space in a building called Highgate Studios in Kentish Town, north west London, between Camden and Highgate. Of course, we had a Coffee Nation machine and one of the new concessions installed in the office so we could all drink our product every day.

It really was a terrific time. Scott and I were busy recruiting the early team. Tim from Scott's village wine shop joined us and so did Toby, Del, Shane and Richard. Shane planned the installation schedules, ensuring that the space had been allocated, previous fixtures removed and that power, mains water and waste drainage plumbing were all in place prior to Coffee Nation's arrival. Toby, Tim and Richard were all Brand Guardians, and Del was administrator for this group. We didn't pick anyone based on education or qualifications. We chose people for their energy and their enthusiasm for what we were doing. We didn't have to pay anyone more than their previous roles and were able to maintain this style of recruitment for some years to come.

The culture of the organisation was so desperately important to us all. My primary leadership task was to communicate our vision and align the whole team to deliver on that goal. We were going to be the leading self-serve gourmet coffee brand in Europe. We were able to attract great people because we had energy, a clear sense of purpose and we offered the chance to work with the board of the company and influence its direction. If people delivered they would get on in the company. I also think people had the chance to grow and develop more in this kind of environment than in a more compartmentalised larger business. Salaries had to be competitive but this was never the driver in people's decision to want to join us.

Over the years, visitors often commented on the easy yet professional feeling in Coffee Nation's offices. To be honest, we did have plenty of laughs although probably not enough. Friday nights were often spent in the Highgate Bar literally just opposite the office. Despite the playful side, we were serious, intense and focused. First impressions could be misleading. People either fitted in or they didn't. It was that clear, there was no in between. People learnt quickly that no one was going to do it for them, if they had an idea – great, go make it happen. The high-growth entrepreneurial world isn't for everyone and that's fine.

Scott and I also debated at length an employee share option scheme which other members of our board were ambivalent about. We did implement this under an Enterprise Management Incentive Scheme (EMIS) and a number of our early team members got to own a small slice of the company, which we celebrated with them. Upon reflection, I don't think these guys worked any harder or were any more committed or loyal for having these options, but it was good to reward our founding team for their enormous contribution.

Scott developed the site operations manuals and the site audit for our Brand Guardians to use. We decided to call this our Quality

Crusade as we would live and die by the quality of every drink we dispensed. If this was to really take off we had to make sure our self-serve coffee bars were kept looking as good as high street coffee bars. Vivien got to work on office set up and IT as well as putting into place the management accounting and reporting systems.

There was a frugality about the operation. We all mucked in together and made do. Rather than splash out on expensive office furniture we bought a boardroom table on the cheap from a business that had ceased trading just down the corridor. Eight years later we were still using the same table.

ROLL-OUT

We started our roll-out in September and by December were achieving monthly sales of £100k. Our concessions proudly stated "Europe's Leading Self-Serve Gourmet Coffee" across the top. My chairman questioned the statement, given we had less than ten machines trading at that time, but for me it was all about a sense of authority in our category and communicating the vision. We had to convince retailers that selling gourmet coffee in a self-serve format could be a highly profitable operation, provide great customer service and potentially attract more customers to their location.

I was right to continue to worry about this as it was to take much longer than any of us had anticipated to secure the next major customer. That is part of the challenge with disruptive start-ups that take consumers in a new direction. They can take time to gain momentum and this phase can often take much longer than anticipated. If you have a winner it will take off, but enormous patience is needed by everyone.

Around this time, someone picked up a weekend copy of the *Telegraph* to see our first mention in the press. There was a full-page article called the 'Froth Report' with a journalist giving his verdict on the growing number of coffee bars springing up across Britain's high streets at the time. We got more stars than Starbucks or Caffè Nero and only Coffee Republic's drinks were rated higher.

The piece said: "You'll find these vending machines appearing in more and more petrol stations serving espresso (£1.20) that is actually better quality than most of the coffee chains." He didn't rate our cappuccino though, saying it was "scalding and thin on foam." Fun, and of course all completely subjective, but we hated the "vending machine" statement. This was anathema to us. We'd need a public relations firm to manage our message.

The year drew to a close. Installations were going well and we gained agreement to trial with Focus Do it All DIY stores and Megabowl bowling alleys just before Christmas. We really went for it at our inaugural Christmas party. We laid on a limo to collect us from the office to take us to the bar and restaurant in Soho. We were on our way!

LEARNING POINTS

- Start-up business plans are notoriously unreliable as indicators of future growth. Whatever your planned growth rate, build up the timetable line by line and challenge yourself as to its realism.

- Take time to articulate key future risks to growth and talk these through with your incoming investors. How will you respond to each of these risks? It's your response to these risks that will most likely determine the outcome you get with investors.

- Don't oversell or avoid discussing weaknesses and threats with investors for fear you will put them off. This is far more likely to undermine their confidence in you than an honest appraisal of the challenges ahead.

- The greater certainty you can put in place around the first year or so following investment the better. It will help you build your investor's trust and confidence in you.

- Exploit your unique advantage. Success usually follows from repeating this over and over and getting better and better at this single line of attack. The more you stand for a single thing, the less you have to stand for everything.

- Define the financial critical success factor for your business. Do not take your eye off this.

- Private equity funds are invested during the first phase of their life and then realised during the second half, with the aim that the entire fund has been realised by the end of the period, usually ten years. The later into this cycle your business receives investment the less time you have to grow the company and realise an exit.

- It will take you considerable time to get to really understand the business you are in. Any company seeking to compete and enter your space will have to climb the same learning curve.

- Substitutes adjacent to or from outside your category are as likely to be the significant threat to your growth as direct competition, certainly in the early days.

- Recruit for where you want to get to, not for where you are.

2001 – A YEAR FOR LEARNING

A PRESSING MATTER

WHEN WE WERE testing the market and before we'd raised our roll-out funding we were paranoid that someone would notice what we were up to and enter the market alongside us. We kept things quiet; we didn't want to draw attention to our business model.

Now we had the opposite problem – nobody knew what Coffee Nation was and we needed to change that if we were going to reach our ambitious growth targets. We needed publicity. I rang up the Public Relations Consultants Association, explained who we were and told them we needed a PR firm to help us get our message in front of the right audience.

The firm I chose was one of the UK's biggest PR agencies. They fielded an account director and their managing director, who were both great people. We had two battles to fight:

1.   Get noticed by more companies who could offer us tens or hundreds of locations.

2.   Start to register in the minds of consumers. We needed to educate them as to what we were about.

We spent time educating our PR team on what made Coffee Nation unique. They needed to understand it if they were going to succeed at pitching the story to the media. With PR you have to drive the process and the agency, or nothing happens. They can't do it for you. They are the conduit to the media and you have to feed them the raw material that they can turn into compelling news.

Our agency didn't let us down in our attempt to punch above our weight. One of the first pieces of press coverage was a full-page article in the *Sunday Express*. The headline was 'Cream of Café Society' and the sub-headline was 'The founder of Coffee Nation aims to be a big hit with his caffeine-loving customers by providing a machine drink that actually tastes good'.

None of us liked the "machine drink" reference because we wanted to be understood as an unmanned coffee bar, not an upmarket vending machine, but these were early days and the journalist had a good point. Almost everyone has had a dire cup of coffee from an office vending machine.

We also worked with the PR team on crisis management procedures. We were selling a food product and consumer safety and wellbeing was critical. We had to consider everything from a customer being scalded to the caffeine content of our coffees and the ethics of our coffee roaster. It was good to be able to point to Coffee Nation in the press when we were talking to potential customers.

PR was undoubtedly a useful part of the mix in those early days, although it is very difficult to quantify any tangible commercial benefit we gained from that coverage at the time. What I did realise was that all of this activity needed to be sustained over a long period if it is to be of real value; it is easy to be forgotten by people if your press coverage does not continue.

SEEKING NEW LOCATIONS

The urgent priority now was to secure more locations. We had launched in a second tranche of Texaco sites, although all was not good. Early indications were that they weren't selling the quantities we had expected. Site selection was still an inexact science at this stage.

Our monthly reports included sales statistics so we could see how many cups per day each site was generating. It built up into a valuable picture of winners and losers, seasonality and like-for-like growth rates from one year to the next. It was a document that was eagerly awaited and read in detail by all.

Fortunately though there was some good news coming out of our estate. Our machines at Oxford on the M40 were going from strength to strength, reaching 2000 cups sold per week. Welcome Break told us that this meant our *regular* and *large* drinks were now the first and third highest selling products at that location, which at the time was the busiest petrol forecourt in Western Europe.

We also started to experiment with locating machines in the lobby areas of Welcome Break motorway service areas. The staff from the retail shops would clean and fill these machines each day and these became our first installations with a cash mechanism so the customer actually paid at the machine. Over time these became successful and made a useful contribution. It showed us that in large sites we could have multiple touch points with the customer, maximising convenience and delivering incremental sales growth.

Expanding on motorways beyond Welcome Break was always going to be tricky, particularly at this early stage. They wanted us all to themselves. Discussions with other petrol forecourt operators were at an early stage and lead times were long. Most other oil companies were quite disorganised when it came to their retail offer, so unfortunately it wasn't as simple as just knocking on other forecourt company doors for our next big break. In addition, big companies rarely move fast. We had to find another market sector, prove it and add the next roll-out customer to the roster, not just to underpin the next stage of the company's growth but also to reduce our reliance on our two launch customers.

Unfortunately it didn't take us long to realise that bowling alleys were not it. Megabowl already sold coffee in some of its sites but no more than a couple of hundred cups per week of instant coffee and from behind their fast food counter. Our shared belief was that by offering a self-serve premium quality coffee in a highly visible location we could grow sales substantially. To add to the customer experience we built a bar with stools to create more of a café-style feel.

It looked great but it didn't work. We started to understand just how vital the position of Coffee Nation in any environment was. This wasn't the only problem. These machines were remotely sited so they were installed with cash mechanisms which were less reliable than the espresso machine itself and had to be regularly emptied. The single biggest issue was one that, with hindsight, was perhaps most obvious. Bowling alleys are loud leisure and entertainment centres. Adults drink beer and the kids drink Coke. Sure, they could sell a few coffees, but that equipment was already there, behind the counter and part of their fast food offer.

We had installed an expensive piece of kit front of house and it had to perform. 'Reason to buy' was a new column that we quickly added to our site selection checklist. The trouble was that installation, de-installation, delivery charges, plumbing of water and waste and refurbishing the equipment after removal all added up and became a hefty cost. Finding and proving our next breakthrough sales channel was an expensive affair and we hadn't budgeted for it at this level.

We were continuing to talk to Waterstones, who already had coffee bars installed in a number of their bookshops. Coffee and books seemed to be a combination that worked for the consumer. Waterstones were able to furnish us with footfall data and weekly coffee bar sales from which they took a percentage margin. The percentage of customers in a forecourt that we were capturing gave us a rough guide as to how many cups we might sell in a bookstore – probably a worst and best case. From our work with our launch customers we knew that we were generating up to 50% of the sales of a coffee bar but in only 2% of the floor space. A trial contract was prepared, but soon after my contact at Waterstones called and told me that the both the managing director and operations director had left the company and inevitably that put new projects such as ours on hold. It never saw the light of day again after that.

Our original business plan target of 135 locations by the end of March 2001 now looked ambitious given that our roll-out had not started until the previous September and installations had taken longer with Welcome Break and Texaco then we or they had anticipated. We knew we needed to reach monthly break-even as quickly as possible so that we were no longer burning through shareholder funds. Despite these frustrations we were making great progress. In March we sold 115,000 drinks from 48 sites and by April we had 100 sites trading or committed to do so, albeit the majority of these were Welcome Break or Texaco and then other trial installations.

REFINING OUR OPERATING SYSTEM

Aside from new customers and new locations we were busy developing our operating system. This was what we called everything that went on behind the scenes to ensure we could deliver a great cup of coffee to our customers time after time and with minimal hassle for our retail partners and their staff on site.

The software system that allowed machines to communicate with us directly – allowing monthly invoicing and fault troubleshooting – was taking shape. Scott and I worked on the site operating procedures which were to be so important in delivering consistent standards across our estate. We called these our *How2 Guide* and *Expressions Manual,* which were always kept inside the concession unit to aid fast and effective training of shop staff.

Our Brand Guardians did an amazing job of training and supporting each site to deliver the high standards we needed to reach. It doesn't sound difficult, but we were operating in very busy petrol forecourts and motorway locations and had to contend with all manner of operational challenges such as whether there were there sufficient staff to look after Coffee Nation and man the checkouts. Sometimes it was a choice between the two and we suffered lost sales as a result. Milk availability was another issue in the early days. Sites increased their orders of fresh semi-skimmed milk so that some could be diverted to our machines, but from time to time late deliveries meant no milk in the chiller cabinets, let alone in the Coffee Nation machine. Despite these challenges our Quality Crusade audits showed we were achieving at least 80% compliance with our set standards which, only six months after having started to roll-out, was a great achievement.

Culturally it was vital that the team in our Kentish Town head office recognised that the business was out there on site, with each machine trading reliably 100% of the time. Everyone who joined the company spent time out in the field with our Brand Guardians. Our job was to support them in keeping our planes in the air.

The business was moving so quickly that effective management controls were vital. We established a fortnightly sales forecasting meeting. We also looked at unplanned expenditure and worked hard to eliminate budget overruns. Other members of the team would come in to provide their updates on installation costs or opening dates of sites.

Once in a while I took my daughter to work – she was six at the time. She'd play in my office, help our office manager Kate or count petty cash for Sue, our credit controller. She'd heard about these "forecasting" meetings that her daddy was in; it was only some years later that I discovered she thought we'd been discussing the weather!

The disciplines that our finance director put in place were quickly recognised as vital in our ability to measure progress and maintain effective control over the business. She would always err on the side of caution and that meant we always had a little more financial headroom to play with. Her reports were always accurate and thorough and as a board we always knew exactly where we stood financially.

Another discipline that we set up from the start was a remuneration committee. This meant that on an annual basis each director would consider the performance of each person in their team and then set out their proposals for cost of living salary adjustments, merit-based pay increases due to exceptional performance within their role and then promotions. These papers would come to me for review and authorisation.

The remuneration committee comprised Derek, Neil, Martin (until he stepped down from the board in 2002) and myself. I would present the paper setting out what I was proposing across the company. I was then asked to leave the room whilst my own remuneration was reviewed. Once the proposals were agreed by the committee each director was then free to conduct performance reviews and inform each person of salary adjustments for the year ahead. This whole process took a year or two to bed in but was valuable in helping us to define roles, responsibilities, internal structure and eventually HR policies.

Board meetings were held monthly without fail. We took these meetings seriously, although for the most part they were an enjoyable experience. I think on the whole we looked forward to this opportunity to stand back and discuss progress once a month. We each prepared a detailed report and talked through it, starting with mine, then Scott's operational update and then Vivien with finance. Neil from Primary would attend and Derek would chair. Again, debate was rigorous and anything was open to question. Knowing the next meeting where we'd be reporting progress to the board was only four weeks away ensured each of us maintained focus.

INFORMAL CEO AND CHAIRMAN MEETINGS

Meanwhile, Derek and I started to meet once every couple of months or so offsite, to discuss progress and strategy. It really gave me an opportunity to stand back from the day to day and talk through the issues with him away from the business. He'd been through most of what I was experiencing running a high-growth business, so the benefit of his experience was most welcome. We'd usually finish our meetings in his local village pub over a beer and some supper.

One subject we knew would need considering at some point was that of our coffee machine supplier. The danger was simple. Were that business to fail then our supply line of new machines would dry up, as would the supply of spare parts to maintain our existing estate. We had discussed this with them prior to our fundraising and whilst they appeared in reasonable financial health there was still a risk. There was also a risk that they could be bought by a company not keen to see us succeed. We thought this less likely, but either way there was a risk.

Of course, we could simply identify another suitable machine and either buy some from each company or have the second supplier as an alternate in the event of our doomsday scenario coming to pass. In reality this was not as simple as it sounded. Our concession units were designed around our coffee machines. We had a contract for machine maintenance with the UK distributor. If we had another machine we would need a second design of the concession unit, probably another maintenance provider and all of that was before we even got on to communications software. Running two machines in parallel would increase the cost base of the business and would add to our operational complexity. We needed an alternate solution.

This got us thinking about various ideas for how we could develop the Coffee Nation concept further. I envisaged a touch-screen display that was more like an ATM – this would be intuitive and accept cash and credit card payment. It would include a one-stage hot chocolate drink that didn't require the customer to move their cup from milk to chocolate powder. To get a third-party machine manufacturer to develop all of this would require a huge order commitment.

AIRPORTS AND OFFICES

We pushed on with plans for new openings. We had been introduced to Alpha Retail who operated convenience stores at some UK airports. This lead had come via an article about Coffee Nation so it was great to see us getting some direct commercial return from our investment in PR. They were interested in adding takeaway coffee to their store offer.

We were also excited about the opportunity in offices. We met with a company called Regus that provides managed offices to companies on flexible terms. They were a fast-growth business and liked the idea of being able to offer premium coffee to companies occupying their locations. There was a gradual move away from providing full catering services in offices so we saw this as a good shift in the market that could support our growth. We started trials with Regus and whilst there was no shortage of demand there was already a coffee offer provided that was heavily subsidised by Regus themselves. There were also challenges of who would clean and fill the machine and collect cash from it. Despite the apparent attraction of offices we did not proceed with Regus beyond the trial stage.

The old saying *the devil is in the detail* comes to mind when thinking back over the challenges we faced in proving the viability of some of these new market sectors. We had fortunately hit the jackpot back in 1999 by picking up the phone to Welcome Break and Texaco. Imagine if we'd started with offices, bookstores and bowling alleys! Fortunately, I had stayed true to my original vision from 1996 and my trip to America. This was takeaway coffee from convenience stores and in the UK the best of these were petrol forecourts and motorway services.

There was another self-serve coffee company that set-up in the early 2000s. They followed us with a similar model but started with offices as their focus. I discovered that they had invested heavily but ultimately couldn't crack the office sector and the business failed. It was only because we had already established an operation with substantial cash flow from our motorway and forecourt locations that we could support the continued set up, operating and removal costs of trials in other locations. There but for the grace of God, as they say.

ANALYSING OUR ESTATE

We agreed to maintain a core of ten machines that could be used for trial purposes and which would be reported separately from our core estate. Our monthly management accounts were being skewed negatively by the low initial sales and high set-up costs of trial installations.

We started to develop our thinking around acquiring new locations. The three critical success factors were:

1. Ease of entry into that sector.
2. Operational viability.
3. The scale of opportunity.

A small opportunity was fine as long as it was easy to manage. Difficult opportunities, but with the potential of hundreds of locations, were great too as long as *difficult* did not mean *impossible*. For example, despite the apparent scale of opportunity with London Underground, the operational challenges with installing self-serve fresh coffee making equipment in ticket halls appeared insurmountable.

We further analysed our estate and broke it into four categories:

1. Profitable locations achieving our 12-month payback target or sales quickly approaching that level.

2. Sites with growing sales, not yet achieving our payback target but of significant importance to us as a company.

3. Highly speculative where the payback model had yet to be proven.

4. Sites that had to be removed.

Our intention was that our estate would always be heavily populated by profitable locations, with expanding sites supplying us with growth, with then a small number of speculative trial sites and, ideally, no sites that had to be removed.

Around halfway through the year we had a breakthrough with what we saw as a major strategic opportunity – airports. The private equity owner of Birmingham International Airport at the time knew Primary and so made the introduction for us. We saw this as a great opportunity to prove what could become a very lucrative sector. There were so many potential locations for us in an airport: departure gates and lounges, groundside, airside corridors, maybe even baggage reclaim. Soft drink vending machines were dotted around airports including at departure gates where there was a captive audience waiting for their plane. Discussions started and the guys at Birmingham were a joy to work with.

All the machines were to be installed with cash mechanisms and we also had to make a significant change to our business model. There was no one on site that could clean and fill our machines each day so we had to recruit a dedicated Brand Guardian to look after these installations, which significantly increased our operating costs as the cost of one employee was spread over our four trading machines in the airport. Our model normally saw us allocate one Brand Guardian per

40 machines. Despite this, it was an important test of demand in this new channel and we installed a machine in each of two departure gates, one in international baggage reclaim and one on an international pier connecting the main airside retail area with the departure gates.

Regardless of what we had achieved to date, we were of course still an early-stage business with sales of less than £5m. Getting a fair hearing with potential customers was often a challenge, particularly as our target market was almost exclusively risk-averse large organisations.

A good example was a meeting with a large pan-European multi-billion turnover contract caterer in the autumn of 2001. We had taken them to one of our Welcome Break locations. They appeared interested and even impressed but then added: "Of course, Nestlé or Kenco are the real threat in this market." They were a potential customer with many locations that would be suitable for us and so the conversation continued politely whilst underneath I was gently seething at this corporate short-sightedness. After a few minutes I interrupted the chat, looked them square on and said, "No, gentlemen, we're the threat to them in this market."

BUSINESS DEVELOPMENT DIRECTOR

A common characteristic of high-growth, early-stage businesses is that the founder is often head of business development. This usually happens naturally as the founder is so experienced in explaining their new concept to a wide range of audiences – customers, investors, suppliers – that they carry on with this as the business starts to grow beyond just themselves.

I was no exception and loved talking to potential customers about Coffee Nation, what we could achieve together and then closing the contract. Despite that, there was only one of me and to manage a long list of targets and bring some of them through to trial and then to roll-out meant many follow-up meetings. The business development cycle involved a long lead time and it often required simultaneous nurturing of multiple prospects.

We agreed that it would make sense to boost the senior management team with a business development director (BDD). We would offer that person the chance to buy in to ownership of the company and once they had proved themselves they would take a seat on the board.

We lined up a headhunter and were soon looking through CVs. It was critical to find someone who got what we were about and shared in the vision and passion of Coffee Nation. With fresh concepts that can steer a market in a new direction it is often down to sheer force of personality in getting through the door. If the concept works you'll be heard if you persevere. I called it the need to not just win but *over*-win. It was someone with that spirit that we needed.

As our target market was mostly large companies we also figured recruiting someone that either had experience selling into that market or had come from it would be sensible.

Our shortlist included a selection of terrific candidates and we really took our time making the decision – it was a critical appointment. The successful candidate had previously held a very senior position within one of the UK's major supermarket chains, but was keen to move to a smaller, more nimble organisation. We thought this was great; he'd know how to relate to big companies and particularly supermarkets when we came to speak to them.

90% SAID THEY'D BUY AGAIN

Part of opening doors to new customers and accelerating growth would be to get our customers who were buying our coffee to do the talking for us. Whilst in most locations the results spoke for themselves we hadn't commissioned any formal independent research. This was unbudgeted but we felt it was worth the investment.

The results were a great endorsement:

- 70% of customers interviewed said they thought our coffee was as good as or better than that from Starbucks or Costa.

- 90% said they'd buy again.

- 40% said they stopped at the store because of Coffee Nation.

- 67% said they compared us to high street coffee bars, not vending machines.

- The average spend in a basket containing Coffee Nation was £1 above average, which was a 30% uplift per customer.

This research demonstrated for the first time that our product was standing up in the customer's mind as equivalent in quality to a coffee bar. Slowly we were throwing off the association with poor-quality vending. Whilst our name was little known and we were nowhere yet as a brand, our product was doing the job.

The annual CEO's conference for all of Primary's investee companies came around in October and I was able to report that we were trading from 85 sites and were now at cash breakeven. This meant our risk profile to Primary, its investors and all other shareholders was declining. I also didn't waste the opportunity to share the public's overwhelmingly positive response to our product with this audience.

We did look at raising conventional asset finance to pay for more machines but we were still considered too high risk at this stage by the banks we talked to. They described the issues as:

1.   Our business was still loss making.

2.   We were selling a niche product.

3.   Our machines were sited on third-party premises, so there was a higher risk of damage.

Primary completed their investment in November with the final tranche of £1m in preference shares. This now meant we could order more machines and this gave us sufficient funds to see us safely through to being able to fund future growth from bank debt or leasing of machines once we were a little bigger.

As 2001 drew to a close we were nudging 100 trading sites. It had been a year of digging deep, learning about our business, what worked and what didn't. It had been tough on our small team and everyone had worked incredibly hard.

LEARNING POINTS

- You'll have more bad days than good. You have the luxury of today's issues to deal with because you successfully dealt with yesterday and the day before.

- Don't mistake press coverage as a sign of a successful business. A vast quantity of news and magazine articles is not the same as profits and growth.

- Early growth is often characterised by significant improvisation and little standardisation. The balance between these will alter as you come to understand your business, revenue and operating models.

- Allocate time and budget in your business plan for learning how to grow your business once funded. This enables you to develop solutions to each challenge. You can then standardise and replicate.

- Seek quantitative data to support your business development activity, strengthen existing relationships and underpin your vision.

- Share great news with your team. Being able to say we were the number one selling product within Welcome Break forecourt shops after only one year of trading lifted the entire company.

- Managers leave companies on a regular basis and often with little or no notice. Build strong relationships with your customers from the top down and then across organisations at a senior level.

- Find out what your customers' commercial and strategic priorities are, then align your business to those aims. For example, they may be approaching an exit or refinancing. Coffee Nation became an important profit contributor to its retail clients with zero capital expenditure. Talk their language.

- Regularly consider the size and composition of your board and senior team. Does it match what you need in the market?

- Run thorough recruitment processes. Chose recruitment partners carefully and brief them thoroughly on your company and then the role. Maintain momentum but don't be hurried by candidates or recruiters. If you want the best people get them excited about your business first. Your team is absolutely everything that you have to deliver your plan.

- Everyone in your business is there to support those closest to where the sale is made. Look after your front line.

- Don't avoid administrative matters such as HR policies, performance reviews and remuneration procedures. Early professionalisation will pay dividends as the company grows. This will also be value enhancing upon exit.

2002 – MAKING LIVES BETTER

LIST OF CHALLENGES

As 2002 started I made a list of the key issues and challenges Coffee Nation faced:

- How to gain quicker acceptance and understanding by target customer organisations.

- Our continued reliance on our two launch customers.

- Unpredictable growth forecasting for such a young business with a new concept.

- Reaching a critical mass of locations fast enough in order that we could start to invest in developing our brand.

- Exposure to our single espresso machine supplier.

- How to fund growth.

- Maintenance of our machines by the UK distributor.

THERE WERE SOME major questions here. In the year to March we had sold 2.6m drinks and achieved sales of over £3m. Nonetheless, these questions demanded management time and attention and without doubt new challenges lurked just beyond view to test our mettle.

The coffee market was developing fast in the UK at the time; it was apparently worth over £180m. Starbucks had now grown their estate to 100 locations, we noticed that Ritazza, owned by the Compass Group, was operating cafes in railway stations and Marks & Spencer had launched their Café Revive. I had also spotted a small unbranded coffee bar offer within a Sainsbury's Local in central London. It was an exciting space to be in.

CONTINUED ROLL-OUT

Roll-out sometimes felt like one step forward and two steps back. We had opened locations on the high street in smaller Somerfield supermarkets. Naturally we were keen to see how we could perform in these stores as it was our first foray on to the high street. Results were ok, nothing spectacular. In–store location was critical. Near to sandwiches and pastries was not good enough – only next to these products would offer the customer the convenience of grabbing their lunch and a coffee all in one easy sweep.

There were – even then – so many coffee bars on High Holborn that it was difficult for us to be noticed against this high street brand competition. Camden and Shoreditch were very much secondary high streets, being busy at the weekend but mostly frequented by value-conscious shoppers during the week.

Whilst Somerfield sales volumes had been unspectacular they at least displayed some promise. Birmingham Airport, on the other hand, was convincingly unsuccessful. We had launched four machines with them the previous autumn. The international pier machine sold very few drinks; people barely noticed it regardless of additional signage. The baggage reclaim machine was about the same. We sold a few more drinks at the departure gates but it appeared that by the time passengers got to that point they had drank and ate all they needed.

What made the situation worse was the change of our business model. Having a Brand Guardian dedicated to four installations meant we had to sell over 700 cups per week per machine to achieve our payback target. This meant hitting the ground running at motorway volumes. We tried various initiatives to boost sales but none gave us the required uplift. We exited as professionally as we had entered and maintained good relationships with the team at Birmingham. It seemed the consumer was not yet ready for self-serve gourmet coffee in airports. My father had an irritating saying for an occasion like this: "It's all good experience!" Too much bloody experience and not enough results I thought.

We opened some locations within the leisure sector at Alton Towers theme park. We got off to a great start and they reported that their shop sales had grown by £5k within a week of our arrival. This was split £2k from coffee sales and £3k from related spend (we called this the halo effect) on products such as sandwiches and other snacks. These were great results but we had another learning opportunity in this market as leisure attractions experience large fluctuations in business across the year. We suffered little from seasonality elsewhere, but in the leisure sector school holidays and bank holidays were vital as these were their busiest trading periods by far.

Scott and I were asked to speak at a Welcome Break conference and noticed that we were the only supplier that had been invited to this internal event. This was a positive sign from our largest and most important customer and it made us realise just how essential it was for us to maintain our focus on existing customers in parallel with giving attention to growing our estate. We developed a plan to maximise the opportunity with Welcome Break, including opening more foyer locations, doubling up by installing a second machine where volumes demanded, minimising lost sales through machine downtime and promotional activity to drive sales growth.

MACHINE RUNNING COSTS AND MAINTENANCE

Customers were beginning to know Coffee Nation and trust what we did. Once sales were above around 200 cups per day we could add a second machine next to the first and the best of these twin-machine sites were reaching combined sales of 500 cups per day. We were selling some 3m cups per year through Welcome Break, but were losing some 700 hours of trading per month due to downtime (usually caused by mechanical failure). This roughly equated to one machine out of action for 24 hours a day for an entire month.

Welcome Break had commented that the response time in the event of a machine failure had sometimes "not been what it could be." They were voicing a concern we knew privately we needed to address. We had to be the first priority of our machine maintenance provider, without question and every time.

We were equally focused on controlling the running costs of our machines. With over a year of trading history in high-volume locations we were starting to get a good feel for what components failed most frequently. Unfortunately not all of these fell inside the terms of our warranty agreement with the distributor. Out of warranty parts were a constant headache for Scott as it meant endless discussions and ad hoc negotiations. It was equally frustrating for Vivien in the accounting treatment of them. We moved our ingredients supply to a larger logistics company which reduced costs and developed a repackaged cleaning kit with the machine manufacturer, which gave us a further cost reduction.

Scott and I visited our machine manufacturer in Seattle in the spring. We knew we needed to get closer to them, both in terms of future direction of machine development and our need for an ever-higher standard of machine maintenance. Our machines were across the UK, looked after each day by people not employed by Coffee Nation and many of the machines were trading for 18 or even 24 hours a day. In terms of machine maintenance we were a new industry.

We had a good relationship with the manufacturer and were one of their most important global customers. We discussed machine developments with them and addressed the sensitive issue of how we could continue if for some reason they were unable to supply us at some point in the future. It was agreed that the blueprints and designs including part numbers and supplier lists would be held in escrow and kept up to date. We would have automatic access to all of this in the event of their demise.

This meant that at the very least we would be able to maintain continuity of supply for key components and keep trading. It wasn't quite the whole solution but it went a long way. We also explored bringing maintenance of machines in-house to Coffee Nation and setting up our own dedicated function to look after our estate.

Whilst the service we had from our distributor meant we weren't carrying an inventory of spare parts or employing technicians, we were paying towards their overheads and their profit margin. If we could maintain our growing estate of machines better than a third party then it had to be looked at. The machine manufacturer agreed to support us with this and train our team on their equipment.

TESCO
DEVELOPING A RELATIONSHIP

Back home I got a call from our PR team to say that Tesco was interested in meeting us. I had previously approached them in 1999 and there were some positive early signs but I received a letter a few months later saying that they wouldn't be progressing discussions. Added to this, our results with Somerfield had been mixed, which had dampened their enthusiasm and my board was wary of getting closer to the grocery giants.

I was aware of other suppliers to supermarkets that were run ragged trying to meet the constantly changing demands of their buying departments and in return having their margins squeezed ever tighter. This didn't sound like fun but we needed that next breakthrough. As far as we were aware at the time there was no other company that could do what we did, so maybe this would strengthen our position with Tesco. I went to meet them at one of their head offices in Welwyn Garden City and took them through the Coffee Nation concept. They were receptive to what we did.

Over the coming weeks and months we invested considerable time and effort in planning a programme of trials with Tesco in their various types of stores. We couldn't be sure what the outcome would be but we did know that the footfall of a typical Tesco was much larger than any other supermarket we had traded from, so if we could capture the same percentage of people coming into the store we might just sell enough to make it work. Return per square foot was the critical performance measure and we knew that this was our trump card as long as we could sell sufficient coffee per installation.

Tesco wanted to create new demand for takeaway coffee, innovate in customer service, provide a further point of difference from other supermarket chains and make a trip to Tesco better for the customer. All good stuff, but why would people buy a coffee in the first place? If we failed at that first hurdle our association with Tesco would surely be short lived. Slowly but surely more and more people within Tesco met us. They were great to work with and we received positive feedback that we were regarded as a highly professional organisation with a very interesting concept.

We worked on in-store location and reason to buy. Each store format had a different shopping occasion or need. In Express and Metro stores we would be a convenience takeaway product and needed to be positioned adjacent to breakfast and lunch products. This felt the most familiar to our existing business.

In the larger stores the decision was between being located in a visible position between checkouts and entrance or even as a pit stop at a mid-point in the store. Our idea here was to make the weekly shop a little more pleasurable with the opportunity to pick up a coffee *whilst* shopping. We needed early success and proof in at least one format in order that Tesco were encouraged by the trials.

There were further hurdles we had to cross before we could trade from Tesco. Our operating system and in-store routines came under close scrutiny and we had to be reviewed by their trading law department. This process covered everything from our food hygiene COSHH (Control of Substances Hazardous to Health) procedures through to risks of hot coffee cups in the store, including them being put on checkout conveyor belts.

PRICE POINT

Before we could finalise plans for trial stores we had to agree on price. Across our estate we sold espresso for £1.30, a regular drink for £1.70 and a large at £2. There was some variation; prices at motorway services, for example, being a little higher, but our aim was to maintain consistent pricing. Whilst there is often some variation in price across different channels we wanted our customers to be encouraged to buy wherever they saw the Coffee Nation sign, not discouraged because of price inconsistencies.

Coffee Nation's position in the minds of the consumer was – as increasingly evidenced by the market research – a premium quality takeaway version of what they could buy from the major high street coffee chains. We had never had any issues with our prices and maintained a small price difference below our high street competitors (Starbucks was £1.85 for a regular and £2.19 for a large at the time).

Of course, Tesco was used to delivering exceptional value to its customers and we understood that. However, within the gourmet coffee market we were not a value proposition – we discussed this with them and made the point that really the comparison should be with their Finest range. We had been gradually increasing our prices to bring them closer to the coffee chains and whilst I had always believed we should be significantly cheaper in the early days of the business – as we lacked the stores, seating, staff, muffins, biscotti, etc. – I had recognised that premium quality coffee was in fact quite price inelastic, meaning volumes sold didn't fall if prices went up (within reason). More importantly I had begun to realise that the consumer didn't perceive our coffee to be any lesser than a coffee bar product. They didn't expect to pay less for the same product from Coffee Nation.

It was important our pricing didn't devalue our product and it was conceivable that too low a price could put people off as they might question whether it was authentic and it was certainly not the case that if we lowered prices people bought more coffee. With Tesco this was an argument that, at least at this stage, we were not going to win and we agreed that espresso and regular would be £1.30 and large £1.60.

ADDITIONAL ISSUES

Tesco presented us with other problems too. Whilst the scale of the potential opportunity was enormous, neither we nor they had any idea how successful self-serve takeaway coffee would be from any of their store formats. When opportunity knocks it's not always in the convenient shape one would hope.

A real danger for small companies is that they land a really big customer – that opportunity could take them to the stars, but it could also kill them. Of course, the executive side of our board tended to look at things more positively, whilst the non-executives were more guarded. Our private equity backers had plenty of experience of some of their other portfolio companies working for the big supermarket chains and not all of this had been positive.

We could also see another challenge looming. Our in-store concession was 1.5 metres in width. It was purpose designed to be this size to give us as much visual clout in-store as possible. Tesco challenged this and said that whilst they would be happy to run trials and perhaps early growth with this unit, we would need to have a 1 metre-wide unit available quite quickly. The design of retail stores, particularly supermarkets, is based around linear metre bays. Our 1.5m unit made it difficult for store planning teams to fit us in.

This was another cost we would have to bear if we wanted to develop our relationship with this retailer. Satisfying their requirement for a 1 metre-wide unit became the immediate priority and we set about identifying a suitable design company and manufacturer. History proved it to be a wise move but at the time it felt like another big commitment to make given many uncertainties about the opportunity with Tesco.

SMELL THE TELEMATICS

Our original vision was to have a team of Coffee Nation Angels based in our London office, providing telephone support to sites to ensure we were always trading. Once we really got into the detail of what they would be doing it was clear that the cost of employing and equipping a team like this, full-time and in-house, far exceeded the benefit. The vision was sound though; we needed a dedicated resource that would prevent a call-out to our third-party maintenance provider resulting in a site visit by one of their expensive technicians for the many routine issues that could be easily dealt with by staff on site.

We found a company based in Cambridgeshire who were leaders in the use of telematics to monitor vehicle movements and worked with them to develop a specification for a remote fault monitoring platform. They would be able to monitor each location remotely and call someone on site in the event of a problem – for example, if the machine had run out of milk. Sites could also call in if they had an issue. Putting this infrastructure in place helped underpin our position in the marketplace and it helped us maintain our unfair advantage.

By April we had also connected 72 of our machines back to our central server. This meant we could see what was being dispensed and enabled us to build a comprehensive sales breakdown by location each month. We could track sales trends, accurately forecast sales growth of new installations, closely match consumables ordered with actual usage and improve the accuracy of our month-end invoicing.

Whilst we had taken considerable steps with our coffee roaster to select a great blend of Arabica beans for our mass market proposition and worked hard with our equipment distributor to calibrate the espresso machine, we had a nagging feeling that, as a team, we didn't actually know enough about our coffee and how to get the best out of the beans that went in the hopper at the top. Our Brand Guardians undertook their Quality Crusade Audit at each site, focused on three planks of drink quality, availability and station cleanliness. What we didn't know enough about was what we meant by *quality*.

We turned to our coffee roaster and asked for help. They introduced us to an independent guru of espresso coffee who had worked with many coffee bar operators worldwide to develop their recipe and get the most from their coffee. We invited him to visit the company and he ran training sessions which everyone in the company attended. It was remarkable what an improvement we were able to make to what was already a good coffee.

Brand Guardians now felt more empowered to actually have an influence over the quality of drink at each of their locations and whilst standardisation across our estate was important they were able to make minor adjustments. We equipped them all with a set of shot glasses so they could measure the thickness of the crema on the top of an espresso. This often became a talking point as customers would ask them what they were doing, presenting a great opportunity to talk to people about our product.

Our PR focus shifted from the early press coverage we had secured on the concept of squeezing a coffee bar into a box, to more tactical stories covering the opening of new locations or securing new customer contracts. Even the remote monitoring system made its way into the press. "Wake Up and Smell the Telematics," they said. We also started to focus more on activity designed to drive people to our locations and grow sales. For example, a cut-out coupon in the *Sunday Express* for a free coffee at any of our locations saw a good take up. I got out and did some speaking at entrepreneurial conferences and we entered our first awards.

One of the constant challenges we faced was the threat of losing that entrepreneurial edge that had got us to this stage. We always had to be thinking as if we had just started, we needed to keep our message fresh at all times, creating renewed momentum for our category and our brand.

CUSTOMER FEEDBACK

Slowly but surely we seemed to be getting noticed by those who mattered most. We had a customer feedback page on our website called Express Yourself and more and more people used it to get in touch with us. Most importantly we heard from those we let down – when the machine didn't work for them. Scott or I always endeavoured to reply within 24 hours. To get a response from the CEO or COO of the business was not what people expected and we always invited them to call us if they wanted to discuss further. We often asked for a contact number and called them ourselves.

Emails like this became more common and they were a good way of keeping score that we were on the right track:

> "The coffee from the M62 service station shop was the best coffee I have ever tasted. I usually go for a latte in Starbucks as there is one on our local high street. I thought this would take some beating but the coffee I had from the Coffee Nation machine surpassed this."
>
> "I was amazed that fresh coffee could taste so good from an automatic machine."
>
> "I will certainly be keeping my eyes open for more of your machines and telling my friends to look out for them. I have to say I'm not easily impressed but I was so impressed that I felt you deserved to be congratulated."

We liked this one even more:

> "You make my life better."

I milked this for all it was worth in every customer and investor presentation I could. It was the first time a customer had communicated with us not about the coffee, but about what that did for them.

INTERNAL CHALLENGES

All of this made one of my internal challenges all the more baffling. Our business development director had joined in the autumn of 2001 and had made a great start. He'd opened doors and we'd made good headway in discussions at senior level in some big contract catering companies (for offices) and quick service restaurant brands (high street locations).

He was a confident man and had come from a senior position in a major supermarket brand. But by the summer of 2002 I was starting to become concerned and had mentioned it quietly to my chairman. I started to wonder whether, despite the phenomenal workload, it had been too early to start to delegate the business development function. I felt there was too much intellectual debate with potential customers and our BDD was conceding contract points to customers where he didn't need to.

It had dawned on me that we were living our halcyon days. If we had to cave in to customers at this point what the hell would life be like when we had competitors breathing down our necks, as surely one day we would. I just felt he wasn't grasping the opportunity that we had. We'd got this far through a combination of vision, passion, solid execution, self belief and determination and I needed to see more of these qualities in him.

We met to discuss this – I wasn't sure he would even be able to see what I could see. The trouble was he was used to negotiating over minutiae in big deals, but they were *steady state*, as I called them – more about maintaining what had gone before than breaking new ground. We were all about doing new things, we had to punch above our weight to get noticed and be prepared to fight hard to do deals that were good for the customer but also good for us. How could we build and lead this category and invest in its future if we were on wafer-thin margins?

Success in that role was so much about attitude and we just couldn't get there. He left the company on good terms just under a year after he had started. I bumped into him a couple of years later. He was on good form and agreed Coffee Nation had not really been for him. Nonetheless, it was a stark reminder that new recruits had to fit with our culture.

Putting together a plan for the roles needed to take the business to the next stage became one of my biggest ongoing priorities. We recruited a project manager (responsible for management of all machine installations) who reported to Scott and a financial controller as Vivien's number two.

MONTHLY SALES HIT 400,000 CUPS

By June we had sales of £6m and were just edging into profitability. By September our run-rate was £7m sales, we were operating from 122 locations and our sales had grown 53% since April. We were also achieving our 12-month payback target on average across our estate. We sold 407,000 drinks that month. It was our best ever month and our annualised volume was almost 5m drinks. In the year we had raised our funding our sales had been £650,000. We were now doing almost the same per month. Furthermore, we could say that shareholder funds had been used to acquire revenue-generating machines rather than to build overheads or for working capital.

Despite this progress our history of losses meant we had limited scope for securing bank funding – banks don't want to lend to loss-making businesses. Until our cash flow and balance sheet strengthened further they continued to see Coffee Nation as an equity funding story.

Meanwhile, Scott had presented a paper to the board setting out the merits of bringing machine maintenance in house. We could see that whilst there was a significant upfront cost we would move to a lower cost level maintaining our estate ourselves than if we continued to contract this out. With everything else to manage this would be no light undertaking but the board signed it off. Scott would lead this and once up and running we would recruit a head of maintenance.

Whilst very funky, our North London offices were wholly impractical for running a maintenance operation of this sort. We therefore decided to look for new premises – with room to grow and suitable for setting up our machine maintenance operation. We used the same property agent that had found us Highgate Studios and by September we relocated to our new home in High Wycombe.

We had two floors, our own car park and it was just off the M40, so easy to access. Ironically, I had just bought a flat within walking distance of our existing Kentish Town address but I quickly found the drive out of London in the morning to High Wycombe a great start to the day; I was going against the traffic and I could make good use of the time to speak to Scott, Vivien or Derek before I even reached the office.

In October we finally sold our first coffee from a Tesco store. We had four trial locations. Tesco Eynsham was just outside Oxford on the busy A40. It was an Express store with an Esso petrol forecourt. This was a success from day one, with sales starting at almost 80 cups per day. We also opened in Oxford and Leamington Spa Tesco Metros and the petrol forecourt at the Cardiff Extra supermarket.

Tesco's internal research revealed: "Coffee Nation is easy to clean, fill and maintain, customers like it and it's good value compared to Starbucks and Costa." That was great initial feedback. We also had some issues – kids pressing buttons and hence wasted drinks and our hot chocolate was a two-stage drink (first stage was the chocolate powder then the hot milk), which confused some people. But overall we had made a great start.

As the year progressed we further enhanced our operating model. We were rolling out an automated stock reordering system to simplify this process and we also installed remote monitoring so we could now see – all via a dial-up BT internet connection – when the machine had last undergone its cleaning cycle. This Big Brother tool became very useful in policing site standards and homing in on problem locations. We had also finally agreed with the manufacturer in Seattle that we could now buy machines and spare parts direct from them rather than having to go via the UK distributor. This would save time and money.

IDEAS FOR A CUSTOM-MADE COFFEE NATION MACHINE

By sourcing a third-party supplier's machines our own plans were inevitably closely linked to their own product development agenda. Despite the fact that we had opened up a new and growing niche we were not able to influence how they wanted to develop their own range of machines.

It set us thinking that perhaps the future lay in us having a machine designed from a blank sheet of paper for Coffee Nation that we could then have manufactured wherever we chose. Plus, of course, we would own the intellectual property (IP) for the machine.

We wondered what a machine that was developed specifically for Coffee Nation would look like. Could we make it much easier to use and so overcome the ongoing niggles and complaints we got because people found the layout confusing? Could we make it lower cost and therefore profitable in lower-volume locations, expanding the market opportunity?

The coffee machine had up until now been seen as simply that – the box in the centre of the concession unit that delivered the drink. What if it was all one piece – designed from the ground up for the self-serve market? Could we install new features that would make it even more attractive to retailers and consumers alike? Thoughts ran to filter coffee, fully automated cleaning and touch screens that we could configure and change.

The more we thought about it the more this idea made sense. We could have a machine designed specifically for our needs that we would own all the design rights to and could then have manufactured wherever we wanted. No longer would we be reliant on a single manufacturer. If we could incorporate all we had learnt since I had started in 1997 into a new platform it could put us way out front against any future competitive threat. It was critical that we maintained our category leadership and this could help us achieve just that.

LEARNING POINTS

- Watch for overexposure to one or two major customers, or a single major supplier.

- As a management team, balance your attention between short-term objectives and longer-term planning. Distant threats can quickly become today's issues if ignored.

- Balance proven and profitable with constant experimentation. Some risk taking is essential to identify exciting growth opportunities.

- Look after existing customers as well as pursuing growth.

- Watch for the hidden risks of the single transformational customer. Tesco was both a huge opportunity and huge risk to us.

- It can be as challenging to maintain a new market category as it is to create it in the first place. Our drink price provided an important association of quality with high street coffee bars, but was to prove a long-term challenge with Tesco.

- Know everything there is to know about your product. Today's consumer is engaged and knowledgeable. Authenticity and provenance is vital to your brand and relationship with your audience.

- Don't bleed valuable margin points when you are not under any real pressure. It takes courage to stand your ground but always show humility and grace in negotiations.

- Trading experience provides valuable insight to all aspects of your operating model that was not available to you when you constructed your plan.

2003 – ENTER A COMPETITOR

STRATEGIC PRIORITIES

AS 2003 GOT underway we could see that we had made real progress against some of the objectives we had set out at the start of the previous year, but not all. Growth forecasting still seemed more like guesswork than business planning and whilst we had some vague ideas for a new machine that we owned, this thinking was in the initial stages. We also had to consider how to continue to fund future growth. Short-term priorities inevitably trump working on the longer-term strategic building blocks and I was learning this every day. Board meetings provided a monthly reminder that the clock was always ticking.

Our gross sales had grown by 89% in the year to March 2003, we were £0.5m cash positive and Vivien reported healthy levels of reserves and accruals to protect against any surprises in the year ahead.

We were way behind plan though. We seemed to constantly fall between setting an installation budget that was based on what we believed could happen and what we knew was going to happen with contracted customers (maybe as low as 10 or 20 new machines confirmed at any one time). However, we clearly could not ask the board to sign-off on a budget for the next 12 months showing a growth in our estate of only 20 locations.

The financial year to March 2003 ended with 145 trading locations against a budget of 243, although gross sales were within 5% of budget as sales per day, per machine, were thankfully trending upwards at a higher rate than forecast. Gross margin was heading up and we had learnt to be almost forensic when it came to managing variable costs and overheads. EBITDA (earnings before interest, tax depreciation and amortisation) had by now turned positive so the trends were good. We had been profitable on a month-by-month basis since August of 2002.

The year to March 2004 target was now 247 machines, or basically the same target as for 2003, just a year later. We also set a target of £1.2m EBITDA for the year ahead. We narrowed our focus to motorway service areas, petrol forecourts and grocery sectors.

We desperately needed to set a budget and achieve it. In our efforts to find the next major growth opportunity we had an estate that comprised too many trial locations that were unlikely to ever reach our 12-month payback target. Unfortunately we found ourselves putting together a site removal plan. We just couldn't run with a long tail of underperformers dragging down the core estate – for instance, the Somerfield small format urban supermarkets. In these locations we discovered that some people were put off because the machine looked too difficult to use, appeared expensive or they doubted the quality. With Coffee Nation the customer could not possibly know how good the coffee was until they had stood at the machine, taken a cup and pressed the button.

One person commented that we whispered great coffee, whereas we really needed to **shout** about it being great coffee. We had to capture this feedback and keep it on the agenda for future developments of the machine and our customer communications. Out of six Somerfield stores we withdrew from two. We even had to remove machines from some early Texaco sites that had never hit the required sales level.

At this year's Primary Capital CEO's conference I was able to report sales had doubled from £3.1m to £6.2m from 2002 to 2003 and our payback was on target at 12.3 months, but I also made the point that the inertia of large organisations meant growth forecasting was highly unpredictable. By September 2003 our monthly sales were nudging £0.75m and in the quarter to end September we had delivered £250k EBITDA.

There was always more to do than available discretionary funds permitted. Meanwhile, ingredient costs were running over budget and if installations fell behind plan we could not expect to still spend as if we were on budget. All too often we had to be disciplined and cut previously agreed expenditure if contribution was below forecast. Prudent financial governance was vital.

ORANGE AWARD

There are many highs and lows that characterise the entrepreneur's journey in building a high-growth business. Both are equally memorable and one high came in the form of our first award win.

We were shortlisted as a finalist in the Orange 'Small is Beautiful' Awards and were invited to the awards ceremony at the Russell Square Hotel in Central London. I thought it would be a good opportunity for a bit of fun with some of the team so Shane and Toby came along with Scott, Derek and myself.

When the winner of the award for Best Demonstration of Entrepreneurial Passion was announced I think none of us could believe it – we won! The whole team went up to the stage to collect the award and we were beaming – I was so proud of what we had achieved. After the ceremony Scott, Shane and I headed to the Rockwell Bar at the Trafalgar Hotel and carried on the celebrations. It was great news to share in the office the next day, despite the hangover.

NEW CONCESSION UNIT

We were progressing with the development of a new 1-metre wide concession unit to fit into standard retail bays in Tesco – it was a narrower housing around the same espresso machine. This became known as 2G, or second generation. It needed to be ready this year.

A goal was also set for developing an entirely new product to remove the reliance on our machine partner in the USA and enable us to set our own development agenda. This was a far more ambitious project and we christened this 3G, or third generation. This was confidential and knowledge of it did not extend beyond the board.

Whilst we hadn't yet got our arms around all aspects of maintaining our own machines (spare parts spend was averaging £75 per machine per month versus a budget of £35) we had dramatically improved our uptime compared to when we outsourced this critical function. By the summer of 2003 we were losing only around 80 trading hours per month due to technical failures. This was an 80% improvement and vindicated our decision to develop this capability in house. Not only did this allow us to claim a failure rate of less than 1% (we were approaching 120,000 trading hours per month by this time), but it also meant consistency in machine calibration, which meant a consistency in quality of drink for our customers.

Whilst 3G was the real strategic prize we had an immediate opportunity to enhance our offer to consumers with the development of 2G. A key aim was to make 2G more engaging and easier to use. We also set an objective of designing the new unit to be easier to keep clean. Not to be overlooked was the chance to reduce the cost of the new concession unit as well.

We were really starting to imagine just what 3G could do for us. This could be our chance to make Coffee Nation truly the ATM of espresso. Derek made the point in a board meeting that the initial roll-out and even the new 2G unit were really extensions of our original trial, whereas 3G could be transformational to our operating economics, the P&L of each customer and the experience of the consumer. It was our success to date that would give us the funds to invest and make this vision a reality.

We could see the opportunities:

- Remove supply side exposure to the US machine supplier.
- Our aim of reducing the capital cost of the machine by around 50% would open up many more sites.
- Innovation in retail design and an interface that is easy (not easier) to use.
- An hour per week for site staff to clean and replenish rather than an hour a day would make Coffee Nation even more profitable for retailers.
- Sealed coffee bean cassettes and milk tanks would increase capacity between refills to perhaps 500 drinks – rather than less than 50 – before the milk tank needed refilling.
- A single-stage hot chocolate product.
- The addition of filter coffee for those not wanting cappuccinos and caffè lattes.
- Eliminating the shrinkage, or waste gap, that existed between the number of drinks dispensed and the number that were paid for at the till – this was a cost to the retailer.
- Future developments such as iced coffee to create a new sales channel.

We envisaged the 21st-century unmanned coffee bar – the core architecture could be repackaged into a variety of formats. We would own the intellectual property and ultimately these machines could be produced in low-cost manufacturing regions, bringing us further economic benefit. No other company had yet entered the self-serve gourmet coffee market in an organised way and we believed this development could accelerate our lead.

There was likely to be an investment in excess of £1m to £1.5m and up to two years in time before we would be in the market with this new machine. We identified the leading product design companies in the UK and met with each of them – briefing them over many hours and numerous meetings. It was critical that each of these firms understood how serious we were about this opportunity and how strategically important it was to us – it was equally important that each bidder was as enthusiastic as we were about the project.

Our choice eventually fell to a UK-based product development company with a world-class reputation. Their work stopped short of product design so we selected another organisation to work on the look and feel of the new system.

This was a very ambitious undertaking, although we and our development partners did not believe there was any significant technical risk. Whilst we were building an entire unmanned self-serve coffee concept from scratch, part of the design brief was that there would be no unproven new technology in the system.

By December we had a signed contract and were in possession of a fully costed and timed development plan. A secure data room was established, laboratory windows blacked out and a project launch meeting set up – this was a full day with the entire team. I presented the past, present and future vision of Coffee Nation and how we saw 3G impacting our prospects. Our ambitions were to use this innovation to build a truly global brand. From now on life was never the same. Scott and I made trips to our development partner's facility every week; it almost became a second home.

CORE CUSTOMERS

In the meantime we maintained our focus on our core customers of Welcome Break and Texaco. We were heavily reliant on them and we were well aware of the risk this presented, but there was little we could do about this until we had secured the next customer that combined a large number of suitable locations and high drink volumes per site.

Welcome Break was now nearing an installed base of 80 machines and we had probably reached a state of maturity in terms of penetration of the UK Texaco estate with 50 installations. I had also been progressing discussions with this customer for taking Coffee Nation into Europe. These had been very low-key up to now but we had a strong relationship with Texaco (by then ChevronTexaco) and they were keen to develop this further on the continent.

The region for the European trials would be Belgium, Netherlands and Luxembourg (Benelux). Eating on the go was well-developed consumer behaviour in this region, the forecourts already sold coffee and fuel volumes were very high (a key indicator of Coffee Nation success in filling stations). They were more of the profile of mini-motorway services so we felt confident we could sell a lot of coffee. At the same time, we recognised there may need to be drink menu changes given cultural differences, and pricing may have to vary.

The local operators and management were enthusiastic towards us and had received glowing reports of our success with the company in the UK. The next stage was to make some site visits and plan for trials accordingly. The tentative launch date for trials was autumn 2003.

We had also made progress with Roadchef, back in the UK. They were the third major motorway services company in the UK behind Welcome Break and Moto. We knew this market segment well and obviously had achieved considerable success with Welcome Break. I had met with their board the previous October and their reception had been very positive. They were keen to progress to trials quickly so I prepared a trial agreement and service level agreement. The first machines were set to be live by Easter.

TESCO TRIALS

The other constant was our focus on the Tesco trials. By now we were live in ten Tesco stores. The critical measure of success was profitability per square foot. The arrival of the 2G unit was a positive development in this regard as it occupied less floor space – only 8.5sq.ft., in contrast to 15.5sq.ft. of the original first generation units.

The Eynsham Tesco Express was a runaway success, with sales reaching 90 cups per day. Based on these results we could be rolling out across the Express estate. Unfortunately, this was the high point in the Tesco sales league table. Others showed promise and were growing, but takeaway coffee in Tesco stores (or any other UK supermarket for that matter) was a new concept so a change in consumer behaviour was required. We knew this took time. We also knew that 14m people shopped in Tesco every week, so the scale of the opportunity was tremendous. As we were able to identify the success factors more Tesco Express sites were made available to us.

In an Express location people would stop to buy petrol and pick up a coffee along with a sandwich or pastry from the in-store bakery. The main supermarkets were different though – we couldn't just install, switch on and expect to sell a lot of coffee. These were not forecourts or motorway services. The challenge of getting people to notice the Coffee Nation unit, let alone think, act, stop, put their bags down, pay (machines located near the exit had a cash mechanism for customer payment as there was no till point nearby) and then get a coffee could not be underestimated.

We undertook research in our trial Tesco locations. Feedback was very positive, with 80% rating our coffee as very good and 87% saying the machine was easy to use. Four out of ten were regular buyers and almost one in five did not buy a coffee on their journey before Coffee Nation had arrived in Tesco. This was early evidence we were creating new demand. Almost one-in-three said they had visited the store because of Coffee Nation and almost half drank it in their car. Tesco's own research showed that Coffee Nation added value to the customer offering and more than 80% of people bought other food to go when they bought one of our coffees.

Both companies were finding their feet working together. We had to become integrated into each store, including the required labour hours being allocated to the management of Coffee Nation. Unfortunately, ownership at site level was proving to be a problem. In one weekend I visited all of our ten trial sites around the UK and four of these were out of action because milk system cleans had not been completed.

A marketing plan slowly started to take shape and key performance indicators were thrashed out. I met with Tesco almost every week and slowly but surely we were able to meet more people at a senior level.

We were eventually able to craft a clear vision that Tesco together with Coffee Nation could become a destination for takeaway coffee based on the public's established trust in Tesco initiatives and the growing strength of the Coffee Nation brand and concept.

With sales growth in the Express format, operational procedures gradually coming together and an agreement from Tesco to work with us on marketing activity (they knew their stores better than we did), we eventually gained agreement to roll-out across suitable formats with the new 2G 1-metre unit. By the end of the year we had a signed contract with Tesco. We at last had our next major customer.

In the first instance we would roll-out across suitable Express convenience stores. We were to be positioned next to the checkouts (visible for easy management) and next to the in-store bakery. A standard Tesco sign would be positioned above the Coffee Nation station to highlight that the store sold coffee. Finally, we were starting to see that we would be designed in as a standard feature. We even started to see Coffee Nation mentioned on the 'What's in store?' wall-mounted signage alongside bakery, off licence and National Lottery. Large car park banners were also designed.

Tesco held an annual supplier ball at the Honourable Artillery Company in the City of London and in 2003 we were invited for the first time. It was a black tie affair – Derek and Scott took their wives and Trudi accompanied me. I think we were all proud of what we were achieving with Tesco and also to be associated with one of the world's leading retailers.

BENELUX TRIALS

By late 2003 plans were well underway for our Benelux trials with Texaco. The plan was to open five trial sites, with one having a dual Coffee Nation installation due to expected high volumes. We had been presented with figures by ChevronTexaco of their coffee sales in the Netherlands. It was clearly a well established business and the Dutch drank a great deal of coffee on the roadside.

The local management were initially somewhat sceptical as we explained that Coffee Nation would increase the drink price significantly (they currently charged €0.60, whereas we charged £1.30 in the UK), lower their margin and increase sales volumes, thereby making them more money.

We decided to increase the drink price to €1.60 – equivalent to around £1.14, so still below our UK Texaco prices. In Eindhoven we saw speciality coffees being sold for up to €2.50 and McDonalds were charging €1.25 for a small espresso with powdered milk. We believed that the combination of product quality, the coffee bar experience and increased drink size would enable us to charge a premium price for our product and generate more attractive returns for ChevronTexaco, as had been proven in the UK.

Our customer had approximately 65 locations in the Netherlands. We developed a mini-business plan based on successful trials and estimated that 35 machines across 30 locations was a realistic target to aim for in the first year.

Success would put us on the map in this first European territory and we could then approach other oil companies regarding their forecourts in the Benelux region. It was close to home so we could run the trials from our UK base (we dedicated one of our best technicians to look after the machines) and given progress with Tesco we could then approach Dutch supermarket groups as well.

The set-up costs meant that it would take one quarter to reach breakeven and a 35 machine roll-out with associated infrastructure would require an investment of around £600k. Of course, we would then have a foothold in Europe so this investment was seen as entirely reasonable. Trials were planned to start in January 2004.

A BATTLE OVER MARGIN

Back in the UK, despite great early feedback from the highest level, the trials with Roadchef had followed a somewhat circuitous path. It appeared to be a great opportunity given we knew motorway operations so well. Somehow though I had the feeling that we'd need to let Roadchef take their own time in seeing just how well Coffee Nation worked with their customers and how attractive it was for their P&L.

We started trading from four locations in June and within six weeks had achieved sales of almost £11,000. Downtime was negligible and customer feedback was as we had hoped. A third of customers said they had stopped at Roadchef because of Coffee Nation and almost half said we were their preferred choice of coffee-to-go. Almost 75% said we were their preference to Starbucks or Costa.

Sales continued to rise but we then learnt that Roadchef was also going to trial another self-serve coffee offer called j.j beano's which was a start-up competitor to us. As the weeks went by our sales continued to climb but Roadchef told us that they were being matched by the j.j beano's offer. Was this purely a negotiating ploy? Their finance director admitted to me that we had done everything we said we would and no criticism could be made of Coffee Nation.

In August we experienced zero downtime and based on what we were delivering from four machines we were confident we could deliver £1m annually in clear profit for Roadchef just from their forecourt shops alone. Our position still wasn't clear however. Despite reassurances from their FD that he was in favour of Coffee Nation, the news eventually came that they were going to select j.j beano's, branded Roadchef/j.j beano's and – we believed – serving a Costa coffee product.

Site management had informed us that the j.j beano's trials were achieving no more than 60% of our sales volume. We were capturing up to 17% of forecourt footfall and 11% in the retail shops. Despite our commanding lead in the market the message we were getting was that the competing offer could match us operationally, that it was easy to look after, with minimal downtime, and our brand was not strong enough to outsell the upstart. This left us competing on margin – not a place I wanted to be.

The news of losing Roadchef came midway through a board meeting, which did not make for a good second half. Had we attempted to be too aggressive in our deal with Roadchef? We clearly wanted to improve our terms with each subsequent deal. Maybe our market position was still too nascent to be trying for this? The start-up j.j beano's had zero trading history in this sector. Their proposition mimicked ours and our performance was well in excess of both Roadchef expectations and – we were told – the j.j beano's trial. From our point of view their decision was opaque. After our board meeting wound up, Derek sat on the sofa in my office and said "You've got a competitor." Not a good day. I felt a big lump in my throat. Clearly, we couldn't win everything, but this really did surprise us.

We gradually learnt that this deal had been done based entirely on the margin offered by our competitor, not their ability to deliver a great product to the highest standard. I had previously been asked by Roadchef whether a lower grade of coffee could be used in Coffee

Nation to allow them to receive a higher margin. I'd reacted strongly to this suggestion, explaining that if you cheat the customer you'll always get found out. I could now see where they had been going with this.

We decided to do a formal sweep of all competition in early 2004. This episode just served to make us even more determined to retain our leadership of this category. Neither I nor the rest of the team had worked as hard as we had only to see us lose our pole position to a poor quality imitation of our original.

TAKING A BIG STRIDE FORWARD

It had proved to be a big year. The business had doubled in size and we finally had our contract with Tesco. They placed their first order for 25 machines against an agreed installation schedule prior to Christmas.

The significance of this could not be underestimated. Tesco were the fourth largest retailer in the world and regardless of our confidence in our abilities this was a major endorsement of the company, the concept and all of what the team had achieved. We were hopeful that in time there would be a halo effect with our visibility in Tesco providing sufficient reassurance for other retailers to follow suit and choose Coffee Nation.

Our 3G project was well underway and none of our customers knew about this. Despite the annoying loss of Roadchef, we were sure Tesco and 3G would accelerate our growth and continued market leadership over the next couple of years. We also had the launch of our first European trials to look forward to early in 2004.

We had made some major strides forward strategically too. Awareness of Coffee Nation was growing; an advert in *The Grocer* magazine for Brand Guardians had attracted over 200 applicants. We won the SAGE award for best business leadership in the small business category and we were featured in the *Cafe Report* by Allegra Strategies. This was an annual report on the coffee bar market and for the first time an entire section had been dedicated to self-serve gourmet coffee.

We also heard that Tank & Rast, the German motorway service area operator, could be interested in talking to us. We had a number of major strategic projects underway and a growing estate, so had to be careful not to overstretch ourselves and drop the ball.

LEARNING POINTS

- Our aim was *profitable* growth. Some companies necessarily have to invest more to grow faster and therefore run at break-even or a loss for a period. Others require significant investment in infrastructure up front and do not reach profitability until higher sales volumes are reached.

- We were able to grow before additional headcount was required. Growth in costs followed growth in revenue. What is the relationship between revenue growth and fixed costs in your business?

- Actively manage under-performing parts of your business. Either change something to reach a positive contribution or remove them. Set clear timescales and stick to them.

- If customers are not aware your product exists they cannot buy it. What investment in marketing is required to achieve your required rate of sale?

- Prioritisation of discretionary spend is important to focus limited resources to where they will have the greatest effect.

- Don't hide your vision. We enthusiastically shared ours with Tesco. Their 14m customers per week and our category leadership created a unique opportunity. It's just as important that your customers buy into your vision as well as your employees.

- The arrival of our first genuine competitor raised serious questions. We had pioneered the category and were now paving the way, but we didn't want to lose this position.

- We were playing for success in the long term. Despite the loss of an important contract, to compromise our product integrity in the short term would have been a retrograde step.

2004 – AIM IN MIND

ME-TOO COMPETITORS

WE WERE BECOMING acutely aware of just how long new categories and markets take to develop. Not only were we educating the consumer that coffee from a *vending machine* in a petrol station really could be just as good as coffee from a bar on the high street, we also had to demonstrate to retailers just what was involved in delivering a high-quality beverage from an automated and unmanned kiosk, consistently and with minimal failures. Our operating system in which we had invested heavily was intended to enable us to deliver on our promise for every cup sold. The challenge we often faced was that of disbelief by potential customers: "How hard can it really be to sell a cup of coffee from a machine?"

Over time our determination to stand by our values and the systems we had developed to ensure our product quality were vindicated. The start-up we lost out to at Roadchef never gained any significant scale beyond that first customer. Our *intelligence* (site staff friendly towards Coffee Nation!) told us we were outselling j.j beano's by at least 25% and the reliability of Coffee Nation was far higher. We could never be certain, but maybe we were selling 25% more than the other trial offer but their much higher margin on 75% of our volumes meant the cash profit for the retailer was actually higher than with Coffee Nation. Roadchef management, however, had said that our operating system had not delivered markedly greater availability than our competitor and the Coffee Nation name was not a sufficient pull to outsell the other offer.

We knew for sure that of the limited competition to Coffee Nation that did exist, none of them had anything like the sophisticated behind-the-scenes setup that we did, so were certain this was a red herring.

From our own direct observations it did appear we were selling more coffee. Given we knew we could generate very high sales on motorways we had proposed a deal to Roadchef that would have made our stations the most profitable – for us – out of our entire estate, by far. Wanting to improve on previous deals is sensible but maybe we had been too ambitious with this in an attempt to secure the contract and maximise its profitability. The latter was of course important but only up to the point that we could be certain of securing the deal. We could have offered the customer a far higher margin and still enjoyed a healthy margin ourselves – and within our payback target.

Of course, it was easy to see this after the event, but when pitching for the contract we had probably allowed our objectives to become blurred. We absolutely wanted to win this contract – it would have given us two out of three motorway operators, secure for a long term, and allowed us to further build our market lead. We were in land grab mode and this was the time to secure market share and grow our estate. But we played to maximise profits rather than grow the installed base and we lost out on the contract as a result. Our competitor had no choice but to play for locations rather than profit (they had no other sites) and we could easily have cut them short because by now we were profitable and cash generative, which gave us some real firepower.

Another me-too competitor emerged at about the same time called My Coffee. During 2003 we had been in discussion with Sainsbury about undertaking trials in their Local format of convenience stores. We did not believe the locations they had offered were the best to start with and we were sensitive to trading with Sainsbury given we had not yet cemented our arrangements with Tesco.

Sainsbury therefore decided to forge ahead with My Coffee, although we were keen to maintain good relations with them. In time, Sainsbury terminated its agreement with My Coffee and came back to us. The reason was they did not possess the operating systems necessary to trade from and roll-out across a premium retail business such as Sainsbury. This was so different to our experience with Roadchef. Slowly but surely, our operating standards did set the benchmark for self-serve takeaway gourmet coffee and became an essential element in our growth.

An important issue remained from the Roadchef experience: whilst we had been outselling our competitor, our brand wasn't yet as strong as we had perhaps expected. Unlike a grocery product or bottled beverage, we couldn't simply be listed in every Tesco or Sainsbury, for example. We had to go where we could maximise sales. This of course limited our exposure to the consumer and the rate at which this could grow.

CAFÉ PRIMO

There was one other competitor that was to cause us trouble. In 2004 our contract with Welcome Break came up for renewal. There were further locations across their estate that could benefit from a self-serve takeaway coffee offer and their CEO had stated that Coffee Nation wasn't the only game in town. Welcome Break at the time had developed a Starbucks-style coffee bar called Primo. In conjunction with Kraft, they then installed a Café Primo self-serve unit serving a Kenco coffee bean product next to a Coffee Nation station at one of their locations on the M40 motorway.

I challenged this move and though their CEO said he could not see what there was to complain about, he was keen to find a way forward with Coffee Nation as so much had been achieved together. He and his Retail Director came to see the Coffee Nation operation, including maintenance, to gain an understanding of what we did and how this benefitted Welcome Break. We also gave them some idea of how we were investing to lead the category well into the future, without revealing the detail of 3G.

In the end, this is exactly what ensured the continuation of our relationship with Welcome Break. We were proven – this was an important profit stream to our customer and any other option could not demonstrate the track record we had in managing and maintaining a premium quality self-serve coffee offer in such high-volume locations.

In the January across 82 locations with Welcome Break we had fielded 172 calls in our call centre, 67 of which had been solved over the telephone (Coffee Nation Angels indeed!), 15 preventative maintenance visits were undertaken and only 193 trading hours were lost. Machine reliability averaged 99.6%.

Finally, we had proven that not only could we win major contracts but we could retain them up against some of the largest food companies in the world. In our category we had at last been proven to be the safe option. Despite their claims they could make more profit with Primo/Kenco than with Coffee Nation, we had now demonstrated that regardless of what a company may offer as a margin on paper it is real cash profits that matter. I had first presented that argument to Spar and Alldays back in 1997.

A new long-term agreement was constructed with Welcome Break. We decided it was well overdue that we increase our drink prices (this was good for both parties and still kept us below high street coffee bar prices). Coffee Nation would now be promoted as *the* brand of coffee-to-go in Welcome Break and we expanded by another 20 machines across their estate.

BEING ON BUDGET

Our new 1-metre wide, second generation concession was finalised at this time. We introduced new features such as remote control central locking that meant the whole unit opened with one touch of a button, making it really easy for site staff to perform any of the scheduled daily hygiene and replenishment routines.

The touchpad on the espresso machine was redesigned to make it easier for consumers to navigate (we asked our 3G design team to take a look at this for us), introduced brighter fibre optic lighting to help our *shop front* stand out and various sensors to prevent someone dumping chocolate powder without a cup being in position. It became a natural evolution from 1G – and it provided the mainstay of our expansion for the next three to four years.

At the end of 2003 the last quarter's sales were 32% higher than the corresponding quarter the previous year. We were maintaining a high growth rate, even as the company got bigger, and we were now not far short of being a £9m business. We expected to end the year to March 2004 at around 200 trading locations. This was great, but still short of the 247 we had previously forecast. After the board meeting that month I scribbled on the front of my board papers "budget accuracy – hit it and get rid of unnecessary optimism." There was no doubt we were making progress towards our vision of being Europe's leading self-serve gourmet coffee, but hitting a budget was another matter.

Budgets are important because they present management – including investor representatives – with a yardstick against which progress can be measured. The budgeting and forecasting disciplines we employed were unusual for a company of Coffee Nation's size, but were expected by Primary. I welcomed these disciplines and learnt so much about good business management from our time as a board together. However, at the time the company had simply not yet reached a point of predictability where budgets could be hit plus or minus 5% or 10%. We were far from being a mature company.

In the early days of my relationship with Derek he had suggested slow yet sustained growth that forms a new long-term trend is far preferable to a short-term fad. Starbucks had taken ten years to reach 84 locations, but then only another ten years to reach 1000 sites. Imagine trying to set annual budgets in their first decade!

As we progressed further the company was transitioning from an early-stage venture to the lower rung of what is called the mid-market, that is companies with sales exceeding £10m. With this growth, we were starting to construct a plan that would lead us directly to an exit for Primary Capital and a refinancing of the business to set the foundations for future growth. The aim of this was to put us in the strongest possible position to give us the broadest range of options – for the company, exiting and non-exiting shareholders alike.

The challenge we faced was that with two years to run to the target date for Primary's exit, so much of the growth that went into that plan was still based on as yet unproven assumptions. In early 2004 we drafted a plan that would see us reaching around 600 locations within the next two years – more than trebling the size of our estate.

Some 280 of these locations were Tesco stores (this is what had been presented internally at Tesco ahead of our contract sign off – at 60 cups per day this would at the time have represented approximately 7.5% of the UK take-out branded coffee bar market). A (hopefully conservative) 35 locations were included for Texaco in the Benelux and other UK growth came from a collection of new customers that had or were near to having signed trial agreements.

It was not hard to see where the risks lay. The Tesco roll-out was always dependent on sales volumes per day – we needed to be averaging 60 cups per location, per day. It was also dependent on gaining sign-off from an internal Tesco forum comprising the head of the Express format, head of operations, commercial analysts and marketers. Tesco had taken two years to go from first meeting to signed contract and there were still hurdles to leap before we could start to really grow. Tesco was always going to be a marathon, never a sprint. Texaco Netherlands was yet to launch and other UK was all early stage. By February we had shaved some of this growth off the plan – mindful not to be seen as too optimistic – to just shy of 500 locations. Probably wisely, we had pared Tesco back to around 170 locations.

The other fine line we had to tread was between maintaining an attractive upward trend in profits growth and investing for tomorrow. We knew that regardless of sales volumes, our infrastructure costs would exceed contribution from our European Texaco trials. Tesco was currently loss making for us given the higher than normal Brand Guardian coverage we gave these locations (to support operational integration – key to demonstrate readiness for roll-out) and 3G also showed a loss due to project management costs.

Presentation of management accounts had to change in order that we could distinguish each customer group and their net contribution (positive or negative) to the bottom line. Only this way could we see how each part of the overall was performing.

TEAM DEVELOPMENT

The business needed to be running smoothly day-to-day to allow the board and executive team to be focusing, say, 70% of its time on strategic issues and 30% on routine matters, not the other way around. The lack of a strong leadership team often creates a natural block to growth. We certainly didn't have this problem but we did need to develop our management team's capabilities below the board. This would protect what we had built whilst the board could be free to focus a reasonable amount of time on the future and how to make the big leaps forward. We started to look seriously at how to build a great team immediately below the board.

Vivien had recruited a trainee financial controller who was by now qualified – we had paid for James to sit his accountancy exams. Darren was growing in his role of managing installations and roll-outs to ever-increasing levels of professionalism and time-planning accuracy. Shane – who had joined the company late in 2000 – was now my number two in business development. Scott was looking at his requirements to free himself up from day-to-day operational management and we knew we needed to up our game in terms of dedicated customer management resource. This was a new role that would be dedicated to major customers, working with them centrally to help us grow our category.

We also recruited for a technical manager to lead our maintenance function. This was a difficult role to fill. We needed someone that not only understood espresso machine maintenance, stock management and spares allocation, but also the ideal candidate would have management experience – our aim was to build a world-class function in its own right within the business, dedicated to eliminating failure and maximising quality, consistency and reliability. It took several attempts before we got the formula right for this appointment.

We also needed to think ahead to our people needs if Texaco Netherlands was a success. Again, this was a fine line. We couldn't go ahead and recruit people before knowing we had a business in Europe. Waiting until we knew would force us to delay growth until the necessary people were in place, or divert resource from the UK at increased cost. We often tripped over great people keen to be part of what we were doing at Coffee Nation and we tried to keep the relationship warm with them until we could invite them to join the company.

Coffee Nation was an intensive and focused work environment that all of our team were passionate about. There was energy about the place and people routinely went way beyond the extra mile. As well as awards for growth and entrepreneurial passion, I really did want us to be recognised as a great employer. My verdict is that we did well in this area but we could have invested more in our people and created an even better culture and spent more time together as a team to celebrate our successes.

SEEKING A UK MD

To date we had concentrated on the commercial relationship with our customers, product quality and our operating system – we wouldn't have got to where we were without that focus. We now needed to look at what we did at each site after we had installed – how could we help grow sales and bring more people to Coffee Nation? We needed someone dedicated to our brand in the company.

My focus was driving forward the big strategic building blocks – so major relationships like Tesco and Welcome Break, then product development with 3G, international opportunities, building the management team and ensuring we moved smoothly towards Primary's exit sometime next year or early in 2006. I did not have the time to do all of this and continue to pursue a basket of target companies in the UK. I accompanied Shane on some customer meetings but our core UK market needed someone to lead it and drive its growth to allow the executive team to focus on the next major hurdles we had to deal with.

We agreed to recruit a UK managing director – who would also take over management of our Brand Guardian team from Scott, freeing him up. The UK MD would report to me – he or she wouldn't be on the main board but would essentially lead an operating board with all the major middle management roles reporting to them. They needed to be a sales/business development oriented individual as so much of our focus was on growth. This was a vital appointment – I prepared a brief and set out to identify a suitable headhunter. Our aim was to fill this role by early 2005.

We had to take these big steps if we were to maintain our growth – bringing the right people on board in the right roles almost before they were needed – but this investment in the future was always a pressure on our still infant profitability.

My recruitment of someone to focus on our brand and marketing was proving to be a painful process. No single candidate stood out, so instead of a full-time brand and marketing director, we met with an interim management company and interviewed a number of experienced consumer products marketers. This was an expensive route, as it was based on a daily fee plus a margin for the management company. We could only afford three days a week but we needed a bigger presence on site. It was also what our customers were expecting of us now. Obviously, a single successful marketing initiative could more than pay their fees for an entire year.

The individual we appointed was on contract to LOVEFiLM when we met her. They were growing fast and were highly disruptive in their market. It was likely she'd therefore be a good fit for Coffee Nation. Sarah joined us on an interim basis in June 2004 and hit the ground running.

NO FOOTHOLD IN THE LOW COUNTRIES

Our trials with Texaco Netherlands were finally off the ground in early 2004, with five locations trading across the Dutch road network. We had rented an apartment on a short-term let for Peter our technician, who was going to be based there during the trials to ensure technical support levels were beyond question.

Within weeks of launch we were achieving averages of between 160 and 260 cups per day. There was no doubt that Coffee Nation was working for the Dutch consumer. Customer response to our drink quality and size was positive, with just a little early resistance to the higher price and some customers wanting stronger coffee. Of course, the product was completely different. Our coffee was made from fresh milk and fresh beans and was almost double the size of the filter coffee served in small plastic vending cups from their existing Autobar vending machines.

Feedback from sites was positive, although we had to exceed their average profits for 2003. We were currently around 14% below their average 2003 margin. Our model relied on us being able to charge a premium price, drive up sales volumes and generate a higher cash profit for the retailer. Our sales needed to be about 10% above their previous levels in order to maximise their cash profit and after a month or so of trading we were about 25% short.

Autobar – our competitor in the region – responded with a fresh milk, bean-to-cup machine selling for €1 per cup. We had experienced some initial resistance to change by the local management – they had questioned if an improved product from their existing supplier (who they had been with for 13 years) at a price more akin to what the consumer was used to would suffice.

We were exceeding the Autobar trial results on a like-for-like basis and our superior product quality was acknowledged. Our actual sales volume compared to the same period the previous year was down by around 20%, as customers reported that previously they would have bought two small coffees. One-in-five customers told us they visited the store more often since Coffee Nation had been installed. The evidence was that what we had done in the UK was now happening in the Benelux – i.e. provide coffee-bar quality product in an easy to use, attractive format at prices comparable to high street branded coffee bars and sales will climb.

Despite these positive signs, securing an initial foothold in a European country was to prove elusive at this time. Despite Texaco in London having authority over decisions taken in the Netherlands they did not want to risk alienating local management. In the end the incumbent supplier smartened up their offer enough for Texaco to decide to stick with their long-term provider. Clearly, there could be many reasons why a company was chosen and not all of these were down to quality of the coffee, customer reaction or profitability.

Better news about prospects in Europe came later in the year when I learned that Terra Firma Capital, a London-based private equity firm, had just bought Tank & Rast, the German motorway services company. I met with Terra Firma and a further meeting was soon organised with their MD for Germany. As a private equity-owned business, I felt Tank & Rast would surely be keen to squeeze more profit out of coffee and would likely want to move ahead quickly if there was initial interest.

CRUNCH MEETING WITH TESCO

Following the triumph of the Tesco contract being signed just before Christmas, we now had to gain approval from Tesco Express. This would then unlock their estate and we could start to expand from our trial locations. We needed to demonstrate continued sales growth and operational integration.

We had a new contact within Tesco. Peter was enthusiastic about Coffee Nation and laid out his thinking that an immediate roll-out into, say, the first 100 Tesco Express stores would give us something to really shout about. He also reassured me that the broader aim of Tesco was to see us installed in most of their stores and that this project had the support of the board of the company. I also spoke with Sir Terry Leahy, CEO of Tesco. He was well briefed on Coffee Nation and was very positive about the product, the concept and its future with Tesco. This was good for my own board to hear.

Over two years of hard work came down to a single meeting in early June 2004. This would decide our fate in Tesco. I sent Peter a final email at 2pm ahead of their 5.45pm slot when they were presenting to the Tesco Express forum with all key stakeholders present. I dropped the latest news of sales growth in our locations into the email, as well as other news that we would now benefit from a fixed permanent sign above each Coffee Nation unit announcing coffee-to-go. I also included an email from a Coffee Nation customer who was driving 24 miles to his nearest Coffee Nation station several times a week and described our coffee as "the best thing since sliced bread." Having 100 Tesco locations around the country would mean shorter journeys for people to buy our product.

The Tesco response came a tense day and a half later:

> "After a successful trial and a good presentation at Express Trading we gained agreement to integrate CN as part of the standard Express offer – where appropriate."

We were at last certain of our position with Tesco. We had immediate sign-off into 54 Express locations. Across the summer we received drawings of all these stores with Coffee Nation designed in as an integrated part of the Tesco offer.

Roll-out with Tesco started in September and whilst we had stores selling 100 cups per day from the start, as we added new stores the average sales per day fell from 50+ to around 35. Sarah's priority was to develop a plan to see us achieving the target of 60 cups per day per store as quickly as possible.

We prepared a joint press release and a half-page article under the heading 'Tesco's Take-Out Challenge' appeared in the August 2004 edition of *The Grocer* magazine. The opener read:

> "Tesco is targeting the high street coffee bar market with a major roll-out of Coffee Nation's self serve gourmet coffee units. The concessions have already been installed in 30 Tesco Express stores and the multiple aims to roll them out to 150 by next March, advertising their presence using in store signage and banners outside shops."

By October we were opening two stores a day with Tesco. Trials were also underway in their Metro format (small high street supermarkets in urban locations). We were operating from Canary Wharf and Bishopsgate (near Liverpool Street station), but these were a different proposition to the Express format. Local coffee competition was intense and size and layout of the stores was completely different to Express.

We had other growth opportunities in the UK that we were pursuing, including WHSmith Travel that operated from over 200 locations across UK airports and railway stations. Shane now had a colleague in

Sarah and so once he secured trial locations she would work with him to plan the launch and grow sales as quickly as possible.

Development of 3G proceeded on budget and only four weeks behind schedule. We had developed a specification covering all our requirements, which were then ranked in terms of importance (to consumer, retailer or us commercially) and likelihood of inclusion in the system, based on cost, time to develop and complexity. The big question we always came back to was: what is really important to us commercially and really difficult to copy?

Drink quality had to be consistent with a barista-made equivalent. Coffee bean freshness was another key area for improvement. How could we increase the capacity of cups and lids and again reduce the frequency of staff visits the machine needed for replenishment? We decided on a large, colour touch-screen for drink selection and incorporated cup and cup size sensors to prevent customer mistakes or misuse. In parallel with this, our 3G industrial design partner was working on making the machine intuitive and easy to use.

PROBLEMS ON THE WEST COAST

The core reason for developing our own coffee machine was our reliance on a single company on the west coast of America. In the summer of 2004 one of our nightmare scenarios came to pass – investor support for them was withdrawn and they were unable to continue trading. We were four years in from Primary's investment and seven years in from my founding the business and we were genuinely facing a doomsday scenario – not only would our supply of machines dry up and quickly, but without knowledge of parts suppliers it would take time to organise supply of components to keep our current estate trading.

We faced a situation where growth would be impossible and to continue trading would be precarious. Despite our very close working relationship with our supplier we had not seen this one coming and we had to move fast. Derek and Scott flew directly to Seattle and I coordinated from the UK. All board leave that summer was cancelled.

I enlisted the help of our 3G development team to look at alternative machines, although this was far from ideal as we would then have original US machines, alternates *and* 3G – adding cost and complexity in terms of technician training, site operations, spare parts and so on. We considered building carbon-copy machines using all the information held in escrow that was ours in the event of our supplier's failure. This was possible but would cause a serious interruption to our growth.

Some members of the manufacturer's management wanted to pursue a management buy-out, restructure the company and return it to a sustainable and profitable position. We investigated whether there was a way we could play a central role in facilitating their survival, at least until 3G was firmly in the saddle for us.

There were four key considerations:

1. Our immediate need for machines – this looked like around 90 to 100 units over the next six months.

2. A strategic spares order to build stock and ensure trading of our current estate as far forward as possible.

3. Identification of new suppliers for key components to remove our reliance on the US supplier.

4. An agreement whereby in the event of their demise we would have access to IPR, software code, suppliers, parts lists, drawings and specifications.

Through immense hard work and very late nights from all members of the Coffee Nation board a solution was eventually thrashed out. With advance payments of around $500k for machines and spares, we were able to facilitate a management buy-out and the manufacturer was able to continue trading.

The rescue deal we engineered included securitisation of our prepayments and complete management control by us in certain circumstances. Thankfully this wasn't needed, our machines appeared, as did our spares, and disaster was averted. Vivien made regular trips to Seattle to oversee their operations and go through their finances with a fine-tooth comb.

This had been quite a distraction to say the least, but we had coped and whilst the pressure had shown at times we had come through this real test undamaged. It really threw a spotlight on bringing 3G to market and thankfully the first working prototype was expected in January 2005.

PROGRESSING TOWARDS AIM

Between development of 3G, trials in Europe, expansion of the management team and the deal with Tesco, our finances increasingly came under the spotlight. Our current expansion was being funded directly by cash flow from trading activities. Vivien had secured a package of asset finance and an overdraft of about £500k, but this was certainly nowhere near what we would need to fund future growth. It would not be long before we would need to seriously look at future funding sources and the implications of each route.

Vivien was also hard at work underpinning systems development that would put in place robust controls way beyond the planned exit. This included a fixed asset ledger, ingredient ordering and forecasting, machine maintenance, automated sales invoicing, sales forecasting and disaster recovery.

We were steadily progressing on all the major value enhancing strategic priorities that would lead to a sale or listing on AIM. Primary suggested I learn more about taking a company public so I attended a two-day programme run by Ernst & Young, the accountancy firm.

We met with a couple of corporate finance advisory firms to start to test the water towards an AIM float somewhere in mid-2005. The view was that there would likely be genuine investor interest in the company and the lines of attack we were pursuing (completion of 3G development with first locations trading, renewal of the Welcome Break contract, Tesco expansion underway, Europe, adding strength and depth to management and showing good upward trends in profitability) were all sensible for driving interest in the business.

LEARNING POINTS

- Having reached profitability we could afford to focus more on gaining market share. To ensure we secured each new contract they only had to be profitable enough. By adopting this strategy we could have starved competitors of any foothold in the market.

- We had created a new market category but we had to ensure we did not lose our ownership of it. Initial contract wins were secured against no competition and an unproven opportunity.

By the time contracts are up for renewal, the landscape may be very different.

- Build a broad base of support for your business across customer organisations.

- How can you tighten your grip on your category? Aim to improve contract terms upon renewal.

- Competitors do not need to do everything the category leader does or do it to the same standard to be used as a pawn in contract renegotiations by your customers.

- Knowledge is the most valuable asset in your business. It must be protected and passed on as you grow.

- Build a first class leadership team below the board. Make promoting from within the norm, not the exception. Establish personal development plans for each director and senior manager. Consider the use of external coaches and mentors. Companies that invest in this area outperform those that don't.

- Exit becomes a focal point and creates a short-term focus. This may be at odds with long-term, consistent, steady growth.

- Do not be blind to increasing pressures on your board and other senior managers as the business grows. You will face more complex issues and challenges you have not experienced before.

- Recruit the best leadership team you can – we survived the near collapse of our machine supplier in 2004 because of the combined efforts of our entire board. It could have sunk a lesser team.

- Be careful not to try and run before you can walk. We were impatient to wrap up the UK to allow us to focus on the bigger prize of European expansion but it was our home market that was to create the value in our business.

2005 – GANZ KAFFEE, GANZ SCHNELL

THE NEW YEAR got off to a good start. In January we opened our 100th location with Tesco and our 300th location for Coffee Nation overall. We had increased the size of our estate by 66% since the previous August and during that time had opened up to four stores per day.

We finished our year to the end of March operating from 306 locations. Our sales had reached £11.5m and we delivered £1.1m EBITDA. We had grown by 40% over the previous year. Most importantly though was the EBITDA margin we had reached – roughly 10% of sales. We had demonstrated beyond doubt that the business model worked and was profitable. We just needed more big companies wanting to deploy Coffee Nation at the rate of four locations per day like Tesco.

Despite being able to take pride in these numbers, the underlying picture was one of very unpredictable growth. Our chairman had observed this was likely to be a problem when he and I first met. He had certainly been proved right – the way to describe our growth would be *very lumpy*. We were planning to meet corporate finance advisers with a view to appointing the most appropriate to steer us towards a refinancing and an exit for Primary. It was a concern that this lumpiness could prove to be an issue with the exit.

DEVELOPMENT OF 3G

We had some major priorities with 3G. The first fully functioning prototype was being tested in the laboratory and had been unveiled to me and Scott the day before our AGM. It looked exactly like the foam mock ups but this one actually dispensed coffee. Drink quality was outstanding – way ahead of what we were achieving with the machine we had been using to date. The foamed milk was to the same standard as a hand-produced coffee shop product (although 3G delivered that quality consistently every time).

The 12" touch-screen was easy – almost intuitive – to use and the machine had coffee beans, milk and consumable capacity to sell 100 cups per day without any replenishment required for three days. This would truly transform the retailer's experience. Despite our best efforts to confuse it by trying to dispense a cappuccino into a tiny espresso cup, the machine was always one step ahead. Again, this would lead to a major operational improvement by eliminating wasted drinks.

The *design for manufacture* phase then followed and in parallel we were selecting a manufacturing partner with the capability to produce 3G in – we hoped – large numbers going forward. We also had an eye towards using the architecture of 3G to produce a smaller, lower-cost option (4G) in the future. This would open up locations that would not have sold enough coffee for 3G, let alone earlier versions, to be viable. If 4G could be low enough cost then putting them almost everywhere (within proven sectors) became a real possibility.

One of our first tasks with 3G now we had a working prototype was to test it with the public. Whilst 85% of people we had surveyed in 2003 said they found Coffee Nation easy to use we could see (through filming them) that what people say and what people do are two very different things. People are often reluctant to admit problems with seemingly simple user interfaces and are unable to articulate those problems.

We had also discovered the widespread disbelief amongst consumers that we actually sold fresh coffee made with fresh milk. Many thought it was instant coffee and powdered milk. We therefore had to shift their thinking to:

"Coffee Nation machines make real drinks."

Do this and 3G would not only be easy to operate, cheaper to buy and run, and hassle free for retail staff, but it would also outsell our earlier efforts. Our design partner explained that the product must seduce, the interaction must be satisfying and the participation should be rewarded with a memorable product and experience.

We knew this was important because Tesco had recently commented that we had got it right in their stores in regard to operations, but that we now needed to focus on the user experience. They wanted to see Coffee Nation as simpler for customers to use, less onerous for staff and with less labour budget required per store.

Although 3G was now live in the lab and the second and third prototypes were in build, the project was now running two months behind schedule and £500k over budget. Our product development partner essentially took this half million pound cost overrun on the chin and did not pass it on to Coffee Nation, although the next phase – the final stage before handover to manufacture – would cost us £200k more than budgeted.

It emerged the delays and extra spend were due to an over reliance on off-the-shelf components in the original design and greater technical challenges than had been anticipated. This put the original 18-month deadline under considerable pressure. Even so, we maintained a strong relationship as they were undoubtedly one of the world's leading product design and development companies.

So far 15 man years of engineering effort had gone into 3G's development, 670 detailed part drawings had been prepared and 110,000 lines of software code had been written to run all aspects of the system. We had also invested in patent protection. We had filed a claim for 12 specific inventions with the aim of making life considerably more difficult for future competitors if they attempted to copy or reverse engineer what they could see in the new Coffee Nation machine.

ENHANCING OUR BRAND IN TESCO STORES

Whilst our Tesco relationship was strong we really were now into the detail of how to grow sales store by store. By the end of March we were trading from 150 stores but the average sales per day had dropped to less than 30 cups as new openings diluted the sales of the longer-established locations. This was where we now had to concentrate our efforts.

There was no doubt that word was spreading and we started to get more and more emails from customers delighted that what they thought they could only previously buy on motorways and in some petrol stations was now appearing in their local Tesco. Some examples were:

> "Now I don't have to be on the motorway to enjoy the best coffee I have tasted in the UK."
> "Now I can pop out at any time for my favourite coffee."

Tesco ran an internal staff incentive that rewarded their teams for cleanliness of the Coffee Nation station and sales growth. As we were often situated next to the in-store bakery we discovered that croissants and Danish pastries were the most common item found in a basket with Coffee Nation and for every one Coffee Nation customer there were six bakery customers. Part of our plan had to be to capture more of these people.

We could also see that sales in the original 12 stores we had opened in 2003 had grown by over 40% and were pushing 60 cups per day. We also had nine stores opened late in 2004 that were now trading at 50 cups per day, having grown sales since launch by 58%. Our big challenge was the 56 stores opened between October and December 2004. Sales had grown 14% by spring 2005, but from a very low base of 20 cups per day.

Such growth rates were commendable in virtually any product category but there were noises that Tesco was "neutral" on coffee, given the long tail of slow risers. It was clear that the fast speed of roll-out across an estate where we had limited experience of ideal store positioning, etc., had been a drag on our sales growth. There was no question that sales were growing – we just had to make it happen quicker.

Operational compliance was crucial to growing sales and we could see that there were gaps here. We produced and sent to Tesco every week a report that showed, via our online fault monitoring, which stores were losing sales due to being out of milk or coffee beans, or not having been cleaned. I wouldn't say this was an easy win but there were clear actions that could be taken, store by store, to resolve this. We had been able to define the ideal in-store location and proved that sales where we were best located exceeded those with the worst in-store position by a ratio of 3:1.

Sarah arranged a meeting with a company called dunnhumby that helped businesses achieve consumer brand loyalty through analysis of data from customer transactions. Their premise was that customers tell us what to do through the data they leave behind. They had helped Tesco to great success with their Clubcard. We were told by dunnhumby that they could help us identify the characteristics of Coffee Nation customers in Tesco stores and thus identify new sites based on shopper profile as well as site characteristics. It would also be valuable to see how this could help us grow sales in existing locations.

Initial research conducted by dunnhumby showed we were driving people into Tesco Express stores and driving spend upwards. It also showed that a first time Coffee Nation buyer quickly became a loyal repeat customer and these people were starting to form convenience shopping routines in Express because of us. Furthermore, a loyal Coffee Nation customer spent more on average per visit than someone visiting Tesco but not buying Coffee Nation.

Within the space of a year, the number of Coffee Nation customers in Tesco that had bought our product five times or more went from 5% to 35% of those buying, so more people were becoming frequent buyers. A one-time Coffee Nation buyer would spend on average £14 per week in Tesco Express, compared to £28 per week for someone who had bought Coffee Nation ten times or more. It was possible to identify the products most likely to be found in a basket with a Coffee Nation drink such as croissants, a Tesco Finest sandwich and daily newspapers.

For customers buying one of these linked products, a campaign was devised using a coupon printed at the checkout that would entitle the customer to a free Coffee Nation drink when they were next in the store. The thinking was that this would encourage a trial of Coffee Nation amongst consumers of the profile who were most likely to buy our product and to drive up frequency of repeat purchase for those already buying. The results were impressive, with up to 14% of coupons issued being redeemed and weekly sales of Coffee Nation growing on average in the participating stores by 12% ahead of non-participating stores.

This helped more of our stores reach the initial target of 50 cups per day we had set with Tesco. By now over 100,000 customers were buying Coffee Nation from Tesco every month and by the end of the year we were reaching sales of almost 40 cups per day from 140 stores (there were some locations that both we and Tesco concluded were not locations for coffee, so we withdrew from these).

RECRUITING A UK MD

Late the previous year I had kicked off the process of recruiting a UK managing director who would be able to relieve me and ultimately the rest of the board from day-to-day management of UK operations.

The recruitment firm I hired proposed the best place to advertise the position was in the *Sunday Times*. The response was very encouraging, with 360 applicants. Eventually we got down to four potential candidates. All would have been good choices, but who was the best fit?

Some of the considerations at the forefront of my mind were:

- Retail and brand experience.
- Did they appreciate what had got Coffee Nation to where it was today?
- Did I believe they passionately wanted *this* role?
- Had they been an MD before?
- What experience of a high-growth consumer business did they have?
- Would they be a strong leader?
- What was their track record of delivering results?
- Would they be comfortable working at the highest level in our customer organisations?
- Were they convincing and believable?
- Was this position a logical next step for them?
- Did they have personal presence and determination to overcome the inevitable challenges?
- How was their self-awareness and emotional intelligence?

Our successful candidate was the sales and operations director of a successful consumer retail business in the UK. He had been part of a private equity backed management buy-out team and the company had then been acquired in a trade sale. The role of UK managing director at Coffee Nation was the logical next step for him.

I thought he would work well building relationships with our customers and he was quite different to my more entrepreneurial style. His prior exposure to private equity was useful and his references were excellent, confirming everything he said he had delivered.

Carl joined the company in April 2005 and spent the first month out with our Brand Guardian team across the UK. By June he had secured trials with Odeon and Waitrose and I recommended to the board that we formalise his appointment three months ahead of the end of his official probationary period. His brief was simple – grow the UK estate on gradually improving terms for us, sell more cups of coffee from existing locations and focus on every line item to drive profitability.

NEW OPPORTUNITIES
WHSMITH TRAVEL

WHSmith Travel locations were looking like a good bet for us. I had met with their CEO and they liked the concept. We felt there was more of a propensity to buy a takeaway coffee in a WHSmith store that was situated in an airport or a railway station – they were directly akin to retail shops in motorway service areas.

Every opportunity had its unique challenges and this was no different. Before they could install coffee in their stores, WHSmith Travel would need the approval of its landlord for many of its locations. There would doubtless be other coffee destinations within that location and whilst we were takeaway only with a limited drink range and no food offer, the coffee bar operators might object on the grounds that we could erode their business. Landlords did not want to rock the boat with other tenants.

Our first location with this retailer was at Manchester Airport in their Terminal 2 arrivals hall. We were pleased with results and so were they. We were averaging around 75 cups sold per day and they told us we were the hardest working 1-metre bay in the store apart from the newspaper cube and that one-in-ten transactions included Coffee Nation. At this run rate we would be happy to launch more locations, although due to the perceived risk of cannibalising other's coffee sales we were blocked from two other airside locations at Manchester.

Getting this single trial live had taken a year and was just not a sensible investment in time unless growth in installations followed. The retailer was keen to expand with us although we had to demonstrate our sales were incremental, i.e. Coffee Nation increased total shop sales rather than seeing a net decline as a result of our replacing a linear metre of other products. Many of their stores were very small and every inch of retail space had to be utilised.

SAINSBURY AND SOMERFIELD

We had progressed faster with Sainsbury although of course we had prior experience with them and they had tested the rival My Coffee offer. The team we were working with prepared a paper recommending a roll-out with Coffee Nation to 100 of their petrol forecourt sites that they believed were capable of delivering 50 cups per day. The next stage would be the Sainsbury's Local forecourt sites.

We developed a plan to open up to 25 locations by March 2006. Our first two Sainsbury petrol forecourts at Roehampton and Horley were selling between 60 and 80 cups per day, which was a fantastic start. An even better next step was when we signed a multi-year contract with Sainsbury with the aim of reaching 100 installations across their petrol forecourt (a joint venture with Shell) and Sainsbury's Local formats.

During the year we also learnt that Texaco was selling some of its UK forecourts to Somerfield, including many of our best performing locations. Somerfield in turn planned to sell and lease back 140 locations, which in itself should not have been an issue for us. The bigger question was whether Somerfield would want to continue the contractual relationship we had with ChevronTexaco. Early meetings with Somerfield proceeded well and they were, as we had hoped, impressed by our concept, product quality and consistency of offer. Maybe this could open a much larger opportunity. Our achievements with Tesco surely could not have gone unnoticed.

Somerfield looked like a possible 35 locations for the year ahead and they confirmed that we were to be their self-serve coffee partner. They also agreed that self-serve was more suitable in a convenience store than a served offer and in six of the 35 locations we would be replacing a manned Costa Coffee operation. At last we seemed to be getting the message across – self-serve makes more sense.

EXXONMOBIL

The opportunity with ExxonMobil (Esso in the UK) had been on the radar for some time and could offer significant next-stage growth for Coffee Nation. It offered potential in the UK, Europe and maybe even the US in due course.

Shane had been managing Esso and moving them towards an agreement for UK trials. They were taking us seriously and we had met with their head of food service for Europe, who had been impressed with our product quality, site support through our Brand Guardian network and Rapid Response Technicians, as well as the lack of any need for central management of Coffee Nation by Esso.

Things started to move forward and a meeting was then set up with their worldwide head of food service. Exxon operated thousands of petrol forecourts around the world under a variety of brands. We were keen to meet this gentleman and leave him in no doubt as to our capabilities. We organised a tour of some of our locations and the meeting went very well. He saw a great opportunity to partner with Coffee Nation.

Whilst we got the green light for UK trials they also invited Kraft to trial with their Kenco coffee brand. We had seen off this competitor in Welcome Break and Tesco and we had to stress to Esso that we couldn't drift into an expensive programme of trials without a clear agreement to roll-out on a long-term contract if certain pre-agreed success criteria were met. We had learnt the risks of costly trials in the Netherlands.

There were some important questions that we needed to be mindful of in proceeding with this company:

- We had been described as a "slick system" – there was no question we were slick, but did they not also see us as an emerging brand?

- Clearly compared to Kraft and Kenco we were a tiny company – to expand further into Europe with such a small business could be seen as risky.

- An enormous company like ExxonMobil may see Kraft as a safe option. We knew that *we* were the safe option and we'd have to make sure they formed the same view.

- ExxonMobil had a belief that a staff-served coffee offer was needed in their premium locations (they had Costa Coffee bars in their larger On-the-Run locations) and self-serve would be ideal for smaller Snack 'n' Shop locations. We disputed this strongly and were going to need to help them see and understand why.

It was clear that we would need to treat Esso as a long-term strategic opportunity – they had shared with us that a single coffee offer across Europe was their ultimate aim and their coffee programme in the USA was to be re-tendered in three years, so all was to play for. We must not lose this.

Carl made great progress with them. It had taken an age, but we eventually launched five trial locations that traded strongly and reached an agreement to open a further 50 locations across their Snack 'n' Shop forecourt convenience stores in 2006. Work was also underway on a plan to open up to another 150 stores across 2006-07 and Heads of Terms had been signed to this effect. Given the scale of the Esso opportunity we had agreed to unveil 3G to their European head of coffee early in 2006.

MOTO

We had also been working towards building our relationship with Moto for some time. They were the second largest motorway services operator in the UK and would therefore likely be a similar business to Welcome Break for us. Moto was owned by Compass Group, who could maybe offer further routes to growth.

We had first met with Moto in 2004 and they liked Coffee Nation. We modelled each of their locations based on their existing coffee sales and capture rates and compared this with our motorway experience. We showed a significant opportunity to uplift their sales, even on quite a conservative basis.

We proceeded with discussions and got as far as preparing a long-term contract covering their entire estate. Moto was supportive of a roll-out with us, but the final decision lay with their parent company Compass. Coffee Nation was rejected on the basis that the self-serve gourmet coffee market was too young and potentially too attractive to

Moto/Compass to simply commit to a single external partner, at least for now.

We realised just how serious Compass was about the coffee-to-go opportunity for its Moto motorway services when Carl sent me a couple of pictures he had taken of a new Baristo branded self-serve offer he had seen at a Moto location. It was essentially a large espresso machine with single push-button drink selection. It had quite a retro look and at first glance looked quite smart with a red, cream and chrome colour scheme. If they developed this to a reasonable level of competence then it would likely rule out any deal with Moto for Coffee Nation.

Looking on the bright side, as this was an in-house development it was unlikely to become a mainstream competitor to us. Nevertheless, despite all our success with and for Welcome Break if we couldn't crack Moto it would look like we'd be stuck in only one out of three possible motorway operators. Despite pioneering the category and our knowledge leadership, Roadchef had opted for a Coffee Nation imitation and it looked like Moto would develop their own offer.

This changed later in the year though when good fortune smiled upon us. Certainly in my career I cannot think of a better illustration of why it's always a good idea to maintain great relationships with customers that don't buy from you *today*, because *tomorrow* may be very different.

Compass announced that it was to sell SSP (Select Service Partner) in September 2005. It emerged as part of this deal that Moto was to be bought by the acquisitive Macquarie Bank of Australia. This had the potential to change the game for us and remove the obstruction that had prevented us completing a deal with Moto previously. There was absolutely no time to waste and I was straight back on the phone to their retail director who we had built a good working relationship with 12 months earlier. He agreed that it would be good to meet up again once the deal was completed.

TANK & RAST

We had been progressing with Tank & Rast in Germany. Coffee was an established part of their retail offer but there were numerous machine types, coffee brands, drink prices and variable standards of delivery. They liked our standardised (or homogeneous, as they described it) drink range, product quality, consistency and simplified management for the sites and T&R centrally. They recognised self-serve gourmet coffee was all we did and we would bring considerable expertise to this area. They operated some 380 locations across Germany, were innovative and highly professional. We agreed to an open sharing of information to allow some up-front modelling ahead of undertaking trials.

The triggers for a roll-out would be our standardised offer, clear branding, increased drink price and coffee quality. They had invested in coffee equipment just a couple of years earlier and didn't want to see this written off at significant cost years ahead of time. If trials were successful neither of us thought this would be a deal-breaker.

By mid-year we had agreed terms for a six-month trial and had selected locations. Such were their existing coffee volumes, we were to install dual Coffee Nation stations in their forecourts as well as single machines inside their main building retail shops.

One complication was that we could not use the Coffee Nation name in Germany. A small German coffee business had registered the national mark days ahead of our EU registration and that business had then been acquired by another German coffee company. Instead, we registered as Coffee Rapido in Germany and this was the name we would trial with. Colours, layout and all other elements of our offer were exactly as Coffee Nation in the UK.

We met with the owners of Coffee Nation Germany and our plan was that once we were clear we would be expanding in that territory with Tank & Rast we would seek to acquire the name with enough time to allow our roll-out to start as Nation, not Rapido. We planned for our trials to start in July and budgeted £100k to cover their cost.

Our trials went live in August 2005 under the Coffee Rapido brand we now owned. We had back-lit banners above the machines exclaiming "Ganz Kaffee, Ganz Schnell" (Real Coffee, Real Quick). Aside from the name the machines were indistinguishable from Coffee Nation installations in the UK and it was not long before we started hearing English voices buying our coffee. We had been spotted by UK truck drivers on the Continent who were our fans back home.

Not only did the machines look great, but we felt we had demonstrated a real professionalism to go from initial meeting with the T&R board in April to live trials in August. We did not know when or with which company we would eventually see Coffee Nation launch in Europe, but we were now certain that operationally we were more than ready.

Results in September showed we were selling 49% more cups of coffee than the same sites had during the same period the year before and our like-for-like sales value was up 79%. Our two companies agreed to meet in London in November to start negotiations towards a roll-out contract.

BUSINESS MANAGEMENT

As the business scaled up, management information became more and more important. Without a real grip on the detail it would be easy for cost increases to go unnoticed or lazy assumptions to set in. Milk and chocolate price rises had to be accounted for. These were tiny fractions of a penny per cup, but on the volumes we were now selling they became meaningful. Could these margin losses be recovered elsewhere? We knew what it cost to maintain a new installation, but what about a four-year old Coffee Nation station? What was the impact on the maintenance cost line of price increases on spare parts coming from the US?

Whilst our aim was always to elevate board discussions to the big issues we would think nothing of spending an hour or more of a board meeting poring over a single financial metric that was heading in the wrong direction. Only positive action arrests worsening situations and our monthly board meeting on occasion gave us early warning of dangers ahead if minor issues were allowed to run unchecked. Of course, there should never be any surprises for the board when they receive their papers – good or bad.

Forecasts had to withstand real scrutiny. Our original funding plan of five years earlier had shown a relatively linear growth rate and reality had proven to be very different. We had recently almost doubled our estate size due to our Tesco roll-out, but predicting which new customers would translate into growth stories and which would go nowhere continued to prove challenging. We had to constantly guard against hockey-stick growth curves just around the corner (or "jam tomorrow," as our board called it). It was inconvenient for us that large companies would not move faster, but our inconvenience was not their issue.

The final pieces of the management jigsaw (at least for now and ahead of Primary's exit and the refinancing of the business) were the brand and marketing director and an operations manager. The brand role had been on the table for over a year but in 2004 we hadn't been able to find a suitable candidate. This time round we did find someone who we thought would be a great fit with Coffee Nation.

Charlotte had been working in a similar vein for Krispy Kreme and it appeared she was doing a great job in building the public's awareness of that brand. I was impressed, we got on great and the rest of the board felt the same way. She was set to join the company at the start of 2006 (as Sarah, our interim marketer, was finishing with us at the end of 2005). I was excited because we now had someone on the team who had been highly successful in creating an aura around this US brand that was new to the UK. I set out to Charlotte how I wanted to get us beyond being seen as a "slick system" and move towards being regarded as a hot consumer brand on the up.

The operations manager was to lead the Rapid Response team (technical maintenance), establish the blueprint for maintenance as we expanded into each new country, as well as manage and lead our call centre operations, develop our brand standards across all customers and integrate new products (such as 3G) into the company and our corporate customers – in essence, a technical head of the business.

The role of leading our maintenance function had proved a difficult position to fill successfully since we had launched it late in 2002. We had always wanted someone who could mould our maintenance function into a truly world-class area of the business; expecting to find this amongst people experienced in the hands-on maintenance of espresso machines was unlikely to yield results. By looking beyond the coffee industry we were able to find the right person. Sarah was set to join the company early in 2006.

We had also considered for some time the need for dedicated customer managers. This role was intended to focus solely on working with each major customer day-to-day, whether that was to reduce shrinkage (wasted drinks), work on sales-boosting initiatives or operational matters. We had plenty of talent within the business ready to step into these roles, so we were able to expand the Brand Guardian role to include this and promote from within.

3G WORKING PROTOTYPE

Although behind schedule, by October the first production prototype of 3G had been assembled. The company we had chosen to build production units was based in Aldershot (a lot nearer than Seattle!) and was experienced in the assembly of precision equipment. We could therefore be confident of build quality. It was certainly another milestone reached when we saw a working prototype rather than the original number one lab prototype. Field trials would start early in 2006 ahead of production beginning in the spring.

We had by now unveiled 3G to Tesco and Welcome Break. As our most important customer it would be with Welcome Break that the first 3G unit would commence customer trials in the New Year. We agreed with Tesco to install an early production unit at New Tesco House to showcase our latest development. There could be no better way of exposing Coffee Nation to senior management and board members.

It was agreed we would not open any more locations with Tesco until 3G was available. It was great news in the medium term that they wanted 3G, but in the short term it meant that we'd fail to meet our installation budget – I suppose we couldn't have it both ways.

In the meantime, we focused on relocating under-performing machines to more appropriate stores, we completed the installation of our remote fault reporting software and started the negotiation of a new deal with Tesco. They continued to be very positive towards us, commenting that Coffee Nation was seen as a must-have product in Express stores and they acknowledged we were market leader in our category.

SUPPLIER OF THE YEAR

2005 had been a big year for us. By now we believed we had the largest estate of branded gourmet coffee retail outlets in the UK, aside from the majors of Starbucks, Costa and Caffè Nero. Operationally we had proven we could open up to five locations per day without drama and two years after launching our own maintenance function we were completing over 500 PMs (planned maintenance visits) per year, achieving near to 50 days MTBF (mean time between failure) per machine and an overall reliability approaching 99%.

Whilst we were still behind our forecast for the year in numbers of installations, sales per installation was 16% ahead of forecast and our gross margin was also trading up at 41%, versus 37% budget. Gross margin for Coffee Nation was the last line above the central overheads, so was a true reflection of the underlying profit of the business. It was basically sales, less the margin to our customers, less the costs of our Brand Guardian network and Rapid Response Technicians, along with spares and associated costs. It was the same as store profitability for a retail chain. The higher the gross margin percentage of sales, the more we could afford to invest in our product and brand. In turn this would mean higher sales and more profits for our retail partners.

3G was out of the lab and almost ready to be tested in the real world. We had bolstered the leadership team with three senior appointments. Our first stage roll-out with Tesco had been completed, meaning we now had three major UK customers, de-risking the business a little from our launch partners of Texaco and Welcome Break (this had taken almost five years). German trials looked hopeful and we had encouraging results from Esso and Sainsbury, both of which had the potential to become our fourth and fifth major UK customers.

We picked up some more awards too. We were ranked as the 21st fastest growing private company in the UK by *Real Business* magazine and appeared in their Hot 100 feature. A similar league table in the *Sunday Times* put us at 13th. Neil from Primary had earlier in the year suggested to the board that I should be entered for the Ernst & Young Entrepreneur of the Year Award, which at the very least might offer some free publicity (very useful for private equity investors planning their exit).

E&Y sent their people out to the office to interview me for the award. I never expected to win – I just loved talking about our business, what we'd achieved and where we were going. To be named Entrepreneur of the Year for consumer products and services for the South UK region in 2005 was a bonus. To cap it all we were named supplier of the year to Welcome Break.

LEARNING POINTS

- As a pioneer and category creator you will always need to bang the drum about something. Compliance with daily cleaning and stocking routines was as big a challenge in Tesco as it had been in Welcome Break three years earlier.

- Be wary of what you agree to in order to secure a customer. Some of our customer organisations wanted Coffee Nation to be exclusive to them in their channel, although we never agreed to this. Without certainty of growth from that customer we would be shut off from pursuing other companies in that channel.

- Consumer behavioural data is a powerful technique for finding new ways to grow sales.

- Always keep your vision front-of-mind, including in recruitment advertisements.

- If someone interviews well but then shares details of a higher paying offer elsewhere, ask them to decide first which company they want to join. Do not chase people by offering more.

- Is there any part of your business that is currently outsourced but is really part of your core competitive advantage, so should be in-house? It was proven the right decision for us to bring maintenance in-house.

- Make sure your board takes decisions. A long list of items carried forward each month with no outcome is not an effective senior leadership team.

- Whilst rate of growth of new sites was beyond our control, every line below this in our accounts was within management control.

2006 – TRIALS, NEGOTIATIONS AND CUTS

IN EARLY 2006 we won another business award – the *Sunday Times* Fast Track Award for Innovation – and we were runner-up in the Best Use of Technology Award, both of which were presented at a ceremony at Richard Branson's house in Oxfordshire. Charlotte, our new brand and marketing director, joined me for the event.

Despite my big smile in accepting the award, life felt very different this year. Every company goes through difficult times, although I thought that as a six-year-old, profitable business with over 300 locations our biggest challenges would be behind us. This year was to prove that you never quite know what is around the corner in business. Winning business awards is no assurance of ultimate success.

GOOD OPPORTUNITY, WRONG TIME

Our trials with Tank & Rast (T&R) had gone well and I met with their chief marketing officer (CMO) in Bonn. He set out his view of the trials, talking of our great visibility in store as a destination to visit, *emotional* appearance, good pricing for our product, transparency of operations, organisation from our end, solid operational support and, finally, a good fit with German customers and our overall professionalism.

The period from week three of August 2005 (when the trial started) to the end of that year generated more profit for T&R than they achieved in sales for the same period in 2004. We had matched their forecast profit for the trading period in 2005 as a result of increased sales volumes and increased drink price. We knew that a negotiation would follow, but given the results and the feedback we were hearing we felt optimistic a deal could be concluded. Fundamentally there were three issues, but there were ways around them:

1. Brand – clearly we had proved popular with German customers, but why have a new coffee name when Dallmayr was the established and respected coffee brand across the T&R estate? They were also operating attractive Segafredo and Lavazza cafes in some locations.

2. Our revenue share model – we were told that tenants would not warm to this as it gave them less control. This felt contradictory as the CMO had previously stated on several occasions that one of the key benefits was the greater control we brought and its transparency.

3. Funding of assets – our business model where we purchased and owned the machines was different to the existing arrangement for supply of espresso machines to each tenanted location.

I updated Terra Firma back in the UK (T&R's owners) and they confirmed they had heard good things about Coffee Nation from their German colleagues.

We continued to run the trial locations, although they had by now proved themselves. Given we had relocated a technician to Germany from the UK the trials were actually costing us money so we were keen to move along without delay, hopefully to a successful conclusion. The problem was that it was not simply a case of agreeing a commercial deal with T&R centrally, as there were powerful operators of each location to manage also.

We entered into a complex analysis of 200 of their locations and their retail director shared with me his projections for sales and profits for this network of sites based on their existing sales. Competitive proposals from Tchibo were also set out. I then showed him a financial illustration based on a roll-out of 3G over five years and compared that with his current performance. He acknowledged that with Coffee Nation, financial returns were most favourable over a five-year period, but less attractive in the early years.

There was no doubt that we could and would grow the self-serve gourmet coffee category – I had demonstrated 3G to the retail director at T&R and he had confirmed that, in his experience, we were streets ahead of any European competition. The challenge was simple – margin aspirations would have to be very high in order for us to dislodge the incumbents.

This went well beyond not pushing a deal too hard. Setting up Coffee Nation in another country had major risks and when we took this step we had to be confident it was the right time to do so. Looking hard at the facts it started to seem as if this was not the right time.

Further, there were now no shortage of expansion opportunities in the UK and introducing a high-risk, unknown variable in the form of setting up a major operation in Germany looked distinctly unappealing. Beyond that, we didn't have the financial headroom for this undertaking and we would have to build up our experience maintaining 3G successfully at home before even contemplating running these new machines in Germany.

Strategically it was a very sizeable opportunity to position Coffee Nation right in the heart of mainland Europe with a great company who we got on well with, were highly professional and also keen to introduce us to other European roadside convenience retail operators. It was just, plain and simple, the wrong time.

A PERIOD OF DIFFICULT NEGOTIATIONS

Back in the UK we were working equally hard to move forward with another large and valuable customer, Tesco. We had shown them 3G and they described the inside of the machine as "brilliant for Tesco." It had also been described as "good for customers and good for staff."

We were by now selling about 160,000 cups of coffee per month from 150 Tesco stores and both companies could see the opportunity to gradually phase in 3G. They believed there could be a further 150 stores or so in the year ahead that would be a good fit for us.

I had drafted a set of Heads of Terms for a new agreement with them that would phase out 2G and bring in our new product. By Christmas 2005, most of the terms were agreed. There was only one real issue outstanding and that related to something we had not been able to persuade Tesco of back in 2002 – namely the price at which we sold our drinks.

The terms of the deal worked perfectly well for us if we were selling espresso at £1.30, regular size at £1.70 and large at £2 as we were elsewhere, instead of the £1.30 for espresso and regular and £1.60 for large as at present. Even at the higher prices, the new Tesco terms were not highly profitable for us (given lower sales volumes compared with motorway and petrol forecourt locations), but they offered an *acceptable* return and the benefit of our contract with Tesco went far beyond the income from selling cups of coffee.

Further expansion across Tesco's enormous estate was valuable in enabling us to offer our product to more and more people across the UK. It also sent a strong message to other retailers that Tesco rated our product and our professionalism. They were a world top-four retailer and would be an invaluable reference as we ventured beyond the UK.

At the current substantially discounted prices the terms of the deal did not fly for us, but Tesco did not want to increase them. We could not understand their resistance to a modest price increase that would still leave their customers paying considerably less for a Coffee Nation coffee than the high street coffee bar chains and many other retailers of good quality takeaway coffee. If a Tesco Finest roast beef sandwich was £2.50 it did not seem unreasonable that a Coffee Nation cappuccino should retail at £1.70, but Tesco were very sensitive about being seen to raise prices.

Of course, what we were really tackling here was the fact that Tesco were not used to being unable to set the retail price themselves. Our business model was quite clear and had worked successfully so far: Coffee Nation will recommend the price and agree the appropriate level with our retail partner. The retailer could not change the price – up or down – without our agreement, and neither could we without their consent.

Whilst it was a significant departure from our model, I started to see that perhaps the way through was that we charge a fixed margin per drink size. This seemed to be a genuine win-win for both parties. We could peg this at a level that would ensure our required margin and payback, but allow Tesco the freedom to price as they wished. A condition of this was that the retail drink price could not be lowered from its current level (thereby protecting our price integrity across our estate) and that we conduct consumer trials at the higher prices we charged elsewhere. We further proposed that we would share in the upside if the drink price were increased from its current level.

I set this out in a detailed paper to my board and we agreed that we would be prepared to move forward on this basis. We had also agreed to give Tesco priority with 3G in the grocery market. I went back to Tesco with prices at which we could sell to them. They could then add their desired margin to arrive at the retail price. However, having gained control of drink price, Tesco then wanted to renegotiate on the Coffee Nation margin.

Our experience of Tesco had largely been highly positive since we had started working with them in 2002. However, some of my board were now questioning the time spent attempting to close this negotiation. As much as we wanted to expand our presence in Tesco, it had to be commercially viable. Volumes were way off what we sold in petrol forecourts and motorway services and our drink price (or what we would be charging Tesco) was also way below where we were in other sectors. We could live with this as we were building our estate in Tesco *to create demand*, but any further drag on our income was a blow to our profitability and my board had every right to question the commercial logic.

Time dragged on and we still had no deal. It was now by far our longest commercial negotiation and some of my board were starting to ask questions about how valuable Tesco was to us. It was not helped by the fact that Tesco had by now decided to undertake a trial with a self-serve Kenco machine in one of their London stores. I went to check out their offer and see if it had moved on since our encounter with them in Welcome Break a couple of years previously. It hadn't, it was still just an attempt to have an offer in the category we had created. Staff feedback on site was not complimentary. I was told there had been little support on the ground from Kenco and when I visited I was told the machine had been out of action for some days.

When we still had no resolution by November, one of my board commented, "We don't need to be in Tesco, if we were selling bacon, eggs or bags of salad we'd have to be but we can build our estate elsewhere." He was right, but to lose our Tesco relationship would have been a bitter disappointment having achieved so much with them in the last four years.

I asked Vivien to rerun our forecasts without them in the numbers. We had to assess the impact on the business of the loss of this customer – determined though I was that it would not happen – and look for ways to neutralise the impact. It was a valuable exercise and did not paint a terrible picture in terms of impact on the company (we would survive and remain profitable), although to lose 150+ locations would certainly mean redundancies as we would have surplus Brand Guardians and technicians.

TERM LOAN

Notwithstanding Tesco, 2006 had not started as we had been hoping. We had expanded our senior management group with Carl, Sarah and Charlotte, which increased our overhead base significantly. We were investing heavily in completion of the 3G project and continuing to support expensive trials in Germany. We were fighting multiple battles, all of which put our cash headroom under pressure. I had a new top-gun marketing director but she had no budget.

Whilst we already had an asset financing (for our vehicles and some funding of machines) and invoice discounting facility in place, we were now working hard to secure a term loan from RBS to fund our future expansion. The purpose of the loan was to fund our first order for new 3G machines and related equipment and we agreed £1.3m was required. If approved, this would be repayable over three years.

RBS agreed that Coffee Nation was by now a stable business, beyond the higher-risk early days that Primary's equity injection had funded. When the bank's due diligence report came back it confirmed that:

- We were market leader in our space.
- Management was strong and ambitious.
- Demand for our product was likely to continue to grow.

It also commented favourably on the strength of our finance and accounts function (Vivien and three others, two of whom were qualified accountants) as well as our ability to produce high quality and timely management information. They noted positively that this was highly unusual for a company of our size. They noted our history of delivering on key performance indicators consistent with or better than budget over the last three years. Their overall conclusion was that Coffee Nation was well run and tightly controlled and that a forecast EBITDA of £1.9m for the year ending March 2007 looked achievable and sustainable.

By early February we were in receipt of RBS's offer. Detailed warranties and undertakings were set out in the loan agreement that we had to comply with. We would have to prepare a 'Look Forward EBITDA certificate' signed by and on behalf of the directors of the business that we would meet the financial covenants set when they were tested each quarter.

This was the next step for us in terms of growing up as a business. Ratios were set as a means of financially stress testing the business, for example there was a ratio set for how much profit before interest and tax (PBIT) had to exceed the company's total borrowing costs. Exact EBITDA and capital expenditure figures were set that we had to meet or not exceed, by quarter, respectively. Covenants such as these are there to provide the lender with assurance that the business can withstand normal (or even abnormal) fluctuations in trading and still be able to comfortably meet its obligations under the loan.

There could be absolutely no deviation from the assumptions we had set out in the forecast provided to the bank and there had to be exceptionally tight control over discretionary expenditure, but our finance director was able to report that we could meet the covenant tests and the other areas of concern had been addressed. It was clear, though, that any shortfall in revenue would have to be compensated through cost reduction.

I set the ball rolling by requiring that any discretionary spend of £100 or more had to be signed off by me personally and there was to be no increase in headcount (which did put our maintenance function under some real pressure throughout 2006 as we headed towards 400 locations later in the year).

My level of attention to the smallest financial details stepped up a gear. I would go through our management accounts line by line with Vivien – and look to see where we could release some slack and give ourselves increased headroom for when it came to our quarterly covenant test. No stone was left unturned and, interestingly, I found myself enjoying these working sessions as it taught me more about my business, right down to the ground level. It also gave me more confidence in financial discussions and decision making. By the end of September, Vivien had been able to show we had satisfied our covenant tests for two consecutive quarters.

A covenant worksheet was added to each month's board pack so we could constantly monitor our position. RBS was delighted they had been able to complete the deal and asked if they could write an article on the company for their new *Deals Done* magazine for business customers, setting out how they had been able to help us. They even shot a video at our offices.

Our results for the financial year ending March 2006 were the only set of low growth results we had delivered in the six years since Primary had invested. Every other year we had delivered sales growth of at least 35%. Installations had increased only marginally to 346 and our EBITDA margin dropped to just over 7% from 10% of sales the year before.

Of course, 2005-06 had been a year of readying for the next stage of growth. 3G development, German trials and the strengthening of the management team with Carl, Sarah and Charlotte's recruitment and joining costs had all had a negative impact on our EBITDA performance. The good news was that Sainsbury, Esso and Somerfield were looking like they would contribute significant growth over the next 12 months so 2006-07 should see installations, sales and EBITDA back on a healthy upwards trajectory.

The RBS loan was symbolic of where we had got to. We were finally turning the corner from being reliant on the two customers that had supported our launch back in 2000 and Tesco in 2003. We were reaching a watershed point – we could confidently show that our forecast growth in the year to end March 2007 could all come from existing customers.

REVOLUTIONISE MY DAY

We were now ready to install a 3G preproduction machine into a customer location. Fleet Services on the M3 was agreed as our test site. It was one thing testing a prototype in the lab with family and friends, but quite another to allow the public to put it through its paces.

The overwhelming response was that it was easy for customers and easy for staff. Early indications, even after just a few days of trading, were that we were growing sales over the previous 2G installation. Charlotte undertook customer surveys whilst Darren and Sara managed the technical aspects; 94% of customers described the new machine as "welcoming and intuitive" and 99% compared our coffee to high street coffee bars. The mocha and filter coffee products were also well received. Some customers even described it as the "iPod of coffee."

The Welcome Break staff who were normally forever replenishing our machines with milk exclaimed how we had "revolutionised their day" as there was much less restocking for them to do. The machine even kept itself clean and all of the wasted drink problems were eliminated.

Of course, not everything worked flawlessly – there were component failures and some software issues. In parallel we installed another 3G prototype into our workshop and one of our senior technicians took up the job of writing the technical manual and workshop guides for our maintenance team. A second trial was planned for May in another Welcome Break location, this time with the main focus being on system reliability.

We expected to place the first production order for 50 machines in June, for delivery commencing September. There were commercial pressures from customers to think of. We were fast approaching a situation where demand would exceed our capacity to supply – unless we bought more machines from the US.

The initial estimate for the cost of an installed 3G was more than for 1G or 2G, so there was clearly a big project ahead of us to bring the cost down below this level. The project had by now cost £2.5m, with another £177k to come. The extent to which we needed to undertake field trials had not been known and manufacturing set-up and tooling costs had also exceeded forecast.

DELIVERING FOR MOTO

I introduced a fortnightly meeting of the top team – the executive board and senior management team (Carl, Charlotte and Sarah) – and spent time with our Brand Guardian and maintenance teams. We also organised a round table session with the entire company where we updated them on progress and invited them to share their own ideas on how we could do better, in whatever way and wherever in the business.

We enjoyed fantastic loyalty and commitment from our team, although I learnt that the big headlines were not the major attraction for many, even those that owned shares and options. The greater focus was job security, interesting and varied work, feeling valued, an enjoyable working environment and a competitive salary. Sometimes in our pursuit of the big stuff we overlooked some of the smaller things that cost little or nothing but made such a big difference to people.

It was May before the dust had settled on Moto's sale to Macquarie and their retail director, Tim, could meet me. Given we had built a good working relationship with him back in 2004 when he had been in favour of Coffee Nation, a meeting over supper and a glass of wine seemed more appropriate. I knew a good venue in Chiswick near to where he lived and booked a table.

Moto had committed considerable time and probably a fair amount of money to the Baristo machines which they had installed across 30% to 40% of the estate although Tim commented that reliability was a constant issue. Ensuring the operational disciplines were in place to manage self-serve coffee to a high and consistent standard was an ongoing headache.

He explained they were selling more coffee than previously, but nowhere near the capture rates he could imagine we were achieving in Welcome Break. He has also added that labour costs were a concern and went on to explain that Macquarie wanted to see new concepts creating genuine growth in the business.

This all sounded like a very positive backdrop against which to restart a discussion with Coffee Nation. Moto had recently begun to introduce Marks & Spencer stores into their sites and could see how a niche category leader (like us) and a big destination brand (like M&S) could drive enormous foot traffic into their locations. He also said that they desired a point of difference. That sounded like 3G to me.

He had handed me all the ammunition I needed – Baristo was a pain to operate, labour costs remained high, capture rates had not reached our levels and maintaining high operating standards was a constant headache. What more did I want?

To secure Moto would demonstrate we could win multiple major contracts in a single sector. In the last six years of dealing with large companies I'd learnt just how hard it is to get them to change direction. This was not the time to forget that, but it was also a time to be bold – just like the early days all over again.

I didn't waste any time and went back to Tim the next day. Our 3G trial at Welcome Break Warwick on the M40 was singing and I knew in an instant that we needed to get him in front of it. Our new offer didn't just address the issues he had with Baristo – it went way, way beyond.

The other good point was that Tim was informed from his own Baristo experience – he'd learnt that an attractive and easy to use machine is only a small part of what made self-serve gourmet coffee work. He'd get what 3G would do for his business far quicker than a company without any experience of self-serve gourmet coffee.

My instinct was right. He was open to a commercial discussion around Coffee Nation in Moto. The first step was to agree a trial of 3G in one of their locations. We agreed a single location trial of 3G to run for six weeks. Assuming this was a success and satisfactory terms of a deal could be thrashed out then Moto would become our next major trading partner. The trial was planned for Moto's Leigh Delamere service station. The agreed success criteria were customer and staff reaction and feedback, reliability and technical support, sales uplift, commercial performance and waste/shrinkage. Sales took off and we were soon reaching 200 cups per day, against 135 with Moto's own Baristo offer.

By October we had a draft set of Heads of Terms with Moto for a new contract to be their exclusive self-serve gourmet coffee partner. They operated 56 petrol forecourt stores and this was to be the primary focus. As sales volumes grew we would double-up, adding a second machine alongside the first. Their retail shop estate was the next opportunity after the forecourts.

We debated the commercial terms to propose to Moto. Of course, no one wanted to offer a higher margin than necessary yet at the same time we didn't want to undercook it by a few percentage points only to lose the deal. These were high volume locations – we knew how they'd perform and recollections of Roadchef came to mind. We didn't need to take an unnecessary risk. By the end of the month the Heads had been signed and our lawyers were busy drafting a roll-out contract.

COMPETITOR CUSTOMERS

An unintended consequence of our new union with Moto was the effect it would have on our Welcome Break relationship. Welcome Break had been our launch customer back in 2000 and while we had no exclusivity arrangement with them, they were always sensitive about us appearing anywhere else on UK motorways and it wasn't rocket science to anticipate they wouldn't be delighted to hear customers would now be able to choose Welcome Break or Moto to stop for a Coffee Nation. News travels fast and, unknown to us, Scott had been spotted and overheard in a Moto store discussing arrangements for expansion on the motorways.

From our perspective, though, we had to be very careful that we were not over-exposed to any single customer. Many companies in their efforts to please their largest customers become over reliant on them and chase increasing volumes of business but often at the expense of profitability.

I regularly met with the CEO of Welcome Break and often over a spot of supper. Of course, on this occasion I did have to share the news with him that we had agreed a contract with Moto. I thought I'd leave it until the end of the evening. Dinner and the meeting had proceeded well and was otherwise uneventful until he erupted, revealing he knew about our plans to install in Moto. I could not believe it – he'd beaten me to it and I really did have egg on my face. Of course I was going to tell him, but no matter how much I might protest all he knew was he'd spoken first.

Within days I was back on the phone with him and he was soon meeting us with his retail director to plan how we could do even more across their estate, together, to make Coffee Nation even more successful, including drive-through Coffee Nation pit stops and new marketing campaigns.

He was adamant that a price rise was overdue and I didn't feel on too solid a footing to object. Coffee bar prices had risen during the year and a small 20p increase was not unreasonable as it would still leave us well below all our competitors. As it happened the price rise helped us with our bank covenants, so that was a bit of a result!

500 LOCATIONS IN SIGHT

We could now see our way clear to 500 locations (not including Moto) in the UK with existing customers, although this depended very much on availability of 3G. In June we signed a contract with Esso and the first milestone was 40 machines to be installed by the end of the year. Esso had also gained approval for the capital expenditure to fit out another 75 stores with Coffee Nation in 2007.

Somerfield had Heads of Terms for the installation of Coffee Nation across its forecourt convenience stores. We had trials live with them and had replaced a manned Costa Coffee operation in their Eastbourne, Rochester and Witham stores, and were now selling up to 100 cups per day from each of these. Another UK operator of forecourts, Malthurst Pace, had signed a long-term contract with us in October and we were soon trading well from 23 of their locations.

We had a second customer beyond WHSmith Travel in airports in the shape of World News (Alpha Retail) that operated convenience stores across a number of UK airports – we were in Birmingham and East Midlands airports. It was a different story to 2002 – we were selling up to 150 cups per day (because we were in a convenience store, not trying to stand out on our own at a departure gate). We also had trials with Co-Op, Southern Rail and even Gala Bingo (where, perhaps not surprisingly, sales of our coffee did not take off).

The upshot was the business now looked very different to even 18 months ago. We had contracts in place with Welcome Break, Tesco, Sainsbury, Esso and Malthurst Pace. At least 95% of our estate across these customers was in our well proven sector of roadside convenience retail. Moto and Somerfield were both at Heads of Terms stage, so we were confident that within weeks we would have seven major signed contracts operating in our proven, low-risk market channel.

Welcome Break was approaching maturity in terms of numbers of machines we could deploy and of course there remained a big question mark over Tesco but, other than that, we were at the start of our relationships with all of the other companies.

The new contracts all had considerable upside potential. Malthurst Pace, for example, operated some 280 UK locations and we were in less than 10% of these. At our October board meeting I explained that I was confident we could underpin much of our growth for at least the next three years from contracted (or soon to be signed up) customers.

Our EBITDA target for year end March 2007 was £1.9m and I could report to the board we were marginally ahead of budgeted EBITDA for the first half of the year to end September, with October being slightly up on budget. With five months of the year remaining we had delivered over £1.1m EBITDA and were running at almost £200k per month, so we could be confident of hitting our year-end target.

ESSO OVERSEAS

Esso presented a big overseas opportunity. We were already their exclusive partner in the UK for their Snack 'n' Shop locations and they were keen to standardise and embrace new concepts across their European business. In the summer both their European head of coffee and global group director for coffee and food service from ExxonMobil in the US came to see us.

We agreed that 2007 would be a good time to reconvene to discuss trials on the European Continent. Considering the US, their global head of coffee explained how Exxon had 1200 sites with their Bengal Traders offer, which was a range of filter, self-serve coffees but they had no espresso-based offer. He said 3G was ideal given it needed so little staff attention and took care of product safety aspects so well.

We discussed a pilot programme in an appropriate region of the US (high demand for espresso beverages, tight concentration of sites and probably east coast) – sometime in the next 18 months to two years. He explained that, as they were such a large company, things took time – I countered that these timescales were ideal for Coffee Nation given its agenda closer to home anyway.

Within a few weeks I received a letter from him headed "Potential Expansion to the US". His US colleagues agreed that our offer appeared to be an ideal solution to enter the genuine gourmet coffee market using real milk and espresso. He concluded:

> "...If, measured against pre-agreed success criteria, the program proves to be successful we would then like to work with Coffee Nation as our self-serve espresso partner for North America. Clearly this is going to take time/financial management & resource on the part of both our companies but we would like to aim to have this pilot live within the next 18 months or so."

It would only be a matter of time before Coffee Nation started to expand beyond the UK, but right now our priorities were clear and they were all in the UK. These were:

1. Order 50 3G machines.

2. See 3G safely into production.

3.   Install the first eight 3G machines in Welcome Break before Christmas 2006.

4.   Get the Moto and Somerfield contracts signed.

We had agreed with Welcome Break that they would be the first company to receive the 3G machine. They were our largest and most loyal customer and had also been more than helpful in allowing us to remove high-performing 2G machines for us to test our new product. Our aim was that having run the eight initial locations for some time we could then sit down with Welcome Break and look at how we could construct a new long-term relationship together, using 3G and anchoring them as our most important customer.

FOCUS ON THE PRIORITY AT HAND

Our original thinking back in 2004 was that we needed to expand the management team in order to allow the executive board to prepare the company for expansion beyond the UK, hence Carl's appointment as UK Managing Director. The reality had been somewhat different of course. We had conducted European trials but were not ready to make this leap as a business. There were a number of reasons for this.

First, 3G was not finished and in the market and this delay had put a considerable strain on our financial position. Second, our aim had been to complete a refinancing of the company by the end of 2005. This had not been possible and therefore the company was effectively starved of the kind of investment that would have allowed us to enter Europe on a solid footing. Consequently, Carl could not assume the full scope of his role as UK MD.

Regardless, we still needed to complete one thing at a time and that was 3G. We really needed to focus more than ever and this meant streamlining the business to focus solely on the UK. Carl's role was repositioned as sales and marketing director, Charlotte and Sarah both left the business, and we promoted Tim, one of our earliest team members, to service manager looking after technical maintenance. These losses of terrific people were regrettable but we had to cut our cloth to meet the needs of the business, continue to maintain our bank's confidence and meet the EBITDA forecast of £1.9m for the year to end March 2007.

At our 3G manufacturing company, 96% of all components required for the assembly of the first 50 machines were on order, but it seemed as we dealt with one issue another appeared. This final push for the finish line to see 3G safely into the market had taken so long and cost so much more than originally budgeted that it was frankly an embarrassment. Vivien held a conference call with the manufacturer every day – it was this level of detailed management that was necessary to steward the project through to conclusion.

Just prior to Christmas Moto signed their contract to give us six major contracted customers, and Somerfield was expected to be not far behind in the New Year. We remained within our covenants and finished the financial year with 408 trading locations by March 2007. We hit the £1.9m EBITDA target, which was up 125% on the previous year. Our sales exceeded £13.5m, which was a 17% increase on the previous year, and most importantly the percentage of our EBITDA margin to sales was up to a very healthy 14%. Finally, and most importantly, we had customer contracts in our proven roadside sector that would underpin the next three years at least. We were back on the up.

LEARNING POINTS

- Smile just as much when the going is really tough – I had a desk toy that said "See the fun in being behind the 8 ball."

- Be prepared for commercial negotiations with large organisations to take considerable time to conclude. Work through the various scenarios with your board if necessary.

- The more compliant you are, the further you push the deal away. Be seen to co-operate but don't concede. Only give – in return for something of value to your business. Stand your ground *and* be flexible.

- It is always important to carry your board with you – all have their say but once a course of action is agreed all must support it wholeheartedly.

- You will be amazed at the savings you can make when you have no choice. Quarterly covenant tests really focused the mind.

- Staying in contact with Moto from two years before and the sale of that business in 2006 was a good illustration of luck – this is when preparation meets with opportunity.

- Opportunities that fail to land first time around often come back later when you are building a category for the long term. That was expanding into Europe for us.

- Making cuts can be painful and not what you expect when you are growing and profitable. This must not deter you. Never be in denial of what actions you must take today.

- See award wins as a bit of fun, good PR and a shot in the arm for your team. Nothing more. Keep your feet on the ground.

2007-2008 – COMING FULL CIRCLE

PIONEERING A NEW category is so much about staying true to the core and never being distracted. It's also about telling the story, over and over and over again. It is sometimes said the CEO in this type of business has to be the chief storyteller and I can understand why. As the leader of the company, staying true to your vision is critical.

In 2007 we sold our 40 millionth drink and our machines at Welcome Break Services on the M40 motorway at Oxford met with their millionth customer. We were also generating a net cash inflow each month of almost £250k. We confirmed 101 machines to be installed in the first four months of the new financial year and by August we had opened our 500th site, with commitments underpinned to 540 trading locations.

There were some internal changes too. At the start of 2007 Vivien, our finance director, left the company and was replaced by Simon Vardigans.

COFFEE HERITAGE

There were one or two projects within the business that we were keen to progress but, due to budget or other resource limitations, had not been able to. Our website was overdue some serious redevelopment. The design of our cups was due an overhaul. The other area we believed warranted serious attention was the heritage of our coffee.

Gala was one of the largest roasters in the UK and were also part of the much bigger Dutch Drie Mollen Group. They were responsible coffee buyers but we felt we wanted to play a more active role in ethical sourcing. Working with Gala we were able to develop our own provenance programme.

This was in two stages. The first was to source our beans via the Rainforest Alliance certification programme. This meant that by paying farmers a premium rate we could help ensure dignified living conditions for farm workers and neighbouring communities. This would mean farmers would have the resources to care for their crops and their land, in turn helping to build a sustainable local economy.

The second stage was to engage directly with a local community in a development project. This involved Coffee Nation funding repairs to a local school in San Elisa Village in Guatemala which was attended by 75 local children, as well as improving school facilities and provision of educational materials. We believed this approach was the best combination of improving economic opportunity for coffee farmers, social development and quality of life for their families and communities, and conservation of the local ecosystem. By July we were using our Rainforest Alliance certified beans from Guatemala.

A NEW START WITH TESCO

In March, Somerfield signed a contract with us which meant we now had seven major customers. We had enormous growth potential with most of these, but there was one that remained uncertain. That was, of course, Tesco.

After another heavy board discussion in early 2007 I recall setting out how I saw the Tesco situation with Scott. Our business had changed shape dramatically in the last couple of years and a review of net sales or gross profit by customer would quickly reveal how our operations and profit was now more evenly spread across our customers. As the newer partners grew in size for us, the relative importance of any single customer would decline. Up until recently Welcome Break had been the anchor of our business.

For me, whilst we obviously wanted to see a profitable future with Tesco, that didn't all need to come from the terms of the deal itself. They had committed to a programme of consumer research and we were in dialogue about a retail price increase for our drinks. Sales volumes were climbing and like-for-like growth was clocking up at a very healthy 21%

across the 143 sites we had traded in for more than 12 months. Sales growth and a price increase would both translate to increased profitability and there was no reason to assume sales growth would tail off (our Welcome Break sites were still growing after six years).

A new Tesco contract just had to be profitable *enough* for us to both be able to move forward together and feel good about it. Whichever way I looked at it I could not see any benefit to Coffee Nation of not trading in the UK's leading retailer. I said to Scott, let's just hold our nerve, not antagonise and work towards a positive outcome for *both* companies.

We met with Tesco that spring and started with a clean sheet of paper. From our perspective we needed three things:

1. An appropriate drink price.

2. An agreed plan of action to ensure compliance by each store to operational routines.

3. A set of commercial terms we could both work with.

The underlying question concerned whether Tesco was committed to selling coffee in its stores and, if so, whether they wanted to work with Coffee Nation. I think they also wanted to know we were committed to them.

By the end of May we had agreed a change in drink prices to £1.50 for regular (previously £1.30) and £1.80 for large (previously £1.60), with espresso unchanged at £1.30. This was a very positive step forward and by the end of June we had a loose proposal from Tesco in writing.

From there the pace picked up and on 10 July a new contract was finally signed which brought to a close almost two years of negotiation. It was both a huge relief and a really exciting step forward. This now meant we had seven committed customers and it would be several years before any contracts were up for renewal. This would undoubtedly set a better platform for the refinancing of the business.

It was agreed there would be a relaunch of Coffee Nation in Tesco. They issued a press release that stated "Tesco is delighted to be working with the market leader." This sounded all the better considering they had undoubtedly entered into discussions with various global coffee operators during the negotiations with us.

We immediately appointed a customer manager with an exclusive focus on Tesco. It was agreed that Coffee Nation had to be included on the P&L account for each location – only this way would we achieve the operational compliance that was needed by making each store accountable for its own performance.

Tesco wanted to see us in more locations within the next 12 months and soon sent us plans for a further 72 Express stores for our consideration. Our marketing plan stepped up a gear and Tesco agreed we could use giant Coffee Nation cups outside stores to tell people we were available there, as well as enormous banners that were displayed on car park walls or fences where possible.

We were invited to install a 3G machine in Tesco House in Cheshunt (this had been proposed over 12 months earlier but put on hold during the negotiations). By October we were averaging 40 cups per day across the Tesco estate. By early 2008 we had installed marketing panels above our machines in 90 locations and telephone lines were (finally) installed in all locations to enable our machines to communicate sales and fault data.

EXPANSION WITH MOTO

We had completed phase one of installations with Moto by May and had 53 machines trading. Phase two was an additional 17 machines to double-up alongside the highest performing machines and these were all live by the end of July. Of course, it had been our intention (and stated in our contract) that Moto were to receive 3G, but continued issues with the new machine meant this was impossible. Whilst these issues had undoubtedly dented Moto's confidence in 3G, fortunately it had not dampened their enthusiasm or commitment towards Coffee Nation.

Moto and Macquarie were happy to proceed with 2G and agreed this machine was proven, robust and easy to support. This was validated by what our Brand Guardians reported on site visits. In brand audits 22 Moto sites had achieved 100% availability and we had achieved 99.48% trading availability during the month of July.

We had in fact doubled Moto's prior year turnover from coffee and doubled their capture rate. This paved the way to start discussions about entering their amenity building and becoming a feature of their retail shops, as we were in Welcome Break. It was also reassuring as we knew that volumes were still a long way off what we were delivering with Welcome Break, which gave us confidence there was much growth to come from Moto.

Our new customer was very happy with our operational support, reliability and response times to site issues. They now wanted to see a greater investment on our part in maximising that capture rate and driving sales volume. We responded with a programme of activity including marketing banners installed on their forecourts similar to those used in Tesco with a clear message of "Pick me Up Inside" and "Perfect Every Time". We also ran a summer sales promotion with cash prizes for winning sites towards their staff funds (as well as lots of iPods and iTunes gift vouchers). The simple aim was to sell more coffee across the peak summer trading season.

Retail shop trials in two stores started in November and were planned to run until Easter 2008. Sales grew by 50% and 120% over the previous Baristo offer and by the start of February we had a proposal with Moto to roll-out 51 machines across all their retail stores, comprising a combination of a new BabyG or Compact machine for lower-volume locations and single and dual 2G installations. Moto's final word on 3G was they wanted it when we were sure it was ready but not before. Clearly, we could not risk a failed debut for a second time.

STRIVING FOR 99%+ RELIABILITY

RBS had extended a new term loan (a £2.25m three-year term loan plus £0.7m asset financing and £1m invoice discounting, as well as vehicle financing) to replace our previous facility. This had been contingent on the signing of our Moto contract and now meant we could go ahead with ordering the second production batch of 3G machines. Of course, we had yet to see 3G trading reliably and in production.

We agreed that Derek would oversee the final stages of 3G transfer to production. RBS's due diligence report for the initial loan did note the lack of a dedicated project manager on 3G and relative lack of manufacturing knowledge and experience within the team, which was a concern given the significance of 3G and subsequent models to the future of the business.

Derek was a chartered engineer with an earlier career in manufacturing, so this background was sure to be of benefit to the project. We agreed that he should also set about recruiting a product design manager who would have full responsibility for all product developments within the business, including 3G, BabyG or Compact and beyond.

We had two 3G machines on permanent test at Coffee Nation but these were still operating at less than the reliability required to call this a finished commercial product. The milk, steam and cleaning systems were still not behaving. It was adequate for a prototype but regardless of how carefully these components and systems were assembled they refused to operate reliably. There were other obtuse software and control issues but we were gradually working our way through these.

Version 5.0 was to be the initial production standard and the first step was to transfer all the technical drawings of 3G from our development partner company to Coffee Nation. This meant the purchase of a computer aided design (CAD) workstation and associated Solid Works software.

By July we finally had a 3G machine running continuously for three weeks without any failure. By August the build standard had been frozen and we had received independent confirmation that the machine met with CE product marking requirements as well as NSF (National Sanitary Federation) requirements in the US. The latter was essential if we were to use 3G in the North American market.

In parallel with this we met with a number of companies to select a maintenance management system. Whilst our technicians and support team did an amazing job of keeping our machines trading, we were aware that we knew very little about fault trends, utilisation of our team, how to optimise stock holding levels or how to ensure the nearest technician was sent to respond to a problem.

We also took the step of bringing in-house our call centre operation that we had outsourced for the previous five years. With the remote fault monitoring capability we now had we could create our own centre of excellence with our own people. There was also an expected cost saving of around £90k per year. Very soon, we were enjoying shorter response times by technicians and Brand Guardians.

From here we were confident to resume production with all of the first 50 machines expected to be installed by early 2008. However, as we progressed – cautiously – with the next installations we found there were still issues to be resolved and minor design changes were required.

By January 2008 we had our full technical team in place; they were on a steep learning curve but making great progress.

A third field trial was added but the pace of roll-out was slowed considerably to only two machines per month throughout much of 2008. Downtime on the trial machines was declining steadily but our quest for reliability in the 99%+ region was the top priority and until we achieved that 3G could not be declared fit for purpose.

This project had been far from a success – every deadline and budget had failed to be met, costs had spiralled and reliability had for so long proved just beyond reach. The three-year plan prepared in January 2008 showed the first 50 machines deployed on a trickle basis through the year. No more 3G machines were forecast from there. Until we could demonstrate a reliable product in typical conditions at a forecourt or convenience retail outlet, 3G would remain a trial product. Given this shift of focus RBS agreed that the new loan could be for 75 2G machines instead of 50 3G units. A £1m interest rate swap agreement was also part of the new package, designed to offer protection against future interest rate rises.

There was brighter news elsewhere on the product front, as 2G would remain the workhorse of our growth for the foreseeable future. With a fully resourced technical team now in place we would be able to bring some of the 3G functionality to future versions of 2G without the need to use costly third-party designers and mechanical, software and electronics specialists. We also took the opportunity to expand our head office space, specifically taking an adjacent unit to our existing premises in High Wycombe and dedicating this to product development and the technical team.

BABY G

We also progressed with a smaller, lower-cost offer, this being the Baby G or Compact machine. At its heart was a smaller, lower-capacity espresso machine from our original supplier on the west coast of America. It lacked some of the functionality of its larger equivalent in 2G, such as the ability to communicate remotely and detect low milk and coffee bean levels, but these could be incorporated with little difficulty.

The product range was limited to cafe latte, cappuccino, Americano and a single-stage hot chocolate. We had a smaller concession unit designed, taking some design input from 3G so that it looked like a one-piece coffee station rather than clearly a coffee machine in a box. Other than that the brand imagery and overall appearance was as 2G. Coffee Nation but smaller! The great news was that the drink quality was to 2G standards but the whole set up cost less than half the price. This meant we could provide a complete solution going forward from the highest to the lowest volume locations, so more and more people would get to enjoy Coffee Nation.

We undertook trials in Esso and Somerfield locations where the new offer was well received by staff and customers alike. This quick, low-cost development had almost overnight substantially increased our ability to trade from many more locations right across our customer base. Many of our customers had raised the concern of how to offer a solution in low-volume sites. Just because fewer coffees would be sold it did not mean the quality should be any less. We now had the answer for this challenge. By the end of 2007 we were ready to start rolling out this new offer as the network solution for both lower volume Esso and Somerfield locations.

Somerfield had acquired much of the old Texaco estate and over 60 of these were to be knocked down and rebuilt, meaning that Coffee Nation could be designed into these new stores from the start. Somerfield also recognised the importance of in-store positioning, so vital to maximising our sales opportunity, and agreed that all future installations of Coffee Nation would be at *gondola end*. This meant we would occupy the entire end of a fixture with the machines facing towards the till-points, completely un-obstructed, adjacent and highly visible to people standing in line to pay and also those entering the store.

Esso had showcased Coffee Nation at its annual retail conference and told us that it was the highest selling product in store – our regular drink was first and large was the third highest selling product. Our new Compact machine meant Esso could now see Coffee Nation as their self-serve coffee partner right across their estate, with 3G ultimately replacing their manned Costa Coffee shops in their flagship On the Run locations. Between Somerfield and Esso alone there was an immediate potential for 80 Compact machines across 2008.

Of course, between 2G and Baby G we were suddenly becoming a major purchaser of machines from our original US supplier once again.

This was somewhat ironic given the single biggest objective behind developing 3G was to remove this reliance on a third-party manufacturer and their machine lineage. We agreed that the next priority after seeing 3G operating reliably would be to develop a stripped-down, lower-cost version using Coffee Nation intellectual property. This was to be the 4G we'd always envisaged based on 3G's architecture, developed in-house at Coffee Nation and using our contract manufacturer.

FUTURE GROWTH UNDERPINNED

We were aware that a review of the Welcome Break estate was needed, given many machines were now fully depreciated. It was agreed that we would *re-life* the Welcome Break estate where any machine was more than four years old. This meant replacing the concession unit with a new one and a complete refurbishment of the espresso machine so everything was as good as new.

Plans were also progressed for a *series two* 2G machine with increased milk capacity, flavoured syrup dispense, credit card payment and single-stage liquid hot chocolate, although it was agreed that bringing the Compact machine to market had to be the immediate priority.

In the early years of the business, no matter how many companies we were talking to or trialling with, our growth never seemed to match up to what we had budgeted on paper, but for the last year or so we had been faced with the opposite problem – demand was exceeding our ability to supply and this was compounded by the ongoing setbacks with 3G. Esso, Somerfield and Malthurst were all offering up more locations faster than we could finance new machines – particularly given the prudent limitations set by our bank covenants.

As 3G expenditure drew to a close and we had new banking facilities supporting the next phase of growth in installations, we could motor on towards 550 installations. We also had new trial customers, some of which we had been progressing slowly with for some time. We opened two locations with Sodexho (the world's second largest contract catering business) in defence establishments and agreed to open in Relay convenience stores on London Underground. They operated from 1100 locations but were new to the UK. We were also progressing with SSP, who had previously owned Moto and operated most of the catering on UK railways and were also present in more than half of the UK's airports.

We often found ourselves trying to prove new channels in which people might want to buy a takeaway coffee and these locations were themselves part of a much bigger picture of an ever-changing retail, property, travel, transport and consumer behaviour landscape. Even high sales volumes were no guarantee of success.

Despite selling almost 200 cups per day with Alpha Retail at East Midlands Airport there remained too many insurmountable issues preventing us from really proving we could not only sell coffee but scale up our operations in airports. Turnover rents were typically 20% to 28%, airports want people to sit down and eat rather than eating and drinking on the move, and the hand baggage, liquids restrictions and increased security measures had all influenced consumer behaviour and changed habits in a way that was not conducive to what we were trying to achieve.

We finally replaced the My Coffee machines in Sainsbury and where we had replaced the Costa manned coffee bars in Esso our sales were soon reaching 90 cups per day. The business was changing in shape as we were approaching a point where non-motorway business in the UK was going to be the biggest part of our sales.

A number of Malthurst Pace operators ceased trading and left us with some unrecovered debts, so contracts with individual operators and direct debit mandates had to be the way forward. Somerfield posted a £600m+ loss in 2007 and whilst this made us a little nervous we had never lost a contract (or an entire customer!) since the company had been formed.

Trials were then started with Spar – one of my first customers back in 1997 – so the business had really come full circle. They operated 300 Spar branded forecourts around the UK and a trial agreement with them was signed in October.

Coffee Nation edged towards 50 employees and we expected to end the year to March 2008 just shy of 560 locations, £20m sales and £3m EBITDA. A new service manager joined the company to pick up on the excellent progress Tim had made in the role and a national operations manager, ex-Automobile Association (AA), joined in February.

Regional north and south Brand Guardians were appointed, new business development resource was recruited to focus exclusively on the independent sector and the service director role was fully implemented, allowing us to optimise our maintenance effort. Some of our Brand Guardians were promoted into customer manager positions and Chrissie and Dominic were promoted to roles as marketing specialists.

Sixty-five Compact machines were scheduled for installation in Esso, Somerfield and Malthurst locations in the first quarter of the 2008-09 financial year. At the February 2008 board meeting Carl was able to report that our installations forecast to the end of March 2009 was confirmed and installations for 2009-10 were broadly underpinned.

★ ★ ★

I reflected on the journey we had undertaken. Coffee Nation was no longer a small business – it was now firmly in the mid-market league with growth in sales and profits set to accelerate further over the next few years as we expanded across our contracted customer organisations. We had a committed team and real expertise and depth of capability across the business and we kept our promise to our customer of giving them a great coffee, wherever they saw the Coffee Nation name. Of course there had been setbacks, disappointments and blind alleys along the way but we had remained true to our goal and finally delivered our vision.

LEARNING POINTS

- We should have employed an experienced project manager with the relevant technical and engineering background to oversee 3G from the concept stage. They would have ensured project vision, budget and timescale were aligned from the start.

- The 3G project was far more than our proprietary design matched with third-party manufacture. It changed the business in ways that we did not imagine when the project was started in 2003. We developed all the capabilities of a coffee machine company, minus the manufacture.

- When building visionary businesses do not over estimate what can be achieved in the first five years. Expect it to take ten years as this is probably nearer the mark. If investors require an exit along the way this could be at odds with your wish to continue leading the business in to the future.

EXIT

TIMELINE & PROCESS

June 2000 – Primary Capital invest in Coffee Nation with the aim of exiting (trade sale or listing) before the end of 2005.

January 2005 – Deloitte (already the company's auditor) are appointed as advisers and begin an intense period of site visits and management meetings to understand the business in greater detail. Deloitte comment that the business is a great investment – clear strategic vision, management integrity and ability to execute. The exit project is christened 'Vanquish'.

June 2005-August 2005 – An Information Memorandum (IM) is prepared setting out in detail the company's history, unique positioning of its offer, consumer and corporate client attractions, trading performance, operating model and future projections. First meetings are then held with potential investors/acquirers. These included private equity houses with a specialist focus on consumer, food and beverage sectors, global coffee companies, UK and European food service companies, vending operators, debt providers, AIM advisers and family investment vehicles. Second round meetings are held in August.

August 2005-December 2006 – Initial offers received. Specifically these include a US family fund investing in high growth consumer businesses (Party A) and two UK based consumer focused mid-market private equity firms. Party A is an all equity offer including a further £5m to invest in the development of the business whilst the private equity offers are competitive but include substantial portions of the headline price payable as earn-outs subject to future performance. An AIM float is also considered but not progressed as valuations are below competing offers at this stage and cannot be certain without clarity on Tesco, Tank & Rast and 3G.

Party A is chosen as the preferred bidder. An exclusivity period is granted to complete commercial, financial and legal due diligence and complete the transaction.

During this period they request the term of Coffee Nation's Tesco contract is extended to reflect the strategic value of this customer, particularly in North America. They are concerned that the loss of the Tesco contract would be damaging to Coffee Nation's reputation and prospects going forward and advise the Coffee Nation board that they will not complete the transaction without the revision to Tesco terms. They subsequently withdraw.

A US beverage company (Party B) wish to acquire half of the company with a call option on the balance. Management are required to roll forward their shareholdings. This offer is rejected as there is no certainty over the ultimate exit timing or value for ordinary shareholdings.

January 2007 – We decide to put the exit process on hold and focus on further development of the company's commercial position, achieve budgeted EBITDA performance to financial year end March 2007, clarify Tesco position, complete the 3G project and underpin performance out to the financial year end March 2008.

June 2007 – Exit process re-commences. We appoint independent specialists to undertake financial and commercial due diligence of the company.

July 2007 – Tesco sign new commercial agreement with Coffee Nation. New IM and teaser document produced.

September 2007 – Deloitte re-engages marketplace. Project name Columbia. Ten organisations (four trade and six financial buyers) receive the IM and full letter disclosing the exit process. Data room prepared.

October 2007-December 2007 – Three first round trade offers are received. Specifically these are from a US based operator of retail kiosks and two European companies within vending and food service. Start of what was then being termed the 'Credit Crunch'. Some parties express concern over ability to deliver a debt package (in the deteriorating market), given the level of capital expenditure required to fund growth. All three parties subsequently withdraw citing growing uncertainty in economic outlook going into 2008.

January 2008 – London-based private equity group Milestone Capital and another recently formed London-based consumer focused private equity group, recognising inability of trade buyers to complete given market uncertainty, come forward with strong offers and stress their ability to complete quickly.

February 2008 – Milestone Capital offer £23m for the entire issued share capital of the company and are granted an exclusivity period to 20 March to evaluate the company and negotiate terms of the proposed purchase. Coffee Nation reserves the right to cancel the grant of exclusivity if Milestone indicate any reduction in the purchase price.

March 2008 – Milestone Capital complete with purchase price of £23m.

March 2011 – Whitbread/Costa acquire Coffee Nation from Milestone for £59.5m.

MY EXIT EXPERIENCE
UNSUCCESSFUL NEGOTIATIONS

Despite commencing the exit process in January 2005 it was March 2008 before a satisfactory exit was achieved. None of us could have imagined this would be the case when we granted party A exclusivity in autumn 2005 to complete a deal by the end of that year.

It appeared we had found a bedfellow that shared our dream of building Coffee Nation into a global business, with the depth of pocket to support this. The buyer could see the potential to roll Coffee Nation out internationally and were prepared to make further funds available to invest in the development of the company. The other members of the board, including myself, could realise some of our equity stakes and keep going in the business. It looked like we'd pull off a pretty finish and give Primary a great result.

Most things happen in life when they are meant to and not before and the sale of a company is no exception. I think I had laboured under the false assumption that if you build a great business, show good historic trends with big future upside and appoint professional advisers, this will automatically equal a great exit result. Sure, all of this is de minima, but it is no guarantee of success.

We had a great company going places but it and our personal shareholdings would count for nothing if we could not deliver a successful exit. Like most entrepreneurs pretty much everything I owned amounted to Coffee Nation paper.

DIFFICULTY OF TIMING

A challenge to our exit came from what we could say about the business as a result of the timing of the exit process. Starting the exit process early in 2005 meant by the time we were presenting to would-be buyers and investors we had only four full trading years of audited management accounts to show them.

At the start of 2005 we were approaching the end of our first year of real profits but had only 300 installations. More significantly, our anchor client Welcome Break had relatively little potential for further growth, Texaco was similar and Tesco had enormous potential but it was taking time to unlock. It was hard not to get excited at the potential for the business but this *potential* was too much of what we were presenting to would-be buyers.

Our difficulty was that the timing of the exit dictated we had to say something. We could not say: "We have three contracted customers, 300 sites and enormous potential for growth but right now we cannot tell you where from." As a result, value was attributed to Tank & Rast or Tesco adding more locations, and 3G's market entry. In the end none of these came to pass during the 2005 to 2007 period, meaning not good news for potential investors when we re-engaged with them later on in the process.

Potential investors expected to see us having delivered what we said we would, but in fact we had not. Many more trials did not result in roll-out contracts for all sorts of reasons. We presented too steep a growth curve only to have to backtrack later on. In some ways this took the shine off the genuine contract wins we went on to deliver. If we had presented exactly what we knew at the time in the summer of 2005 we would have received a very different reaction for we had no future contracted growth in installations at that time and I would have been encouraged to present a more exciting growth plan.

We had to – as a board – take our best view of what was likely to happen. Not exciting enough and we'd have little interest in the business.

We probably leant too far the other way, were too optimistic and focused too much on what the business could be and not what it was at that time. I think this is a key lesson that I learnt – deliverability ignites value, not opportunity. We had no shortage of opportunity but when and if it was all going to land was anyone's guess.

THE WINNER'S CURSE

I placed too much emphasis on selling the future opportunity out of a genuine belief in what was to come. This may be helpful in maximising the exit price, assuming the future goals can be delivered, but unfortunately this was of no use to me unless I was cashing in my stake in its entirety at that time. No buyer would allow that because for this size of business and stage in its history the management team and the company are one and the same.

This is described as the *winner's curse*. Let us suppose you've built a successful business. Then, come an exit or refinancing, strong interest from multiple bidders drives up the price, giving the exiting groups a bumper payout. This burdens the management with heavy expectations to create upside going forward and maintain the rate of growth of cash flow that underpins the price already paid and the considerable debt taken on to finance the deal. I and the rest of the management team focused way too much on this headline value that only benefitted exiting shareholders. The higher the price paid to exiting shareholders at that time, the higher the hurdle that has to be jumped before Party A recover their cost of buying them out and can then share the upside with the management team on a subsequent refinancing. Alternatively, if there is no pressure on timing you have no issue; just park the exit and come back to it when the company is bigger and better established. We did not have that luxury.

We had jumped at Party A's offer as their global ambitions and willingness to invest £5m of new money into fuelling the company's expansion was attractive. We committed to exclusive negotiations with them before knowing what they would be like to work with day-to-day, the terms of the management deal for going forward or what other yet to be revealed terms would appear. They subsequently revealed that they were unlikely to ever sell Coffee Nation, rather they wanted to build portfolio companies for the long-term benefit of their controlling family shareholders. I would be able to sell approximately one-sixth of my shareholding at that time which meant I would be rolling forward five-sixths of my stake into a privately owned business with no intention of ever selling Coffee Nation.

As time went by I could see that I had considered thoroughly what was in the best interests of the company. Who would be the best buyer to take the business forward? However, I had not thought through whether they were the best for me and other members of the management team before we committed to exclusivity.

The deal going forward for management has to sit square alongside the headline price today and must be commensurate with the risks being taken going forward. I was risking five-sixths of my shareholding – kind of rolling the dice again – so should have seen an increased upside down the line to balance out this risk. Put another way, the sale to Party A would not see me benefit from the value I had created to date and I could not realise more than one-sixth of my stake at that time.

With the help of Ashurst I had to negotiate a complex mechanism whereby – after five years, if I wanted to sell my remaining shareholding – their principal and I would agree on a price per share. If we could not agree then I would be able to trigger a full open market valuation of the company (not an accountant's valuation, but rather a full exit process). If this yielded a higher price the principal would buy me out at that price, but if it was lower than the original price then I would have to take it, accepting the efficiencies of the market. Derek had counselled me not to let the deal fall over because of a personal issue and I heard him.

I realised that at the stage the company was at in 2005-06 a sale to a family fund, a trade buyer or any other strategic purchaser probably meant there was little chance of a further exit in the future, thereby severely limiting my opportunity to create value for whatever equity I was not able to sell at this interim exit stage.

This was not what I had wanted and not what I had set out as my intentions late in 2004 to my chairman and later to Deloitte as the process got underway. I wanted to take some cash out now and roll the rest forward with new investors on the basis we were really just getting going and the big exit would come down the line when we had built a much bigger business. This required a financial buyer but none had been forthcoming on attractive terms at that time.

TESCO

The final sticking point was our deal with Tesco. Party A wanted to see a much longer term contractual commitment from them. We did too, but it was just one item on the agenda and I had to let the negotiations with Tesco run their natural course.

Our potential buyer saw this as important to help us create leverage for a Coffee Nation entry into the US grocery market. A successful alliance with Tesco would make for a good opening in discussions with any US supermarket operator. They also argued that if we were to lose our Tesco contract the reputation of Coffee Nation and our ability to gain new customers, particularly in international markets, would be significantly impaired and they were not prepared to take that risk. All this we agreed with, but our entire board were unanimous that we should not risk damaging or destroying our commercial relationship with Tesco in order to meet a *potential* buyer's requirements.

There was nothing more we believed we could have done to conclude a transaction by the end of 2005. Even the week before Christmas we were working late into the night to finalise the legal aspects to complete the deal.

I believed the buyer had messed us about with a poorly planned due diligence process and their wish to see revised terms with Tesco prior to completion had only been revealed after we had committed to an exclusive period of due diligence towards a planned completion date of 15 December.

SALE TO MILESTONE

With Party A out of the picture, it increasingly looked like we would be acquired by a US beverage company (Party B) late in 2006 and lose the independence we had enjoyed with Primary.

On the one hand I was excited about what this could do for the potential of the business, but equally life would change forever. I didn't want to work for a global corporation. At this stage, I had no certainty over realising some of my stake in the company, what would happen to the balance of my shareholding or even in what capacity I would continue to be employed by the company.

I started to re-evaluate my own position. It appeared that a trade buyer looked the most likely route (this was Primary's expectation too) and this probably meant I would have to roll forward most of my equity in the company. Regardless of my personal feelings, if this generated the maximum return for exiting shareholders then I would need to support it, but where would the future liquidity event come from to turn my long-held stake into cash if Coffee Nation was by now part of a much bigger company?

In the end that transaction never happened but in September 2006 in a dinner with Neil from Primary I proposed I exit alongside them. This was not what I truly wanted; I wanted to cash out some of my stake and roll forward the balance confident there would be another open market exit process in another three to five years, by which time we could be delivering £5 to £8m EBITDA.

Unfortunately, there was no way of gaining any sort of assurances that this would be possible. If another private equity house had been the lead bidder then I would have felt differently but this had not happened. I became non-executive at the end of 2006 and Scott took over day-to-day running of the company, being appointed CEO in the summer of 2007.

Back in 2000 Neil had written "I look forward to exiting on the same side of the table as you Martyn," in the menu of our completion lunch. I'm not sure I understood this at the time but since we completed the sale in 2008 I have reflected much on this and learnt a great deal from my experience.

The founder of the company naturally wants to lead their company and in the first couple of years or so it would be anathema to most entrepreneurs to seriously consider not being in charge of their baby or that at some point someone else may be better placed to take the business to the next stage.

In addition, whilst an entrepreneur almost certainly does not start their business with the prime motivation of making as much money as possible, having survived the difficulties of start-up and seen they have the makings of a high-growth company that could be highly profitable, it's a great feeling when multi-million pound valuations start to be mooted. The founder has invested so much of him/herself and likely sacrificed much to achieve this; they will certainly want to see their stake sold for the highest possible price eventually. This may be their one shot at financial independence and greater choices in life for them and their family.

All this should be straightforward if the founder can retain majority control of their business but what if, in order to realise the potential of the company, external investment is required and the founder loses control over decision making in the business? This can place their desire to remain as CEO *and* make as much money as possible under great pressure.

Entrepreneurs face a dilemma and it is one that many are not aware of at the start. They create an opportunity and then need funds to grow it. If they meet the right investors financial gains will soar. If they give up equity to attract investors and high calibre senior managers who share their vision, they will build a more valuable company than one who parts with less. But, to attract all of this they will have less control over most decision making.

This dilemma can result in a tension between the possibility of becoming rich and losing control, or staying in control but accepting they will build a less valuable enterprise. Overlay the likely not inconsiderable ego of the founder (after all they had to take the risk in the first place) and there's a real possibility this rich versus king scenario (see *Harvard Business Review*, 'The Founder's Dilemma', February 2008) can result in the entrepreneur neither maximising their financial potential nor retaining control of the firm they created.

If you have a tiger by its tail and are considering your funding and growth options then take some time to think about who you are first and what you are motivated by most; control or money. The danger is you end up rich (or not, multiple fund raisings can be highly dilutive) but no longer running the company you founded and love *or* you fail to step down from running the business, stifling its growth potential.

Whilst becoming non-executive at the end of 2006 was not what I wanted, I had absolutely no assurance of life beyond exit if I were to remain CEO. I could realistically be faced with a deal that would give Primary a great exit but with my shareholding being wrapped into some giant corporation's stock or transferred into some form of pseudo-management bonus. At least if I exited alongside the controlling shareholder I would benefit from the same terms as them and I knew their motivation was to exit at the maximum price.

The eventual transaction in March 2008 was a good result for all concerned but it was not the exit I had dreamt of. For me, there was no just keep going – it was the end.

Contrary to expectations, the company did pass to another private equity owner, Milestone Capital, and the management team (Scott, Simon and Carl). For the company this was not the end of the road; it was able to remain independent in the way I had hoped. The irony was I was not there to lead it.

Completion occurred on 31 March 2008. A year earlier Alistair Darling had announced that from 5 April 2008 capital gains tax paid by exiting entrepreneurs would now increase to 18%, not the 10% I was expecting (this 10% maximum rate of taper relief had been introduced back in 1998 subject to length of time holding the shares). If there's a good illustration of the importance of timing in business this must be it. It had been ten years since the 10% taper relief had been introduced and now it was going to almost double! You can imagine I didn't think we'd complete in time and we only made it by five days.

I spent most of the day sitting around in lawyers' offices chatting to Derek. It wasn't until early evening that everyone was assembled and the formal process of signing what seemed like endless documents could begin. Between us, Primary, Ashurst, Deloitte, Milestone, their lawyers, advisers and so on there were probably 25 people in the room. Beers started coming out of the boardroom mini-bars and there was the mandatory champagne and congratulations when all was done. We actually finished at around 11.35pm. I flagged a cab and headed to Trudi's. It was almost 12 years exactly since I had started work on the Coffee Nation idea. Job done, the end. Success can look very different to what you imagine when you start out.

The next morning I switched on my phone to see that Derek had sent me a text on his way home the night before: "Thank God that's over." I felt the same. It was the Easter school holidays so I took my daughter down to Bournemouth to visit my mother and sister.

MY FEELINGS ON EXIT

My feelings at this stage were mixed. I was relieved for all our employees – who had worked so hard and demonstrated such loyalty and commitment over so many years to building Coffee Nation – that this seemingly never ending period of uncertainty was at last behind them. I was relieved for all the other shareholders, particularly the business angels who had been brave enough to see my vision and share in my passion when they backed me in 1998. They all made good returns. I was relieved for Coffee Nation, the brand and what we stood for and that the company could continue to bring great coffee to people out and about every day.

I was also pleased for Primary Capital. I had made a commitment to Primary and sincerely wanted to see them do really well from their 2000 investment in me and our tiny business. We did not hit our business plan that formed the investment case for Primary, as our target was to be north of 1000 locations across the UK by the end of 2005, whereas we got to more like 30% of that. However, every aspect of the business model, product, and retail and consumer proposition stacked up exactly as we said it would. The simple reality was retailers took time to recognise the commercial opportunity that squeezing a coffee bar experience into a square metre offered them.

And for me, personally, I realised that to have come all the way and create a business from a blank sheet of paper through to successful exit was something to be proud of. It was also good to see some money in my bank account. I had no immediate plans and for the first time in my life I was in the position of not having to work – at least for some time. I had just turned 40 years of age.

I was relieved that we had achieved an exit full stop and at a decent 8x multiple. Over the following months so many people commented on the good timing of our sale. Any longer and we may not have got a transaction away at all during 2008.

Coffee Nation went on to achieve everything I as its founder said it would. It did eventually reach 1000 locations – sometime in 2011, so just six years later than I said it would back in spring 2000 when I wrote the business plan. Our brand became well recognised and well loved up and down the UK. We did not need to deviate from our original business model, pricing or operating system. The quality of the business was recognised by Whitbread when they acquired the company in 2011 and started to rebrand our concessions as Costa Express.

On the one hand we had sold the company and all shareholders had made money. I had played one and won one but was disappointed the company was moving forward without me.

LEARNING POINTS
PREPARATION FOR EXIT

Given we had an institutional investor from essentially day one and had a limited window of time in which to grow the company and secure their exit, I was less prepared for it than I could have been. Entering the deal with Primary at the turn of the millennium I should have been asking many more questions about exit, how to balance management and exiting shareholder desires, and so on.

The money is made (or not) on the exit, but so much of this is underpinned by the shape of the original deal. The professional investors are seasoned at their game and fresh on every deal. The first-time entrepreneur has never done this before and is all too often simply relieved to have an offer of the money and thinks no further than money, equity stake and maybe good/bad leaver provisions.

Knowing your business inside out is very different to negotiating a deal with professional investors. Back then I should have appointed an experienced adviser to look after my interests who knew private equity as well as I knew Coffee Nation. They could then have stayed with me and helped me shape my thinking around my own priorities as we approached exit. I did appoint an adviser in 2006 but it was late on and I know I relied too much on the general advice of Deloitte and my chairman. An independent adviser can ask some important questions, such as:

> "Are exit timescales realistic given the company's stage of development?"
>
> "What will happen if you miss that timescale, regardless of how well the company is doing?"
>
> "What happens if we grow well but miss our plan?"

Think through the deal you do from every angle, not just how it will be if everything goes according to plan.

An adviser's fees during the exit process may be the best money you ever spend and you'll pay their fee out of your exit proceeds anyway. It'll be one cheque you'll be glad to write. Make sure they are with you through every step of the process and included in all key meetings. Don't let your investors or other shareholders intimidate you.

As a friend of mine said in relation to being prepared for exit negotiations – "the best weapon to bring to a knife fight is a gun." In other words, get the best lawyers and advisors money can buy.

MANAGEMENT TERMS FOLLOWING SALE

If you do not control the board you may have little leverage on any exit deal. Once an attractive offer is on the table that catches the eye of the controlling shareholder there is a real momentum gathering pace and the challenge for the management team is to negotiate their terms for going forward right upfront – so the buyer's offer must include these as well as price.

We granted the buyer an exclusive period in which to undertake their due diligence and complete their negotiations based on the original offer letter, which merely set out the headline price they said they were going to pay, what they would invest in the business and what each member of the management team could cash in at that stage. The intention was that the detail of the management terms would be agreed during the exclusivity period.

The reality was that discussion of management terms took second place to due diligence, preparation of the sale and purchase agreement, management warranties and so on. As the planned completion date drew ever closer we were still trying to complete the detail of the management terms.

Don't commit to a single purchaser until you have agreed the fine print of the management deal. Offer letters are flattering but worthless. Negotiating management terms can tell you a lot about what life will be like with a future owner of the business.

PAY OFF TICKING BOMB SHARE CLASSES

If you are faced with potential *ticking bomb* share classes, such as preference shares with special rights, pay them off and get rid of them. To be able to put yourself in a position where no other shareholder group has control of your destiny (even though you may not have majority control yourself) is far better than a single shareholder gaining the one extra vote that puts them in control of the board.

Instead, we elected to invest our free cash flow into 3G with the (perfectly sound) thinking that this could add a premium to our exit value on the basis that it would be so far ahead of any other entrant into the self-serve gourmet coffee category and its future iterations would underpin our market leadership for years to come. At the very least, 3G would protect us against the loss of our US machine supplier and help ensure our survival (we all thought our decision to develop 3G had been well and truly vindicated during the summer of 2004).

In isolation this was all valid thinking but it failed to take account of the risks we may encounter along the way. Development of 3G was far more complex than we had expected, more challenging, cost more and took longer. A buyer could (and not unreasonably) regard it as a promising albeit unproven new wonder product upon which so much of the upside they were being asked to pay for was based. Investing in a complex and costly new product innovation only three years from an exit deadline (so two years before the exit process needs to start) is potentially high risk and may have the opposite effect at exit to that which is intended.

TIMING

Timing with exits is critical. I have a friend who is the CEO of a fast-growth technology company. Three years ago they rejected an offer of £75m as their shareholders were confident a far larger sum could be achieved if they waited. Today market conditions are very different and it may be worth a third of that figure – all for three year's more work on his part mind you.

Equally, another friend attempted to sell their business in 2004 and received offers well below £10m. The founder decided to put the exit on hold and construct a business plan for growth. In 2008 it was sold for £20m, the majority pocketed by the entrepreneur.

There are factors when funding an early-stage company that – at the time – may not seem important, but may conceal unintended consequences down the line. Coffee Nation was an investment from Primary's no.1 fund which was raised in 1997. This was a ten-year fund and my understanding was that all investee companies had to have been disposed of within that period. The fund was already into its fourth year by the time of Primary's investment in Coffee Nation, giving us six years to build and realise an exit. Their aim was to see the business sold or floated within five years which we understood and were happy to accept. Clearly this did not happen as we did not leave their books until March 2008. Of course, these timescales would be far less of an issue with management buy-outs of established businesses. Primary informed us of seeking extensions to their fund to permit an orderly exit process for the company.

Building a company virtually from scratch and delivering a good private equity level of return all inside five years is almost unheard of. Apart from the odd exception, a sensible period to expect to be holding your business from start-up and building real value would be anywhere from seven to ten years or more. My friend who sold his business in 2008 for £20m started it in 1991!

We had the time we had to build the business and achieve the exit. We had to take our chance and often business is like this. Run with what you have.

EXIT AND YOUR TEAM

As we had progressed with the original buyer towards the end of 2005, I had agreed with Scott and Vivien it was time to reveal what was going to happen with the team at large. We invited the whole team to meet with us and we explained that our original investors were going to sell their stake and a new investor was coming on board. We explained they would be investing further in the company to accelerate our growth, particularly overseas. For those people that owned shares and share options they would be able to realise the value of these.

Of course, the three of us were terribly excited and thought everyone else would be. As a small company, most employees knew we had external investors and many had seen Neil in the office for board meetings. Many also understood that at some point those investors would be selling their stake. Everyone was pleased that the company was going to have new investors but we had failed to anticipate that what we told them probably raised more questions for people than it answered. It all boiled down to change and most people don't like change. They like things to stay just the way they are.

As that deal never happened and the exit process continued for much longer than anyone had anticipated the company felt like it was in a state of perpetual suspension. Outside of the board no one really understood what it was all about and all our attempts at well doing had achieved was to create a sense of uncertainty and anxiety for some of our team. The first anyone should have known about a change of ownership was after it had happened and then only details relevant to the day to day running of the business should have been shared.

FINAL THOUGHTS

The footnote on the exit must be that we did achieve so much and the scale of the achievement was way beyond what I could have imagined when I installed those first Nescafé machines in Spar back in 1997. We had built a fantastic business with a great product that people loved, provided jobs and careers for 50 people, made money in the process and had fun along the way. The business continued to prosper and was sold again successfully in 2011 for more than double the price of the first exit.

One of my realisations after exit was that in many ways I probably achieved as much from selling Coffee Nation in 2008 as I could have done. The timing of Primary's investment, our need for substantial funding early on and the time in which we had to build the company were all factors in this.

Had we been able to secure investment at the start of a fund's life we would have had a nine to ten-year run at it. The preference shares could have been refinanced in due course and we could have exited when the company was much larger, more profitable, the brand better known and the category better understood. So we and I probably made as much of our opportunity as we could.

Exits are often challenging and painful. Trying to marry the needs of the company with the needs of different shareholder groups and matching this with an appropriate funding and capital structure can be immensely complex. The journey towards exit may just turn out to be better than the destination.

TRANSITION: LIFE AFTER EXIT

THERE ARE MANY practical challenges and dilemmas post-exit, but for me the first thing to tackle was how I felt about myself. For a considerable time after my exit from the business I was constantly asking myself: "How did that happen?"

When I exited from Coffee Nation I had just turned 40. Not bad for a beginning. What would Act II bring? It would have been convenient if I could simply have got back to work after the exit, working on the launch of some new venture. In fact I had said to my family that I would take three months off and then get back at it. But I was far from ready and did not appreciate quite what a journey of transition I was about to start.

In the summer of 2006 and after nine years apart (and having divorced in 2004) I proposed to Trudi that we give it another go. She accepted and by September 2006 we were together once again.

So, company sold, new relationship, no job, what next?

COMING TO TERMS WITH SUCCESS

For all the success of the business and having achieved a good exit, at a personal level I felt I had fallen short of what I had hoped to achieve. I was no longer running the company and my own exit came at an earlier stage in the company's development than I had expected.

Other entrepreneurs I knew at the time were delighted to hear of our successful exit and it also appeared good timing – the collapse of Lehman Bros was just a few months away – but it can be pretty miserable when all around are congratulating you while inside you feel you've fallen short of goal. I convinced myself that to build a company in around seven years to £20m sales, £3m profit and sell it for £23m was no great achievement.

I have come to realise with time that I did succeed. It didn't look quite as I had imagined, but knowing now what it takes and having lived the entire journey end-to-end, I can appreciate the success – it does feel good and that comes from knowing that we did beat the odds. Most do not.

As I never spent much time with other entrepreneurs whilst I was running Coffee Nation I had little sense of how we were doing compared to other businesses. If I had stopped to look around and hear others' stories I would have realised that for all our twists and turns we were growing quickly, there was a real need we were satisfying, we weren't being eaten by our competitors and I was having a pretty good time. I subsequently discovered over many suppers, round tables, drinks receptions and networking events that we were one of the few that made it.

There are millions of entrepreneurs and business owners in the UK and most would dream of achieving what we did. This journey taught me that despite falling short of the huge vision I had for my business, very few entrepreneurs achieve something on the scale of what we did with Coffee Nation. The company is still growing today!

EXPANDING MY NETWORK

In 2007, as non-executive director, I decided that whilst we were going through the exit process I wanted to expand my business network. I had a reasonable rolodex but they were mainly contacts and associates directly related to the building of my business. I wanted to expand my connections beyond this, particularly in light of whatever new life awaited me post-sale. I had a sense that serendipity would play a part in presenting me with whatever I was meant to do next.

So I set about this and have since met many, literally hundreds, of other entrepreneurs. I was invited to join Young Presidents Organisation (YPO), a global network of some of the world's most successful entrepreneurs and CEOs. I would have been eligible to join YPO back in 2002-03 and would have learnt much about leadership, management, myself and preparing for exit (as well as being one of the youngest members) had I done so. I was invited to become a board member of the London Westminster Chapter of YPO, serving as

Education Chair in 2010-11, then Chairman in 2011-12. I have also undertaken a variety of advisory and non-executive roles with various growth companies. It was fun to help other entrepreneurs, make a contribution and earn some money again.

As I spent time meeting others within YPO and beyond I started to give what became a very familiar account of my career. The story ended with the sale of the business and me saying "I'm now looking for my next opportunity." Despite what came out of my mouth there was a distinctly hollow ring to my plans. There has to be that spark of passion and sense of optimism that the next opportunity is just around the corner, after all it'd taken no more than six months to arrive at the Coffee Nation concept from a blank sheet of paper.

What I knew about myself was that the passion and ambition that I had thrived on from my early career was strangely lacking. I questioned where this drive and determination had got me. For the first time in my life I felt my personal compass was spinning but I had no clear sense of direction.

I realised that when talking about my entrepreneurial journey the "I'm now looking for my next opportunity" almost eclipsed the degree of emphasis I attached to the achievements of Coffee Nation. It was as if I was saying that I had come close, but didn't quite make it, suggesting that I would need to hurry up and find the next big thing and do it all over again.

I was caught emotionally in describing my life and defining who I was as merely a series of past achievements and looking forward was all about more of the same – I would have to achieve more to compensate for my feelings of disappointment with Coffee Nation. However, there was no imperative to start another business – as friends reminded me, I had the luxury of time, money and my health (we often have two of these but not often do we have all three).

In YPO I joined a forum. This is almost like having your own personal board. My forum consists of seven people from varied backgrounds and all successful in their own right. We are a mix of corporate CEOs, second-generation family business owners and entrepreneurs. We meet monthly, no excuses, and update each other on business, family, health and *me*.

Forum provides a confidential setting for people leading demanding lives to share their ups and downs and seek advice and support from others who may have experienced the same or similar. What's said in forum stays in forum, it is not even shared with wives or partners. It is one of the fundamental values upon which YPO is based and that makes it so successful.

My forum and indeed the whole YPO experience has been invaluable in helping me navigate this tricky period I have called *transition*. For a long time after my exit from the business I felt lacking in motivation to go and set sail on some new adventure. It was almost as if I was no longer who I used to be but hadn't arrived at the new version of myself yet. I actually discovered that this transition is quite common in high achieving people. There is often a difficult barren period before the new you emerges and the next stage of life falls into place.

From my late twenties through much of my thirties I had been focused on *making it*. Aged 23 it had taken me less than a week to decide to become self-employed. At age 27 it took a holiday to see it was time to move on from DRC and look for that high-growth business opportunity. Now, in my early forties, with considerable experience and a successful track record, why was it taking so long to find my next big thing?

LIFE AFTER EXIT, OR JUST LIFE

When I had finally arrived at this place I had been chasing I asked myself "Is this it?" So much of what I had strived for I had actually achieved, but it all felt somewhat meaningless. From talking to others in the same position, I have learned my experiences of this transition period are not unusual, in fact it is commonplace. There is a transition network within YPO that members can join to share experiences of moving from one phase of life to the next.

I have realised as of late that the phrase *life after exit* is a bit of a misnomer. There is no life after exit, there is just *life*. I had seen Coffee Nation's sale as something like the sound barrier – something to aim for and once conquered there would be a wonderful new world waiting for me just the other side. My belief was that it was a destination to be arrived at.

My experience is that it's not quite like that; it's really just another milestone in your personal journey. I know many other entrepreneurs now that have also exited their businesses. Some have sailed through the process. Others have had very difficult journeys and experienced bitter shareholder disputes. Others have regretted parting with their companies almost immediately after completing a deal. All have had to work out what to do next with their lives. This has taken considerable experimentation, some failures and a fair bit of trying to hold on to their past success.

What is common amongst most who exit their businesses via some kind of liquidity event is that building a fulfilling life post-exit is harder than many entrepreneurs think.

Coutts, the private bank, undertook research amongst entrepreneurs. They concluded that whilst 88% of those they interviewed ended up satisfied with their life post-exit, many underestimated the challenge of arriving at that point of satisfaction. There were some valuable insights for those perhaps approaching this stage in their career:

- It takes much longer to build a fulfilling lifestyle than many anticipate.
- The process is more challenging than many imagine.
- Living with uncertainty is part and parcel of life post-exit.

Coutts went on to say that few entrepreneurs anticipate the extent to which their plans may not progress as they thought, or the fact they may have to deal with more failure than they did in their previous career.

Gradually I adjusted to life after Coffee Nation. I became aware of and comfortable with the reality of being an entrepreneur *between gigs*. As an entrepreneur you aren't just someone who takes a risk to back an idea – there is an entire lifestyle that goes with it. The material rewards may indeed be potentially greater than working for a company, but that's only part of the picture. An entrepreneurial career may be quite a ride; a very occasional high punctuated with multiple failures or near misses and long fallow periods.

I realised that you don't just conceive, grow and sell a business and then that's it, you're done, regardless of the wealth generated. You are probably the same person and will still have a desire to contribute to the world in some way, maybe by making your mark again with another business.

YPO kept me close to business and grew and strengthened my networks. I attended a mini-MBA called the YPO Presidents Programme at Harvard. After what felt like a painful journey post-Coffee Nation, I can say with honesty that I now feel content. Of course, part of me believes that Martyn Dawes will only truly have his mojo back when he sees the next opportunity that gives him that glint in his eye and knowing feeling that he's on to something. It's the best feeling in the world. But I have no idea when, or if, that will return to me. So I can stop wishing for it and live my life for today and with gratitude.

I have come to recognise that the biggest gift from Coffee Nation has been what I learnt from my experience. I learnt more about *business* – quite distinct from *entrepreneurship* – in the last couple of years when our exit was underway than in all the years preceding.

Entrepreneurs have big smiles, knock down doors and create compelling images of the future that investors, customers and suppliers willingly sign up to. Business is what must run alongside that if the entrepreneur is to succeed financially. Exits are about business, not about entrepreneurship.

Finally, and perhaps most important, is that I have been incredibly humbled by my experience. Success looked and felt very different to what I had expected, but I now have a far more modest and less important view of myself. My own observation is that it requires enormous resolve, determination, self-confidence and total self-belief to see entrepreneurial endeavours through to success. I also see something of a combination of humble and ferocious in the best leaders. Something for me for the future perhaps.

ON ENTREPRENEURSHIP AND THE SALE

I believe there is a deep-rooted insecurity at the core of every good entrepreneur – there's something that drives them to be out of the ordinary, to do extraordinary things, to be big and attempt what others wouldn't dream of. My insecurity had served me well, to propel me to launch Coffee Nation, dream big and give it my all. This raises a question that deserves to be asked – *why sell?*

In some of the most successful businesses I know the founder has long stood back from running the business on a daily basis. They still own their companies but have taken the time to find and appoint trusted replacements for themselves. They recognised the point in time when the skills required to run an increasingly complex organisation were different to the drive, passion and intensity of the entrepreneurial early years. Brilliant entrepreneurs can make lousy CEOs.

I have friends who have unshackled themselves from the day-to-day running of their companies and in so doing have rediscovered their passion for their businesses; often playing a more valuable strategic role, particularly where international development is involved or future product development, perhaps. They may not be working full time, but they know their businesses inside out and can be a great support alongside the new CEO. Some of the entrepreneurs I know that have built the largest and most successful companies are also the ones that continue to own them.

For me, there had to be an exit, as that was the agreement we made with Primary in 2000. But what if you have been able to fund your start-up and then its expansion from its own cash flow? There are many companies like this. One very good reason to seek some form of exit is to protect what has been built and for the entrepreneur to gain some value for that.

If significant additional funding is required to maintain or accelerate growth, invest in product development, geographic expansion, etc., a larger company or a private equity firm bringing fresh investment can be a good option. Beware, though, as this may be the end of your company as you know it. If it is bought by a larger group it will become very different and the culture will change – many of your team that are accustomed to a more entrepreneurial style may find it difficult to adjust to this.

Similarly, a private equity buyer will likely fund their purchase with debt, which could significantly increase the risks to the business in the event of a downturn in trading or some other unforeseen event. Someone recently said to me that it is best to assume that what you take out on exit will be all you'll make – assume zero value to any remaining shareholding.

It may also be that the founder recognises they have taken the business as far as they can and wants to step back from the daily pressures. They recognise that someone else would be better placed to take the business on to the next stage of its evolution. Or it can be that the entrepreneur no longer has the passion or energy to do whatever has to be done every day and meet the new challenges that face a larger business.

If you want to build a company rather than be self-employed running a lifestyle business, the relationship between control of the business, who's going to lead it and how it's funded can be a tricky path to navigate. If you want to stay in control and don't fancy being answerable to any other shareholders, it might be best to find an opportunity that does not require significant early-stage or development funding. Once you have built a successful company, do you really want to sell or merely stop running it day to day? Maybe replacing yourself and keeping the business is what you really want? Be clear to distinguish between the two.

In the early days you will undoubtedly have gone without holidays, time with family and friends, and a good salary, all in order to chase your dream, follow your heart and maybe change the world in some way. You'll be proud of the sacrifices you've made and the grit and commitment you've put in. But again, a word of caution. If it's all about jam tomorrow then you're banking a great deal on a day that might never come. The exit you are dreaming of may not happen and you have to live in the meantime.

If you have professional external investors they will likely want to see you on a salary and benefits that means you are doing all right but that will – in their view – keep you hungry. Of course, there can be no room for enormous salaries in the early days – many investors lost huge sums to first generation internet entrepreneurs jetting around the world first class with businesses built on sand. However, the founder and his management team or co-founders have to enjoy a reasonable standard of living along the way. If the private equity or VC-backed entrepreneur's earnings don't keep up with earnings in other professions then this is bound to dent the entrepreneurial incentive.

The journey to entrepreneurial success is usually a long one and the metaphor of climbing a mountain is not a bad comparison. Perhaps fairly easy to start with, you soon realise that this was beginner's luck. It starts to get harder and you dig in for the final slog to the summit – which with every step you take can seem like it is getting further and further away. You just keep going. I climbed Mount Kilimanjaro in Tanzania a couple of years ago and our guides kept reminding us "Poli Poli," which means "slowly, slowly" in Swahili.

When you've reached the exit and sold your company many people realise there's nothing actually there at the summit of entrepreneurial endeavour. I remember having this conversation with my chairman years before our exit and even longer before I'd set foot on any mountain. He said you climb one mountain, get to the top, realise there's nothing there except a bigger mountain out there on the horizon and just have to climb that one next!

I had certainly lived like this. I wasn't cut out for corporate life and wanted more, so I moved to London and started my own consultancy. As we grew DRC I realised that one day I wanted more so I leapt and started Coffee Nation. I've now built Coffee Nation, come out the other end and… *now what?*

Trudi, meanwhile, had been quietly building DRC. She had no shit or bust, no rollercoaster, no multi-million fundraising. She did not create a new market category and there was no way I was content with steadily building what we referred to earlier as a lifestyle business. But Trudi has built a highly respected organisation that is at the top of its game in helping organisations and their leaders change for the better.

She is passionate about what she does and has led her firm for almost 17 years. In the last five years she has started another related business (Coachmatch) that is growing and profitable. She has had no external shareholders to answer to, no remuneration committees, no bank covenants and no exit. She is a successful independent business woman and highly respected. Along the way, she has built her own balance sheet and in a very different way has made just as much money as I have. She and I have joked about the hare and the tortoise! The entrepreneurial eco system needs all sorts but recognise that high growth business is not a panacea. You may build a highly valuable organisation – for others.

LEARNING POINTS

Here is some advice I would offer, based on both my own experience and that of other entrepreneurs I have spoken to who have exited.

THINK CAREFULLY ABOUT SELLING

Hard work is a worthwhile way to spend your life and if you're creating something you believe in and which serves people then why stop? De-risk along the way so that you don't have to rely on a successful exit to create real wealth.

Notice that as the company grows where and how you add most value will also likely change. Recruit a great successor to yourself and continue to own the business. Set new goals for growth.

Remember once you've sold it there's no going back. There can be an enormous vacuum post exit; where once you were a leader and CEO now you start your introductions with "I used to be...".

MONEY

If you do sell will you make enough to be able to enjoy the lifestyle you want (or already have) indefinitely? If you plan on retiring and indulging new passions then you will need a lot of money if you want to maintain your standard of living.

Post-exit entrepreneurs are often heard saying "I need to create an income." I did well financially (I did get my Aston!), but I didn't make enough to never have to create an income again.

Take your time with deciding how to allocate your exit proceeds. It's taken a long time and bloody hard work to make it so be very careful you don't lose it. I recall meeting an investment bank and them talking me through their structured products. I left the meeting fortunately realising I didn't understand this stuff – and if I didn't understand it, why would I invest in it?

DO YOU KNOW WHAT YOU WANT TO DO NEXT?

If selling, what will be your new *purpose*? If you are hungry to start another business be aware that finding the next big thing can take a long time. Circumstances may force your life post-exit to be quite different to what you had planned.

Far preferable is to have the idea already simmering, or at the very least a sense of the direction you want to go in. If not, be prepared to accept a fair degree of experimentation and a few blind alleys.

If you started your business in your late twenties or early thirties you may emerge post-exit over ten years later. Having longer-term plans was probably not high on your priority list when you answered your call to start a business.

What dreams and passions are unfulfilled? You have time, money and presumably you are healthy, so don't hesitate. Why take the risks in the first place if you don't enjoy the proceeds?

When I was a child I wanted to be an airline pilot but could not due to deficient colour vision. This didn't stop me flying privately though and in my early twenties I was a glider pilot. I have reconnected with my passion for aviation and have gained a private pilot's licence and my aim is to gain an instrument rating (the most demanding pilot qualification) and graduate to more complex aircraft.

WHAT WILL YOU GET INVOLVED IN?

Be clear on what you will and won't get involved in. I decided that if I believed in something so much that I was willing to put money into it then I'd want to dedicate a lot of my time to it as well.

For this reason I want to commit my time to perhaps one or two major projects where I can bring my experience, lessons learnt and connections to the table and steer its direction. Multiple angel investments with limited time to spend with each therefore did not appeal.

WAIT FOR THE RIGHT OPPORTUNITY

Don't put pressure on yourself to find the next big thing. I found this difficult. It is most likely that when you founded your business you were not putting yourself under pressure to find a business to start. You probably recognised an opportunity, didn't over-analyse and thought you'd give it a go – all when you least expected it.

Opportunity is unlikely to come your way if you are desperately hunting for it. Relax.

SERIAL ENTREPRENEURSHIP

I HAD ALWAYS imagined that post-Coffee Nation I would do it all again; I'd come up with another idea and run with it. It seems I am not alone. According to research from Coutts, 77% of post-exit entrepreneurs would start another business from scratch if they found the right opportunity, or buy into one if they found one they believed in.

Doing it second time around is quite different to the first time. I don't know of many entrepreneurs who have genuinely founded a business, grown and sold it, and then repeated the process. That's not to say they don't continue to use their entrepreneurial talent, but perhaps in a different way – perhaps buying an existing company, or chairing or investing in early-stage or growth businesses.

The first time around, doing it from scratch, you don't know what you don't know. If the budding entrepreneur knew how tough the road ahead would be I am certain far fewer new businesses would be born.

Having built your first business the considerable experience gained may add to your confidence that you can do it again. It's simply having been through the same or similar experience before that gives us the sense of what to do when faced with the same or similar situation again. The path will feel familiar and if you can identify the template that worked for you the first time it may be that the second time around the odds are in your favour.

The reality may be quite different; every business is unique and you may be starting up again in a new sector. The world will also have moved on. Your experience and successful track record should lead to action, but it can be a cause of over-analysis, inaction and caution. If you don't have that same drive and desire to start another business it may be easy to convince yourself you don't know enough about the space you'd be entering or that the risks are too great in some other way.

It may actually be you've found a lower-risk opportunity with greater upside than first time around, but are less inclined to jump without greater certainty. Looking back at Coffee Nation it was 20% spotting the opportunity and 80% bloody hard work. At some point you have to be prepared to trust your intuition, recognise you know enough to get started and be prepared to work out the rest as you move forward. But all this counts for nothing if you don't take the leap. I've noticed that I get excited about things after I start – the energy comes from my involvement. Action gets me excited and reveals the opportunities.

You'll know *so much* of what can (and quite possibly did) go wrong that your experience may tell you to tread more carefully. It will be a fine line between using your experience to inform and drive you forward rather than suggest you have not yet quite found the perfect opportunity. In this case you could be in for a very long wait.

When I started Coffee Nation a fair few people told me I was mad. "No one will pay a quid for a coffee in a garage!" My mental resolve was just about great enough to shut out these comments and allow in the useful feedback. Doing it all again when you're that much older may be more difficult because you care what friends and family think. You're smart, you're a success. The last thing you want is people telling you how dumb your new idea is.

By now you will be in a different position in life – there may have been sacrifices you made (almost not realising you were making them) first time around and now you want to genuinely be master of your own time and invest in your family and other pursuits. You may have quite literally risked it all when you founded your business and you almost certainly (and quite sensibly) won't want to go there again.

Above all, entrepreneurship is a highly creative process. If we are stressed, fearful, weighed down with mental baggage or simply not in the flow then it's unlikely we are going to be in tune with ourselves and what the world needs – this alignment is necessary in order to focus.

Here are a few pointers I find useful when considering opportunities.

TOP TIPS FOR CONSIDERING OPPORTUNITIES

PASSION

Passion must be there in some form. With Coffee Nation it was the business model that appealed, I then had to find the product to match. I was never a coffee nut and my grandfather wasn't a plantation owner! If I spot something and I'm not still thinking about it 24 or 48 hours later then I have my answer; it's not for me and I move on. When I was ready to start the hunt for my next opportunity my old chairman reminded me not to jump unless I am really passionate about what I see.

RESONANCE

In the mechanical world *resonance* is when a material vibrates at its natural frequency. I think a parallel exists here with the entrepreneurial experience. Are there telltale signs that you have hit your natural frequency with this idea or opportunity? Does it immediately strike a chord with people when you share it with them? Do you have a deep sense of knowing in the pit of your stomach?

This deeply-held belief will carry you through the tough times. This may not fall into place right from the start but as you move forward if it feels right then that's what I'd call resonance. Remember entrepreneurship is highly creative; get in tune with yourself. Another term for this is *mindfulness* or *emotional intelligence*.

KNOW THYSELF

Sometimes I have seen something which I just know will work and lo and behold within months, *voila*, there it is.

I went on a trip to India a couple of years ago. In Mumbai I saw little kiosks called Jumbo King popping up on street corners all across the city of Mumbai. This enterprise was founded by an MBA couple and it sold *vadapav* (a Maharastran spicy deep fried potato patty in a bread roll). They were a branded and hygienic version of the thousands of vadapav street vendors which have been around for years.

This caught my eye and got me thinking about the potential of street food back in the UK. I figured it could be a winner and toyed with the idea, but it just didn't resonate with me. Meanwhile, pop-up restaurants and street food concepts have become hot in London. No matter the logic – if it doesn't light you up personally, drop it.

ALIGNMENT

Many first-time entrepreneurs create their own opportunity by starting a business that does what the company they used to work for did, only they can now see how to do it much better. In a similar manner many entrepreneurs, second time around, stick with the same sector and maybe even the same business model. Their track record, experience and knowledge equips them with an immediate advantage.

I recently looked at an early-stage business that was almost a carbon copy of Coffee Nation; it sold a branded beverage using an unmanned dispense system positioned in host locations. It was remarkable how intuitive this all felt; I kind of knew the steps. My experience with Coffee Nation very closely mirrored the steps this business would need to take to succeed so it put me one step ahead in assessing the business opportunity.

SECTOR AGNOSTIC

Many entrepreneurs spot the opportunity first, with the sector being almost irrelevant – it's the signs of an unmet need that they look for. I'm at this end of things myself – serving the consumer through a combination of product, service and great experience.

Exploit the opportunity, learn all there is to know about your space, move fast and own the category. The sector is irrelevant, it's what you can see that others can't that will set you apart. Spot the gap, meet (or create) the need and get out before you reach the top. Then repeat.

NARROW, DEEP AND GLOBAL

Identify a real need or problem that needs solving for the customer, acquire a deep specialisation within that space and then take it global. There's an elegant simplicity to this: understand the problem at a granular level, solve this problem and only this problem brilliantly, then do it everywhere.

The less you do the more you can own it and the clearer it is to everyone what you stand for. The more you spread out horizontally and attempt to develop adjacent capabilities, the more you divide your power and resources and the weaker you become.

THINK BIG

For me this is a must. It's part of what creates the excitement. Can you prove it and then replicate it on a huge scale? Can this be a £100m business? Is it a game changer? Will your idea become part of how people live their lives in the future? These are rare of course.

I passionately believed Coffee Nation was such an opportunity and time has proved me right – that's why it has been sold twice. It's why Costa/Whitbread bought the company. I certainly think for some people buying a coffee from a hole in the wall is now as familiar an experience as using an ATM.

Look for big product and service categories that have failed to innovate over a long period and that could be shaken up. You need *stickiness* – if you can play in a space where demand already exists but you can offer a clear point of difference then you might just be on to a winner.

Entrepreneurs can sometimes make life difficult by not focusing on ideas and markets that can grow really big. When I started Coffee Nation I was thinking small (tiny tabletop machines, instant coffee, newsagents) so my results were crappy. When I got to think and act big (expensive espresso machines taking up space in major supermarkets, serving fabulous coffee) I got big results.

Sometimes, it's that simple – if we limit our thinking for fear of being too bold we hold success at bay. Shoot for the stars and you might hit the moon. Shoot for the moon and you may not get off the ground.

IDEA VERSUS HARD WORK

Sometimes new sectors develop where there is room for more than one major player. The original entrant is the true pioneer and they sometimes succeed, but not always. Later-stage entrants may not be doing anything particularly different, they are simply taking advantage of the opportunity created by the pioneer.

Assuming you don't want to be working hard going nowhere and you haven't spotted a rising market that you can enter behind the pioneer then you do indeed need an idea of your own. The idea you start with may look very different to how your business ends up, but it is generally big breakthrough ideas that create the real successes. They move society forward.

No matter how good your HR policies, sales management procedures or financial controls, if you are in a low-margin, low-growth, commoditised space then the best you'll ever get is the best of a very limited upside. Working hard on the small details won't create a high-growth, highly-profitable and valuable enterprise on its own.

It is far better to find an idea that can gain traction with people – that way you'll be able to build your own momentum, benefit from some tailwinds and sell your own story. You'll create your own upward trajectory that will reveal new opportunities to innovate further for customers that already love you. You'll still work hard but in order to get somewhere.

THE TYRANNY OF CHOICE

The world is full of opportunity, yet it can be hard to come to rest upon an opportunity that works for you. I have to discipline myself to not compare new ideas with Coffee Nation, but to immerse myself in the beauty of the idea on the table. If it's got legs don't worry about the outcome and just commit.

Remember, *on the plains of hesitation, bleach the bones of countless millions, who, at the dawn of victory sat down to rest, and resting, died.*

EVIDENCE OF A BIG, UNFULFILLED NEED

What can you see in the market that affirms you are on to something? Is there another player already there that you can learn from? If it's a big undeveloped space then there'll be room for multiple players and being second can be a great position to start from. Most markets ultimately end up with two or three major players.

Are there external factors that feed into your idea? Equally, be careful you're not manufacturing a need to convince yourself – don't create a solution that is looking for a problem to solve.

TIMING

I learnt that timing in business is more important than it appears and this can work for or against you. For example, low-cost gyms have launched during the recession and are growing fast. Cutting out costly extras that are under-utilised such as pools and spas, using sub-contracted personal trainers and cutting staff numbers using automated entry systems has meant these start-ups could do away with long-term contracts and joining fees, instead offering low monthly fees, flexibility and 24/7 access.

The recession has worked in their favour, but the underlying proposition appeals to many people so they will be sustained in better economic times. They have created a new segment within the fitness club industry.

ON TREND

Let's pick an example. Clean technology is a mega-trend. The world has to switch to low carbon forms of energy. I believe that will happen in the name of progress, not simply because of fears about climate change. This shift has been dubbed the biggest economic opportunity of the 21st century. It's not hard to see why so many will look for opportunities in this area. Undoubtedly there will be big winners in this space.

What are the big macro drivers of change that combined with good timing will provide strong tailwinds of growth? The more difficult the problem to be solved, the greater the takings for the winner, but beware just how fast the landscape can change in embryonic industries.

BUSINESS MODEL

New business models can be as important as the product itself in unlocking growth. Apple did this brilliantly when they launched the iPod and iTunes. To make use of the low margin music you had to purchase the high price, high margin device. The technology made it easy and convenient to buy digital music. It was the business model wrapper that made Apple so successful – it was more than just having a great product. New business models come into being by gaining a deep understanding of how to solve a really important customer problem and may be counter to established practice.

Zipcar is another company that has succeeded because of business model innovation. They have reinvented the stodgy car rental market by positioning their cars in marked bays in urban locations. This means there is always a car nearby. To join you pay a small annual membership fee and they then send you a plastic card which does everything else. Renting a car is literally a two-minute job online – once the car is selected by location and rental period you walk to the vehicle, hold your card to the windscreen reader to unlock the doors and you're away. Technology enabled a new business model that allowed a tired industry to be overhauled.

IGNORANCE, CONFIDENCE AND NAIVETY

To start a business you need to possess all three of these friends. There is an old saying that "with ignorance and confidence success is sure to follow." Having succeeded in building a business you may be confident you could do it again, but the natural tailwinds of ignorance and naivety are no longer there.

When I started Coffee Nation I took time in finding the product to match up with the business model, and did some research into coffee, vending machines and equipment, but within six months I was off looking for sites for my instant coffee machines.

There has to be a degree of irrational behaviour on the part of the entrepreneur otherwise if they were entirely reasonable they wouldn't do it. This seems less of a problem first time around, but may be more challenging with your second venture. I founded Coffee Nation 17 years ago and I've got to stay as naive at 45 as I was at 28.

INSPIRATION

There is a wonderful quote from the actor John Hurt that, for me, sums up the quest for serial success:

> "When I'm in the middle of a performance and it's going well, I have no idea who I am. My head is entirely with the character that I'm playing. There are a lot of words to describe that feeling, but I like to call it inspiration.
>
> "Everything just takes off and you want to know how you got there – so you can repeat it – but, of course that's the one thing you can't answer. Inspiration is something that you can never fathom. It's rare.
>
> "The only way to be open to it is, quite simply, to forget about it. If it happens, it happens. And if it doesn't, that's where being a professional comes in. You never know when you're going to be inspired. You never know until you start."

DESIGNING A HIGH GROWTH BUSINESS

WHAT YOU SHOULD DO BEFORE YOU START — AND AT EACH STAGE — WHEN DESIGNING YOUR BUSINESS FOR HIGH GROWTH

MY AIM IN this in this final chapter is to give you a head start on what it has taken many before you – including me – a long time to work out. I have distilled my experience into a set of guidelines that, if followed, may increase your chance of success in building a high-growth business.

Let's define what *success* will look like:

- You are fit for the journey.

- You start with an idea that is worth pursuing.

- Research, test and market trials ignite the emotions of your early customers.

- You craft a compelling vision of the future that gets your juices going.

- Your initial vision excites those who join your business and those you need to fund your business.

- This vision is carried through birth, early expansion, growth, navigating the perils along the way to ultimately become a mid-market British success that is poised for the next level of growth.

I am not saying that if you follow these principles you will definitely succeed, but virtually all successful entrepreneurs will have addressed these factors in some way. Most entrepreneurs start from the same place, but over time some pull ahead whilst others fall behind. That's down to many factors including sense of yourself, your idea, the size of your market and whether you hit it at the right time. If you fail to consider the above then one of the following may await you:

- The business fails, now or in the future.
- The business survives, maybe grows, but never really takes off in a big way.

At some point you circle back and see what is missing and are able to plug the gap and complete the picture before you run out of funds, equity or both.

In this section I have focused on seven key criteria that I believe go into positioning a business for high-growth. These are:

1. You
2. Idea
3. Business model
4. Vision
5. Research and testing
6. People
7. Business plans and fundraising

I then discuss early expansion and growth or staying the course.

1. YOU

Why start a business? What ambition does this fulfil? What are your personal goals? Are these goals aligned with what you are willing to risk and with the type of business you are looking to start?

If you are attracted to the excitement of starting a high-growth business and the personal sense of achievement that comes from leading a company that one day may no longer need you at its helm – that one day may net you a fortune – then this will require your willingness to constantly adapt and grow, as well as risk taking over a sustained period of time. Your work will become your purpose and you'll need an obsessive attention to detail and passion to get it right.

You should start a high-growth business because you absolutely have to bring some positive change to people's lives. If this is your motivation then your staying power will not be in question when you are tested. Don't embark on this path if you want to make a quick fortune. Out of 221,000 new businesses that launched in 1998 only 83,000 were still trading a decade later. Out of those, 8600 had managed to grow to employ ten people or more and just under 6000 of these had achieved high growth (defined as growth in employment of 20% or greater) in at least *one year* during the preceding decade.[4] High growth is hard to achieve.

Be honest with yourself before you commit. If your thinking doesn't go beyond "I want to start my own business," then beware. If what you start eventually requires more money than you have available personally to see it safely beyond survival then you may be confronted with the need to seek investors – are you prepared for that? There may be a trade-off between the business remaining in your control and the demands of incoming investors.

Behind a successful entrepreneur there's often a partner who's a strong character, offering support through the difficult times and being there to listen. Is your partner 100% supportive? They'll lift your spirits when your confidence is low and provide a sounding board when you are faced with difficult decisions. What about time with your family? Successful entrepreneurs who feel guilty for not having seen their children grow up are almost a cliché. If stability, routine and certainty are important in your life then entrepreneurship is not for you.

If you want to launch a high-growth business then you must be prepared to listen to advice from those that have been where you hope to tread. You will need to develop a fine sense of judgement of what advice to take and in which direction to go on an almost daily basis. When it gets really tough you'll simply see this as part of the process.

As the game gets bigger and more complex you will relish the challenge of growing as an entrepreneur and leader. You will in time

---

[4] 'Vital Growth, The importance of high growth business to the recovery', NESTA (March 2011).

develop an inner voice that will guide you – you'll learn to know what feels right. You will know the difference between being right and being successful.

Businesses can't be created by committee so you need the strength of conviction to make up your own mind. If you believe (and even better have evidence to prove) you are on to something then don't let naysayers put you off. This can be difficult if it's loved ones and close friends who will tell you they only want what's best for you. Don't be talked out of a winner – follow *your* heart and have the mettle to go for it. Remember that not everyone will want to see you succeed.

If successful, you will be able to look back and realise how little you really knew in the early days about yourself, your idea and what would make your business succeed. Ignorance is one of your vital strengths, don't over analyse and talk yourself out of a great opportunity. Remember, it's 20% the idea and 80% your drive and self-belief that counts.

I regularly reminded myself of this little checklist on my entrepreneurial journey:

effort (1) + excellence (2) + determination (3) + detachment (4) = the reward

1. I am putting my all into this: 150%, nothing less.
2. I strive for excellence at all times.
3. I will let nothing stop me.
4. I stand back and see the inevitable failures along the way as merely stages on the journey.

Be clear on who you are, what you want and what you are willing to sacrifice along the way. Then begin and never doubt for a moment, no matter how uncertain you may feel.

2. IDEA

SOLVING A PROBLEM/MEETING A NEED

What issue or problem does your idea solve? How can you test this without spending any money? It may not even be a problem people are aware they have until you offer them a solution. It may not be an existing problem – it's just as likely you are offering a new way of doing things. How does your idea add real value – what does it *mean* to your customers? Why will people keep coming back? Don't start a business, start a revolution!

Entrepreneurs are optimists by nature so many over estimate demand for their product – a lot of ventures fail simply through lack of demand. To build a high-growth business means demand has to be high and sustained over a long period, and for this the right idea is crucial.

High-growth opportunities are not easy to come by. Don't be afraid to fish where others aren't just because these ideas appear unfashionable or old school. Don't look for what is easy – look for what is hard. If it is a problem that is hard to solve, but it is big enough for enough people in our society and you make it your mission to crack it, you might just succeed. Successful entrepreneurs are able to articulate how their idea makes a real difference and the need it fulfils, or impact it can have. They are able to objectively stand back from themselves and articulate why their idea has the makings of a winner.

You absolutely have to hit people with something that will jerk them off their daily autopilot. It took four years before someone sent Coffee Nation that little email that just said, "Thank you – you make my life better." We had just focused on getting the coffee right, but that lady spelt it out for us.

You have to be utterly dispassionate to effectively assess numerous business ideas. Be rigorous in your approach – if this was someone else's idea and they were pitching it to you, would you invest? Ask yourself whether it is *really* worth inventing if it does not exist already.

Aim to reach a deep level granular understanding of your model and your market. The more you know your space, the more confident you can be that the change you are bringing will resonate with the consumer. Others can offer valuable insight, but it's your understanding and mastery of your market and model that can be so powerful. If you get this right then absolutely everything else flows from it.

If your idea isn't working then there's no point hanging on because you love the concept and it *should* work. Be ruthless, ditch it and start over, or make a big change. Don't settle for starting something mediocre. Avoid tinkering around the edges hoping that the breakthrough is just around the corner. More often, drastic surgery is required. The moment you become emotionally attached to the idea is the moment you stop listening to useful feedback and may start down a dangerous path of attempting to justify why it *will* work. Don't be afraid of critical feedback from others – it may take you closer to what will actually work.

Once you have been able to test and prove that you are on to something and the feedback loop starts to confirm it, then you can start to let your passion surface. So, be dispassionate first – objectively assess ideas and ruthlessly reject those that fall short. Passion comes later. If you allow yourself to get attached too early, there's a big danger you've not done your homework and you're backing a dud.

BE A PART OF A GROWTH MARKET AND/OR CREATE A NEW CATEGORY

If your business is part of a growth market then you will have natural forward momentum. If you demonstrate a strong idea in a growth market then people will listen to you.

The idea itself does not have to be unique; entering an existing market where there's room for multiple players can be a great strategy. Most new businesses set out trying to change for the better something that already exists – perhaps based on the personal experience of the entrepreneur. In this case demand may be more predictable and the opportunity lower risk, but on the other hand the market you are entering may already be crowded.

There's more than one successful coffee shop brand in the UK and more than one successful low-cost airline. They offer the same fundamental product but each is distinctive in some way from the other. Likewise, finding an idea in another country that will translate well to the UK is a sound strategy. Pet superstores are a good example that made the leap from the US to the UK successfully.

In 1997 the coffee bar market in the UK was worth a tiny £50m. Coffee culture was taking off and it was hard to see what would bring this high street revolution to a halt. The talk was of hundreds of branded coffee bars across the UK. Seattle Coffee Co. had started with one store in London in 1995. It grew to 65 locations before Starbucks acquired it in 1998, then a year later they had 97 locations. Coffee Nation was launching into a market that already existed and it was reasonable to expect it to keep growing.

As a growth category I could have entered the coffee market with a twist on the basic theme, but that wasn't what caught my eye. No one in the UK was selling takeaway coffee from convenience stores like I'd seen in the US. I unknowingly created virgin territory to play in that was all mine.

If you cannot lead or be one of the leading set in a growing market, set up a category from scratch that you can lead. If you create a new category you make the competition irrelevant. Companies that own their space are often characterised by having high margins and an emotional connection with their consumers who come back again and again and are willing to pay a premium price. They are highly differentiated, have an unfair advantage and explosive growth potential. They are talked about and are memorable.

Most companies focus on being better than their competition, but very often it's preferable to be first than it is to be better. People want to hear what's *new*, not what is better. This realisation was an overnight game-changer for me back in 1998 and credit for this must go to a great little book called *The 22 Immutable Laws of Marketing* by Al Ries and Jack Trout. This book is 20 years old, yet the core messages remain pitch perfect.

Ries and Trout ask – who was the first person to fly the Atlantic solo? Many know the answer is Charles Lindbergh. Who was second? Very few know the answer to this one. It was a guy called Bert Hinkler who apparently crossed the ocean faster and used less fuel. But no one's heard of him! Lindbergh is memorable. Hinkler is not. Be first into the category and mind of the consumer with what is new. Create what will become the new norm.

Many of the most well-known and successful companies illustrate these simple laws so effectively. According to *Harvard Business Review* of March 2013, out of the *Fortune 100* list of the 100 fastest growing US companies between 2009 and 2011, only 13% of these had created their own category but those 13 companies accounted for 53% of the incremental revenue growth and 74% of the incremental market capitalisation growth over those three years for the entire one hundred companies. Category creators grow faster and receive much higher valuations from investors.

CAN YOU BE MARKET LEADER?

Can your business dominate its market? If you can create a new market category you will be able to talk about your space with real authority. Coffee Nation created the category of *self-serve gourmet coffee*. I couldn't sell Coffee Nation the brand as we had no history or relationship with consumers, but I could talk with passion and intensity about the category. I was emboldened to talk about a new development in retail, a new way of serving people. This fresh approach, innovation and my obvious natural enthusiasm were all attractive to those I was talking to. People were receptive to what *I was saying* not what *I was selling*.

I often said, "Don't take my word for it, but if we don't do this someone else will." This was powerful because it was the opposite of selling. The prospect didn't want to miss out on an exciting development, whoever happened to bring it to fruition. I also genuinely believed what I was saying.

This then gave us an early opportunity to be in a market-leading position. Be careful here though. Do create a new market category, but check that it is within a large enough market for you to build a high-growth business. Although ours for the taking, the market for *self-serve gourmet coffee* was tiny at this time. The reason most businesses fail to live up to their founder's aspiration is simply a lack of demand. If not enough people want to buy your product or service then you're going nowhere. Fortunately for Coffee Nation, the market for gourmet coffee beverages sold and consumed out of the home was growing fast.

We didn't waste any time in claiming that Coffee Nation was the *leading brand of self-serve gourmet coffee.* Whenever we reached the next milestone, for example 100,000 transactions per month, this was more evidence we were market leaders of this new category. It sounds arrogant but there has to be that willingness to unashamedly state you are the standard to which others compare themselves.

Everything we did was aligned to the simple message that we had created this new category and were now leading it. A 2004 article in

The Grocer magazine announcing our partnership with Tesco talked about the category. The retailer stated "gourmet coffee-to-go is an exciting market that is growing rapidly." The article didn't need to say we were leader of this market – Tesco having selected Coffee Nation as a partner established our credentials.

Customers tend to gravitate towards market leaders. Of course, consumers don't care about markets, they care about products. By staying religiously focused on our mission of delivering coffee bar quality coffee with near to 100% availability in a self-serve format we attracted a strong following from consumers which ensured we remained the leading brand of self-serve gourmet coffee.

We made a point of regularly updating our corporate customers with details of how we were continuing to innovate for their benefit. We told them about making our machines easier to use or easier to clean. We told them when we were recruiting and when new funds were being invested into the business. We wanted them to *see* we were leading the category we had created.

A LARGE, ADDRESSABLE MARKET

If you are serious about building a high-growth company that will one day become a mid-market challenger you need a large, addressable market. The idea not only has to work well today but has to continue to attract sufficient customers who are willing to pay a price that means you can make an acceptable profit for years to come.

If demand is limited or fails to grow then you may not have a sustainable business, let alone a high-growth one. This can be for many reasons. Consumer tastes change, your offer may quickly become a standard feature of another company's product, people may buy to try and not make a repeat purchase, or powerful substitutes may steal your opportunity. Technology may pass you by or you may be trying to gain traction in a crowded market and go unheard amidst the noise of all the other players chasing the same opportunity.

Our trial locations proved that people would buy self-serve coffee in high volumes and at a premium price. Sales continued to climb so the prognosis was good. From here it was a simple exercise to scope the potential market sectors where Coffee Nation concessions could be sited and how many suitable locations were available. It gave us confidence we had a large enough market to go after. Appendix 1 in our 1999-2000 funding document showed 40,000 potential locations across 13 sectors.

The word *addressable* is not to be overlooked. We launched off the back of our successful motorway and petrol forecourt trials, confident that other sectors would fall in line, but we did not land another major contract for three years and that was in the grocery sector.

Out of the 13 identified sectors we had only truly proven three after seven years. Three more followed later on (hospitals, offices and universities). Six sectors worked after eight years. Many offered initial promise but couldn't scale up because of operational challenges or customers not wanting to buy coffee in those locations. So, we had a *large market* but it was far less *addressable* than we first thought. This was probably the biggest drag on our growth.

Investors usually like to see a large, growing and profitable market that you can enter and disrupt with a distinctive and compelling customer proposition that can be sold at a profit.

Can you define the size of your market and how much of this can be addressed profitably? Is there a high-growth business here or a niche play in a small, specialist sector? If what you find does not match your business and personal aspirations you may need to reconsider the opportunity.

A SCALABLE OPPORTUNITY

Is your business scalable? In my experience this was the area that was most challenging to pin down at the early stage. We had been able to prove people would buy self-serve gourmet coffee in sufficient quantities and at a retail price that offered the prospect of attractive profits.

We had a good idea of the shape of likely margin deals we would need to strike with retailers. We also had a feel for the volume of potential locations. We knew each site needed the same amount of floor space, mains water, drainage and power. Scaling up the business was about more of the same, replicating this model many times over – it was looking at the market for locations where people might want to buy a takeaway coffee.

In principle this was sound and a key attraction to our investors was the scalability of the concept. The product was always the same and it didn't matter who bought our coffee. Each consumer transaction was homogeneous – we only had to learn how to sell the cup of coffee once. We could see that only a small percentage of sites were needed to create a high-growth business. It gave us a test of reasonableness that in the long-term proved to be accurate.

But we struggled to achieve an expansion of trading locations that came anywhere near business plan. Large companies were slow to embrace the profit potential. The revenue share model was unfamiliar to them so this sometimes hampered progress on securing new deals. Whilst we talked *plug and play* and *fire and forget*, the reality was quite different. We described Coffee Nation as a 'cookie cutter' model but it took at least five years to get there. This can be a key challenge in business planning and fund raising. Our challenge was less getting people to buy the coffee and more about getting into enough suitable locations in the first place. The barriers to scale for your business may not come from where you expect them to.

A good rule of thumb is to ask yourself if you can realistically reach, say, £20m in annual sales within five years. This is an aggressive growth rate but break down your idea into its smallest component parts. Then stress test each part – what do you know to be fact and what assumptions have you made? Finally, ask yourself if your business can reach and exceed that figure. If you need investment to help your business grow then investors will be asking you the same question. If you can be achieving £20m sales within five to seven years then you're firmly in the league of tiger companies, achieving growth of 25% or more per year.

In a conventional company growth usually tails off after a few years, but with a high-growth business it's often the other way around. The first few years need so much fuel, so much energy, before you get any results. Then, momentum starts to build, slowly at first. It's not uncommon for high-growth businesses to take five to seven years to get to the first £20m annual sales, but then by year ten to be hitting £50m and £100m a few years later. You may be committing the next decade of your life to this venture and it will doubtless be a precarious path down which you travel, so be patient to find an idea that has the room for growth.

The hockey-stick growth curve is the norm. Most businesses that go on to become major new permanent features of the consumer landscape start slow, then gradually accelerate over a number of years and then, to the layperson, it's as if they're everywhere. It's the classic ten-year overnight success.

DOES YOUR BUSINESS FIT WITHIN A LONG-TERM TREND?

Businesses that capitalise on long-term trends in society and consumer behaviour are often well placed to achieve high growth. The skill lies in identifying a genuine trend that is gathering pace. An entrepreneur with a bold vision may be responsible for creating a new trend.

By being out in the world, observing and experiencing, you will absorb what is going on around you and orientate your business nose in that direction. Or you could start by identifying a major trend in society and then committing to find an opportunity that fits with that trend.

Good timing combined with being on-trend can make for strong currents that will take you far. When I was looking for what became Coffee Nation, I had a sense that small unit retail was changing in the UK; the National Lottery was a recent arrival and supermarket groups were opening smaller formats. Food-on-the-move was developing, both in terms of quality, availability and range of offer, and of course new coffee bars were opening every week. It was becoming a common sight to see someone walking down the street carrying a cardboard coffee cup.

These trends directly supported the logic and timing of my new venture. The emerging coffee culture in the UK put me in the right place at the right time. An attempt to launch a couple of years earlier may have put me too far ahead of public awareness of the nascent coffee culture. Spar and Alldays may not have returned my calls.

You can absolutely have the right offer but if it's at the wrong time you may be doomed before you start. The classic scenario is the entrepreneur that jumps into the space the moment it becomes visible. This is often too late, particularly today in the fast-evolving consumer technology and digital arenas that change direction so frequently and attract so many start-ups. Great entrepreneurs don't wait for the answer to appear – they find out for themselves and in so doing create tomorrow's new market categories.

Equally, you can start out first in clear skies but if your execution lags and others see the same opportunity then all they have to do is implement better and you're out of the game you created. Someone described this to me as "pioneers with arrows in their backs."

FINALLY, A WORD ON COMPETITORS

High-growth businesses talk about the world in relation to themselves. This is a mindset or attitude. Define yourself by what you stand for, not in relation to your competitors. Talk about what you can do, not what others can't. Ideally you'll be starting in a new space where you have the field to yourself – at least to begin with.

If you've created a high-growth opportunity then you will inevitably attract followers keen to take a slice of the market you have pioneered. You have to make sure these new entrants flatter your original but never more than that. That means they are forced to play by your rules. You have to be the standard by which customers compare any other entrant into the category and you must continue to remain the logical choice. Be absolutely determined to dominate your category.

When competitors appeared in our space and scored a victory we made sure we knew why but resisted the temptation to tinker with our offer (this would merely have served to dilute our focus) or try to sell our brand (we'd have looked like we'd been rattled and would have needlessly handed power to our competitors). We didn't let it knock us off course because we knew we did everything to deliver a premium quality product reliably and consistently. Competitors lacked entire parts of the operating system that was needed to deliver on the promise. Our knowledge of our space (which goes right back to working the idea at the start) meant we had no need to lose confidence or momentum.

It also helped that the enemy could only win the deal by giving the customer a far higher margin than we were prepared to. They'd just launched their business – fresh out of the traps – and all they had to offer was to undercut us on price.

Don't expect to keep hold of the entire market but if you have created a new category be sure not to lose that initial advantage. Many companies have pioneered a space only to find it exploited more successfully by later entrants.

3. BUSINESS MODEL

Rarely does the *better mousetrap* model of business work. We can all have a good laugh at some of the crazy ideas that make it onto the *Dragons' Den* TV series – if it was all good investments and sensible business it would be dull viewing! The reality is that most of the ideas we see on that show are inventions unveiled from beneath a sheet and most of these are solutions looking for problems to solve. A tool that may further increase your chances of success in finding that high-growth business is the *business model*.

This goes beyond identifying a customer's problem, being able to meet that need and turning a profit. A definition of *business model* could be:

> A breakthrough way of solving an important customer problem that unlocks a game changing opportunity and creates a sustained competitive advantage.

An effective business model will link all these together in a way that later entrants may find it difficult to undermine.

The *Harvard Business Review* for January-February 2011 also sets out three characteristics of a good business model:

1. Is it aligned with company goals?

2. Is it self-reinforcing, through virtuous cycles?

3. Is it robust?

My experience with Coffee Nation absolutely underpins the importance of the business model. It was core to our success. The category alone was insufficient to unlock the opportunity. It was the combination of new category plus new business model that enabled us to gain access to lucrative channels we could use to gain momentum.

Whilst I was confident that with the right approach Coffee Nation could be a sizeable opportunity, the issue I faced was that I would never succeed in convincing retailers to pay up front for fancy espresso equipment or pay a monthly rental when they had no idea if they'd sell 1, 10 or 1000 cups of coffee per week. I'd be asking them to take the costs now and hope the sales would come in. By Coffee Nation funding the cost of the asset we broke this issue.

By adopting the business model of revenue share it meant there was no up-front cost risk to the retailer, which in turn unlocked the locations I wanted to get into. It was by adopting a business model from another sector (photocopiers!) that I was able to sign up big-name retailers. Our business model forced a laser-like narrowing of focus down to delivery of every single coffee. We were a *coffee retail business* not a *coffee equipment provider*. By narrowing the focus we expanded our category. The business model I created for Coffee Nation was therefore *aligned with my goal* of maximising sales of coffee.

The retailer's part of the bargain was to look after the stocking and cleanliness of the station. Our part of the bargain was supply of product, consumables and maintenance of the equipment to ensure it was always dispensing great coffee. If we both held true to our commitments then the revenue model would work and both the retailer and Coffee Nation would make money. It did and the business model became *self-reinforcing*. Each element of it complemented the next.

Whilst I had stumbled over the business model first and then later decided coffee was the product to match with the model, I began with the wrong product (instant coffee) in the wrong locations. So business model alone was not enough.

The eventual winning opportunity emerged when I switched to real coffee because providing coffee bar quality with a real espresso machine was hard for a retailer to do themselves. We developed an operating system that enabled us to excel at this. We went deep in our narrow space and became really expert. It was our continued obsession with our product and operating system that meant we were able to sustain our business model's effectiveness over time and fend off competitive threats. Our business model was *robust*.

As the business grew we learnt what was required to maintain the competitive advantage our business model had given us to start with into the long term. Feedback loops from consumers and our retail partners enabled us to grow that advantage. This created a *virtuous cycle* that enabled us to remain at the forefront of our market.

In the last section I set out how the first to create a new market category is usually the organisation that then leads that space. This is not always true. A new product may fail to gain traction but when combined with a transformational business model, it can literally change the world. Apple was not the first to market with an MP3 player. Apple's business model was the real game changer.

A low-cost business model allowed Ryanair, a struggling business 20 years ago, to become the largest and most profitable airline in Europe, offering low fares and opening up air travel across the continent to many more people.

Equally, there are just as many companies with marginal business models that do not deliver a competitive advantage. HMV and Blockbuster are companies that once had highly profitable operations but now find their business models no longer viable.

One of the reasons young companies can gain a foothold in large markets and disrupt incumbents is because they have designed their business model from scratch to target precisely the value they want to add to their customers. Large established companies often miss business model innovation entirely as this is far harder to achieve than it is to create incremental product innovations.

According to *Harvard Business Review*, out of the 27 companies that were born within the last 25 years and have entered the Fortune 500 in the last ten, 11 have done so through business model innovation. *HBR* also quote Bob Higgins of Highland Capital Partners – a venture capital provider – who said: "I think we (venture capitalists) fail when we back technology. Where we succeed is when we back new business models."

4. VISION

We have explored how a strong idea, new market category and large addressable market can come together to offer huge growth potential. The next thing to consider is vision.

If a business can paint a picture of the future that people believe in, rally behind and strive for then it has created a powerful *vision* of where it is going, what it will achieve and how it will change the world.

A vision unites people, it gives them purpose and direction, a sense of personal power and a belief that they are part of something much bigger than themselves. A vision gives a business a cause to fight for and believe in.

For the high-growth entrepreneur, vision is a core purpose that goes beyond just making money. If the core idea is powerful it will trump merely focusing on profit – get the idea right and profits will flow naturally. A clear vision is an all-encompassing statement of what a business, or person, stands for.

As Jim Collins sets out in *Built to Last – Successful Habits of Visionary Companies*, visionary companies achieve extraordinary long-term performance. An investment of $1 in a visionary company stock fund held from 1926 to 1990 would have outperformed the main market by over 15 times. Visionary companies display a remarkable resilience and an ability to bounce back from adversity.

In *Built to Last*, the reader is asked: "Why settle for creating something mediocre that does little more than make money when you can create something outstanding that makes a lasting contribution as well?" I think this is a question every high-growth entrepreneur should ask themselves.

Most businesses don't start with a great idea and a powerful vision. My original business idea for instant coffee machines in traditional newsagents taught me what would not work and there was no way I could have built any sort of sustainable business from that offer. It was a chance encounter with a helpful customer that lead to a realisation – I had been trying to sell the commonplace, the everyday and the mundane, and that instead I needed to create an experience, offer theatre and become a destination for great coffee. This sowed the seed for my first clumsy attempt at expressing my vision:

"The country's first true self-service gourmet coffee concession."

Later on I simplified this and realised the power of owning a single word or phrase that captured all of what we were about:

"Self-serve gourmet coffee."

This said all we ever needed to about why we existed. Anything that did not contribute directly to this vision was an unnecessary distraction and could be sacrificed. Focus on delivering your vision brilliantly and tirelessly. Success does not come from the sum of lots of initiatives, but from the power of a core idea and a great vision superbly executed.

Big ideas that can become big business often require significant external investment. The founder may risk being heavily diluted in successive rounds of investment, or worse still be forced out of his or her company altogether if growth in sales and earnings fails to keep pace with the original vision. The business may never live up to the original vision and this may not become apparent for several years. Even if it does, the founder's slice of the value pie may not feel a just reward for their years of exclusive dedication to the cause.

A compelling vision attracts money and great people. I discovered that inviting business angel investors to be part of a journey, to participate in creating the future, was far more effective in securing their investment than any dry presentation of a business plan. It wasn't the detail in the business plan that attracted great people to Coffee Nation – it was our compelling vision.

These are statements from my 12-minute pitch in Cambridge in November 1998:

> "Smart, urban, gourmet coffee stations – a way of life in 21st-century Britain."
>
> "Coffee bars were the revolution – they awakened people to great coffee. Now we're the evolution – the branded coffee station – creating mass access – putting gourmet coffee in tiny spaces – taking it to the people!"
>
> "Imagine a world where you know that wherever you see the Coffee Nation brand (all 1200 locations) you'll be confident of getting the same terrific coffee. You've used Coffee Nation stations at forecourts, cinemas, at college, at your local gym and in supermarkets. Many are open 24 hours a day. Well, that day is coming."

It was not just that a powerful vision of the future helped me raise some seed capital that day. It had a deep and profound impact on me. I no longer believed I could fail. For an ambitious entrepreneur and their backers this is an enormously powerful construct. A decade later that vision had been delivered.

Some may think it arrogant to appear so audacious and self-confident. Don't let this stop you. Many believed that I would fail within six months of raising that seed capital in 1998. I discovered years later that some in the audience actually placed bets on it. *Built to Last* states that Big Hairy Audacious Goals (BHAGs) "look more audacious to outsiders than insiders." I believe this is true.

Your vision should be entirely self-explanatory. It will be the single, unifying ambition or goal that binds the organisation together. Everyone in the organisation must *get it*. Think and dream big – to own and lead the self-serve gourmet coffee category was my BHAG. We all lived it every day. Everything everyone did directly or indirectly helped us own self-serve gourmet coffee, period. When you have a clear vision it's that simple. We had no shortage of great people wanting to join us.

Energy and motivation across the company were high and sickness and absenteeism were almost non-existent. No competitor ever poached a Coffee Nation employee.

Clarity of vision helps you stay the course because you have a course. In building Coffee Nation there were many difficult times, but we all knew what we were fighting to achieve. No matter what the journey threw at us our core idea and ideology never changed. We guarded it religiously. A great vision should transcend its founder or its creator and our vision was far bigger than me.

Coffee Nation won the Technology and Innovation Award at the 2010 Growing Business Awards and was ranked as one of the UK's top 100 private equity-backed companies with the fastest growing profits in the 2010 Deloitte/*Sunday Times* Buyout Fast Track league table. Both these award wins came two years after I left the board and it was great for me to see the company continuing to do so well. A great vision will pay back many times over when the chips are down. Your vision will help you maintain course when you face adversity.

Live the vision – visualise what it will be like when you are actually there. I regularly used creative visualisation (a powerful technique that uses imagination to create a clear image of something we wish to manifest) to picture hundreds of Coffee Nation stations across the UK and prestigious contracts from major organisations. I would imagine what success would look like and experience it as if it were already happening. Continue to focus on the idea until it becomes reality. Creative visualisation is a technique well understood and used by top sports people, business leaders and high achievers in all walks of life.

Think big every day. When Scott joined me in 1999 we occupied a tiny office together and had meagre resources on every level. When we had visitors I handed out my card that stated "Martyn Dawes, CEO, Coffee Nation Ltd". I introduced Scott as the company's chief operating officer (COO) or operations director. Some years later one of those visitors confessed to having privately ridiculed me for my formal introductions. "I thought you were two blokes in a starter office not big enough to swing a cat in!" He later realised I could see what he couldn't – we were leading a company that was going to become a feature of the urban landscape of Britain. I had a vision.

Be careful to distinguish between high risk and a bold vision. These two do not necessarily go together, but they may. Your vision may offer enormous growth potential but leading the consumer in a new direction may take considerable time and make the risk of failure high. You will need to display enormous resilience and absolute commitment to see this through. Remember to keep in mind what you are starting this venture for.

Finally, there is a practical benefit to a clear and exciting vision. Every day you will face countless issues involving employees, suppliers and customers. In a mediocre business with low growth prospects which has not been able to attract the best talent, this day-to-day stuff can be a real distraction or even worse. In the high-growth visionary business, everyone knows what they're aiming for so these issues barely touch the sides. Everyone accepts them for what they are, they don't dent passion or purpose.

5. RESEARCH AND TESTING

There is a balance in a new venture between research, investigation and actually beginning. A hasty start may squander your precious reserves. When I started Coffee Nation I probably spent too little time identifying the killer questions I needed to answer before starting the business. With a little more thought invested at that stage maybe I could have saved some of the time, money and pain that it took before I could see that the original product and location combination was not working. It may have also saved me from some early dilution of my equity. By the time the answer appeared I was virtually broke. My first external investor was an absolute necessity rather than an option.

By the same token, a new business cannot be *researched* into life. At some point you must take the plunge, commit and begin. There is a power and boldness in beginning. Up until that point there is always a chance you will back down, talk yourself out of it or be influenced by other doubters. Once you have committed there is no turning back. It's how you take that leap of faith that will be so critical to your survival prospects.

My early assumptions – that people drink instant coffee at home in the UK so I should offer the same product to takeaway and people will not pay for a real cappuccino in a newsagent/convenience store so I should offer a mock version at a lower price – caused me to lack an awareness of the bigger picture. These assumptions were dangerous and almost cost me my business.

My mistake was that whilst I had identified a plausible idea and there was some supporting qualitative background evidence (people bought takeaway coffee in US c-stores and speciality coffee shops were opening in London) everything beyond these observations were assumptions. Whatever was not fact remained an assumption which had to be proved or disproved.

The US consumer was completely different to the UK counterpart. Most bought a coffee to drink in their car. Most people visit a newsagent in the UK to buy a newspaper and a pint of milk and walk home. If the US consumer drank their takeaway coffee in their car where would I find UK consumers in cars? Answer: at petrol forecourts! One single trial machine at one UK forecourt could have saved so much wasted effort.

I rejected the idea of primary face-to-face research with consumers on the basis that they couldn't tell me what would become the norm in the future, but there were useful questions I could have asked them – such as what type of coffee (instant or real) they may buy from a convenience store if it was available. Single machine trials would have limited my expenditure; instead I had a network of underperforming machines around the UK before I had solid evidence that demand for takeaway coffee existed. I could have been more organised and disciplined in my approach.

Given the high failure rate of start-ups – around 60% of venture capital investments in early-stage businesses return less than they invested – I am curious how many businesses fail because they begin with flawed assumptions that severely constrain their ability to prove demand with the limited time and financial resources available. Undoubtedly, many fold just as they're about to make it.

There are some common themes in early-stage ventures and entrepreneurs that serve against them:

- Entrepreneurs are optimistic by nature and get caught up in their own hubris.

- An objective assessment of major risks is omitted in early-stage planning or is undertaken poorly.

- Entrepreneurs try to prove they are right, often ignoring early warning signs.

- Many entrepreneurs misinterpret critical feedback from peers, friends, family or potential investors as reasons why they will fail instead of taking these thoughts as pointers towards helping them narrow in on the idea that will bring success, as the feedback is intended to. Instead the entrepreneur defends their idea as it stands.

If you can reduce risks before making any significant financial commitments to your new venture then the chances of survival go up (see 'Beating the Odds when you Launch a New Venture', *Harvard Business Review*, May 2010). It is important to identify risks and eliminate them in the correct order:

1. Top priority must go to deal-killer risks that will undermine the venture if left unchecked. These will be the unchallenged or unexamined assumptions that may be almost indistinguishable from the seed of genius which is the idea itself – e.g. self-serve takeaway coffee from convenience stores, but what type of coffee and what type of store?

2. Next are path-dependent risks where the entrepreneur, confident they are heading in the right direction, commits significant financial, human or time resources to a particular target customer group, channel to market, technology, manufacturing process or business model. This path may later prove to be the wrong choice and either kill the company because the right one appears only when money has run out, or force an expensive rethink. If external investors are onboard by this stage, life could be very uncomfortable for the founder.

3. Risks that can be resolved without spending a lot of time or money. Look for risks that are quick and cheap to resolve. How much risk can be resolved for each pound spent?

Removing risk increases value and takes a business in the right direction. Use early funds sparingly to reduce or remove the deal killer and path-dependent risks. Identify the most important uncertainties and don't focus on one risk to the exclusion of all others. Don't become invested emotionally in confirming your assumptions – use low-cost experiments, mock-ups and rapid fire testing to prove *or* disprove a concept before it is too late.

PROVING THE MODEL

A danger for an early-stage entrepreneur is to mistake early proof of concept from trials and experiments with a proven business model. Evidence of early demand for a product may have been demonstrated, but this will be just one element of what has to be proved. Dangerous path-dependent risks may be lurking at the next stage.

The entrepreneur has to hold back their desire to expand their business and focus on the questions that have to be answered in order to identify a business model that can become a scalable venture. It serves us well to recognise that 93% of businesses ultimately succeed by doing something different to what they started out doing.

My journey with Coffee Nation demonstrated this, as summarised in the table below.

Plan	Date	Business plan	Funds raised	Result	Outcome/ next step
A. Instant coffee – newsagents	End 1996 to summer 1997	Yes/Not required	£50,000 founder seed capital and £30,000 bank overdraft	Fail	Trials in neighbourhood convenience store chains
B. Instant coffee – convenience store chains	Summer 1997 to end 1998	Yes/Not required	None	Weak sales/nil growth	Real coffee trial in neighbourhood convenience stores
C. Real coffee trials – neighbourhood c-stores	Summer 1998	No/Not required	£30,000 from business angel	Partial success	Product demand proven. Prepared new business plan to seek funding for initial expansion in same channel with other channels identified
D. Expand in neighbourhood c-stores and investigate other channels	November 98	Yes/ Required	£100k business angel and £90k SFL	Change of strategy post-fund raising	Need to prove business model
E. Trial of new equipment in high foot traffic forecourts and motorway services	Mid-1999	No/Not required	Rights issue, around £150k from business angels	Success	Business model proven. Expansion capital fund raise.
F. Expansion Capital Fund raise	January 2000 to June 2000	Yes/ Required	£4m total available	Funding and roll-out contracts secured	Business starts to grow

Plan A didn't work – the product and location were both wrong. The cost incurred was limited at this stage.

Plan B also did not work – instant coffee was not an enticing out-of-home product and Nescafé is a grocery at-home brand. Consequently sales were weak and would not grow. Cash burn was significant due to the capital cost of adding more machines and operating costs of a larger estate. Also, I attempted to grow the business at this stage, recruiting an operations manager.

It is difficult to separate out exact costs for each phase but I burnt through my original £50k seed funding and was through the other side of a £30k overdraft. At this point there was a real danger my bank would pull the plug. The £30k business angel investment I landed at Plan C saved my skin for a while.

Plan C was a successful test. Note there was no business plan. It was a rapid pivot from gaining the insight to having the new product in front of consumers. It did much to prove the essentials of the offer; we were now selling fresh coffee with fresh milk, the drink price had increased by 50% and sales volumes had doubled, but it was as yet unclear whether this would be attractive to retailers.

I was able to raise a further £100k later that year (for 20% equity, excluding the £90k loan). The intention had been to attempt to grow the business from this stage (Plan D), but a change of strategy was required. The platform wasn't robust and proof of the business model was needed before business growth could be planned.

Plan E took me into high footfall roadside locations and out of suburban neighbourhoods. The combination of an increase in drink price and high sales volumes proved the economic model. I replaced the previous equipment with a heavy duty and easy-to-maintain espresso machine.

No business plan was required – this was a test market using the funds that had been raised. Plan E proved the revenue, gross margin and investment models as well as refining the operational model and product offer. Two distribution channels were also proven, which generated two launch customers.

The business model was now proven:

- *Revenue model proven* – a trial of 150 trading days with sales volumes across three locations of 2300 cups per week. These results secured a commitment to as many sites as economically viable from our launch customers.
- *Gross margin model proven* – our net revenue was £250 per week per machine. This was referred to as gross margin.
- *Investment model proven* – gross margin x 52 approximately repaid the capital cost of each installation inside a year.

Now was the time to write a business plan, raise expansion capital and start to grow the business (Plan F).

The assumptions tested and proven in the 2000 business plan mostly held good for the next seven years. If this plan was followed through the business would be high growth. Everything in the plan had been underpinned.

Had I been disciplined in my approach, this could have been only the second and not the fourth business plan I had written. Plans A, B and C could all have been funded comfortably from my own start up capital, avoiding the early dilution and saving at least a full year of time, operating costs and enormous drama. I wasted so much time and money writing, rewriting and amending countless business plans and attempting to secure investment from numerous individuals, business angels and suppliers.

I almost accepted investment from a small coffee equipment company that was attracted to my business model and saw the potential for big sales of their equipment. This was for a stop-gap amount of money so I would have been back out seeking further funds soon after. Whilst well intended, they themselves were not a high-growth company. A tie up with them would most likely have severely limited Coffee Nation's appeal to institutional investors a year or so later. Early deals of this nature – whilst offering a temporary lifeline – will soon be outgrown by the ambitious entrepreneur, but will prove difficult if not impossible to unravel.

I came perilously close to oblivion because I did not understand that the start-up imperative is to spend a little, test and retest, and prove the business model before contemplating attempts to grow. Beware the many perils of writing business plans and attempting to raise money at the wrong time.

All early-stage efforts need to be directed towards minimum cash burn to prove the concept and reach the point at which the business model can be proven. Proving the model pulls everything together – it gives you the real evidence that you now have a business. Up until that point the journey has all been about getting to this start line.

6. PEOPLE

HIRE THE BEST

Someone once said to me that if you refuse to accept anything less than the absolute best this may be what you get. Nowhere is this more important in business than in the people that you invite to share in your vision and make it happen. The idea can be great and the business model proven, but if you recruit badly then don't expect to succeed.

If you can't get the best, don't recruit, because if you start off with mediocrity then your business will at best be mediocre. If this is where you start then you'll never attract great people beyond that. By attracting the best people you unleash a multiplier effect that will allow an acceleration of progress and upward momentum. Of course it's harder to find and attract the best people, while it's easy to find and recruit mediocrity.

You need leaders at all levels in the organisation who build teams which are then capable of accelerating the growth of the business. At some point the founder has to stop being the nexus of all decisions taken. The immediate questions will be who, when and how?

How does the barely-trading business recruit the best people? There are two answers:

1. *The entrepreneur.* You are it. You are who others are considering joining and switching careers for. It is your character that will attract great people or not. Do you display a calm self-assurance, a complete grasp of your market, business model and opportunity? Are you convincing without needing to try? Do you display an almost arrogant and unshakeable self-belief?

Do they see a passionate entrepreneur but also someone with a fine sense of balance, intuition and good judgement? Can they see that you have a grasp of the challenges as well as the opportunities ahead? Are you pragmatic, commercial and focused? Will you listen and put up your hands to admit when you are wrong?

What kind of leader will you be? Some entrepreneurs are not prepared to listen to anyone else – all success is down to them. They will only recruit people who tell them what they want to hear and will not be willing to recruit people who may be better than they would be at their job. At the other extreme is a weak leader that buckles under pressure, is indecisive or tries to please all. Talented people will assess you as a potential leader. They will be assessing you as much as you are assessing them.

2. *Vision*. There was no cup of coffee that those who joined Coffee Nation in the early days could pick up and hold. The vision for Coffee Nation had to come alive through me. Can you tell the story and bring it to life? Is it believable – a challenge, but achievable? Does your crusade get their juices going? Do they want to be part of where this could go? It's not the absolute scale of your vision that's important, it's how you say it.

Being a credible entrepreneur with a great vision is how you recruit the best people at this early stage. It's all that is needed and it's also all you have. There is no certainty but a great entrepreneur with a captivating vision can entice great people to leave big salaries, corporate bonus pots and long lists of benefits.

QUALITIES TO LOOK FOR

For the first-time entrepreneur, formal recruitment processes such as headhunters are likely to be financially beyond reach. As the vision becomes clear and your confidence grows you will find that you attract people. You may then find yourself in the networks or in the right place at the right time where the people you need to connect with happen to be. That was my experience.

From then on, at first interviews we always talked about Coffee Nation *first*. This was a different conversation for each person and each role, but it was as much started by the candidate as it was by us. Sometimes it would be five minutes, other times it was 45 minutes, before we got to talking about them. Regardless of the role, people were attracted to joining a high-growth business.

Many of the characteristics of the entrepreneur should be similarly displayed by those they are seeking for their leadership team or board, such as a determination to succeed and a willingness to listen and admit when they are wrong. Do they grasp the strategic and tactical, the big picture and the detail? Can they cut through the noise to focus on what is really important? Will they do what the business absolutely needs rather than what they enjoy or feel at their best with? Are they self-assured and decisive?

Will they be there when progress feels remote and the bad news just keeps coming, or will they jump ship for an easier life? Are they self-aware and open to personal development, or heavily entrenched in their own view of themselves? Will they make great leaders and build strong teams? Will they learn from their mistakes? Will they go beyond their comfort zone and thrive in the constant uncertainty of the entrepreneurial environment? Will they reassure or rankle with other board members and investors? Are they at ease with minimal infrastructure and support around them? Do they display an esprit de corps, honesty, integrity and an empathy with their colleagues?

Like you, are they demanding of themselves and others? This may make for a more challenging day-to-day, but it is what you need. Great people are what great entrepreneurs need to help them turn their promising, early-stage ventures into high-growth category killers. They will need to be highly entrepreneurial to flourish in this environment as well as bringing additional skills to complement the founder.

You will have shaped the values of your business and you must recruit first and foremost people who share in those values and perceive them to be as important as you do.

How do you know when you have the right person? It's just as important they feel the same way about you. Spend time together to get to know each other, your backgrounds, previous highs and lows, successes, failures and aspirations. What are they prepared to sacrifice in order to join you? This may be fundamental to knowing they are serious. Do you trust each other? Do you share similar values? Will you enjoy working together?

This stuff is often far from easy to judge but what you feel is not usually far off the mark. What does your gut tell you? You will be spending much of your life with this person over perhaps the next decade. There will be intoxicating highs and crushing lows. You will probably get to see the best and worst of each other.

Relevance of their background is important but far less than their hunger to join you and sense of chemistry in being able to work well together. I never looked at educational background unless this was directly relevant to the position. I don't think I am unique amongst entrepreneurs in caring little for someone's academic achievements. If someone is the right person for you and your company *and* they happen to have a great educational track record then that may be a bonus, but nothing more.

In this order of priority, look for people who:

1. Share in your values for your business, how you do business and how you treat others.

2. Get the vision.

3. You get on with and with whom you share mutual respect.

4. Are prepared to make the leap and join an early-stage business, invest their own money and commit 100%.

5. Have prior industry or sector relevance.

6. Have been successful in a similar role before.

7. Have some connections that could be helpful.

Things often go wrong with senior hires when points 5 and 6 are allowed to outweigh 1, 2 and 3. Technical competence is worth nothing if the new hire does not believe in the vision and does not live the values. Equally, just because all is good at point 4 be prepared to walk away if you cannot honestly answer yes to point 3. It is so easy to store up trouble for down the line.

I appointed a chairman early on in Coffee Nation's cycle of development. Derek brought valuable experience of nurturing early-stage growth businesses into full bloom. Without doubt we would have been flying blind without his valuable and objective perspectives on many occasions. First-time entrepreneurs get out of their depth on a routine basis, which is inevitable as they have no previous experience of what is involved. His background was more tech and telecoms but he understood the concept, was inspired by the vision and we got on well. It doesn't have to be with a chairman, but build a trusted inner circle of a small number of valuable advisers that bring a wealth of experience and expertise.

Our finance director was the final member of the executive team and was hands on in every sense, which is exactly what the young business needs. She had come from a much bigger company (industrial, so again a fairly unrelated background) but was thrilled to be part of an early-stage business with all to play for. She joined immediately following the private equity investment in Coffee Nation. She managed the office move, IT, payroll set up, supplier contracts, and the preparation of management accounts, forecasts and budgets. We never lacked accurate financial information upon which to base timely, informed decisions.

EMPLOYMENT TERMS

Reward must be linked to the long-term performance of the business, which boils down to growth in the value of the company, which in turn comes from sustained and growing profitability. The leadership team within the company (usually the board) must be completely aligned in what they are seeking to achieve. You will attract and retain the best if you are prepared to offer some equity participation in the company. It makes sense that at least some of this is paid for as it is a clear indication that people are committed and believe in the potential of the business. If the core team have a meaningful share then the road ahead is worth the toil for them.

Be wary of over promising on career progression potential – even in high-growth businesses there are relatively few top slots and not everyone wants a high flying career. Ambitious start-ups are always high energy but growth invariably takes a long time and the path can be hard. For the ambitious in your team, not all will want to stick around if upward progression is blocked.

7. BUSINESS PLANS AND FUNDRAISING

PLAN EARLY TO ENCOURAGE INVESTMENT LATER

Business start-up is often a messy affair. My first business plan for Coffee Nation came off the printer around September 1996 but it was almost four years later in June 2000 when I finally raised the funds required to grow a business.

It is not possible to see around corners, but much early-stage disappointment can be avoided if you start from the right place. I was lucky (it certainly didn't feel like it at the time) that my idea did stack up – I just had to tweak the product and where it was sold from. That still took three bloody years!

Many entrepreneurs start down path A only to find that route will not work, no matter what they do. Reality forces a total rethink. Someone offers a lifeline: "I won't buy this but what I really need is X." Path B emerges and the entrepreneur pivots in a new direction. This is very common.

The starting path for most entrepreneurs looks something like this:

1. They have an idea – they believe it to be an identified need or gap in the market.

2. They undertake some rudimentary research which in their eyes confirms the opportunity. They may receive expressions of interest, letters of intent from suppliers or customers, or even land an early customer.

3. By now they are committed to their idea and start work on a business plan which will take hours to prepare and include detailed financial forecasts for at least three, if not five, years.

4. They start the business, committing themselves to spending money following their business plan and/or looking for investors.

5. Early customer expressions of interest evaporate, fail to grow as predicted, or an initial customer win cannot be replicated. Meanwhile cash runs short.

6. Warm noises from investors fail to turn into cash so more is sought while trying to keep the business afloat. It's the perfect

storm. Through desperation the entrepreneur sees the investor as someone who will buy them time to figure out what to do next.

7.   Realisation dawns that more of the same won't bring the breakthrough – the answer lies somewhere back up the chain between the first and second stages.

You get the picture, hopefully. I managed to make all these mistakes – it's so easy to do.

Let's look at what should be done instead.

The starting point has to be an idea. Until this is known to work, everything is an assumption or a guess. There is nothing wrong with this, except don't mistake the two. Most do and they gamble finite resources on a dash to get trading before they know anything.

Great entrepreneurs are not gamblers; they take managed risks. They realise there is little to be gained by throwing everything at the wall and hoping something sticks. Better is to start with an open mind. Be excited by the prospect of your idea succeeding, but don't be attached. Maintain a flexible approach – your aim is to build a successful business, not to rigidly stick to a view of what this looks like.

Then be curious and set about investigating the assumptions you are making. Get out and talk to anyone that can help you to form a view. Solicit as much feedback as possible – all feedback is good feedback. You are risking nothing at this stage and have everything to learn. All of this is costing nothing but time, some shoe leather and maybe a coffee or two here and there. Keep asking yourself the question "What do I know?" and "Is this a fact or an assumption?"

If you stick to this process then you have nothing to fear. The path forward will emerge. You may be wary of feeling humiliated in some way if the answers to your questions show there are major flaws to the assumptions you have made, but this is smart. You have conserved your cash. If this idea isn't the one, there'll be another.

From there experiment and test, on a low-cost scale, every key assumption so that they can become facts. Start with the most important ones – those that relate to sales. Understand the customer, who they are and what will work for them. When will they buy and what will they pay?

Some assumptions will inevitably remain until tested, for example with Coffee Nation we did not know what the customer would pay until we put the product in front of them. Business plans and fundraising usually fail because the entrepreneur has missed out these entire steps along the way. They have gone from idea to writing a business plan and attempting to raise money with little or no evidence that their idea will work.

With investors it is always no until it is yes. If it's not yes then it means you have more work to do. It's that simple. You have to systematically remove the reasons to say no. Investors invest in sound ideas and great entrepreneurs who've done their homework. They will not hesitate at that stage for fear of losing out to others. It's up to you to get in good shape before writing a business plan and attempting to raise money.

Most start-up entrepreneurs think they need money when in fact they need evidence. Money is the last thing they need. The availability of money at the wrong time forces the inexperienced entrepreneur to commit to what may be a deeply flawed plan. They think:

idea + start the business + write business plan + seek investment = success

In fact the formula they should be following is:

idea (1) + research and test (2) = evidence and proof (3) = confidence (4) = business plan and investment (5)

At 1 there is an idea and a set of assumptions which are then tested at 2. Circle back as many times as required between 1 and 2, refining and/or pivoting the idea in a new direction.

Arriving at 3 there is real evidence that people will pay for the product because it removes pain or makes their lives better in some way. Trials also need to test key assumptions and give you an understanding of what is required to scale the business. They have helped confirm there is a large market that can be reached. This period should also have equipped you with a good appreciation of the key challenges to growth. Confidence at 4 continues naturally to success at 5.

If you follow this approach, preparation of a business plan becomes easier; you are able to speak as the objective and informed entrepreneur and what goes in the business plan is what you know to be true. Your plan is based around evidence, not hope.

Remember, smart investors want to invest in businesses that are ready to hit the road and start growing. When you meet potential investors they will be impressed by what you have achieved and all the more if you have done this from limited resources which have been carefully managed. This will reassure them as to how you will run the company and manage their money.

In one of my early business plans I included some *quantitative* results from trial machines but the sales numbers were far from convincing. In fact, a quick glance was enough to show I did not understand how to unlock this opportunity, if indeed there was one. The body of the plan was largely *qualitative*, describing routes to market and supply chain (machine, ingredient, maintenance details and so on), but was of little interest to the reader given the disappointing numbers and trends at the front of the document.

A letter of rejection for a Small Firms Loan at the time had spelt it out in black and white. It noted the unproven nature of the product and a requirement for further credence to the assumptions in my business plan.

A later plan formed the backdrop to my presentation in November 1998. The plan was mailed to those who had pledged to invest that day or who had expressed a strong interest. All those that had heard my pitch and pledged did indeed invest. The plan on its own attracted no new investors.

My pitch was effective and well constructed, providing key evidence-based statements for each of the following and in this order:

1. Growth of US and now UK coffee bar market along with independent growth projections.

2. Coffee Nation is part of this emerging/growing trend – same product but new route to market.

3. Clear unique selling points (for consumer and retailer).

4. Positive *qualitative* feedback from customers actually buying our product.

5. *Quantitative* results from four-machine test market that had run for a combined 40 months.

It finished with an exciting vision of the future. This was all delivered with confidence, energy and pace.

The audience's mental checklist went something like this (some of them told me afterwards):

Positive attribute	This gives confidence to
Trials have been running for some time with people returning to buy the product regularly.	This idea satisfies a real need and people are willing to pay for it.
A confident entrepreneur with some prior business success, sells himself well and has taken personal risks to fund the business.	Management.
It's a simple concept and a product that is understandable.	Others will also understand it (customers, future investors, employees, etc.).
Operating in a growth market.	Part of a growing and visible trend – growth less likely to dry up.
No shortage of possible locations.	Large addressable market.

The business plan included all of this, although the key evidence that should have been right at the front was buried on page 9 – this was that the latest sales from the four locations averaged 900 cups per month per machine and were growing.

I realised that central to successful business plans and investment pitches was to *think like an investor.*

My final plan was the one that launched the business as you see it across the UK today. Get help from those that have helped others develop business plans through to successful fundraisings – they will know what good looks like from an investor's point of view.

We had appointed Deloitte as our advisers and the plan had been prepared with their assistance. It was mailed from them to a shortlist of agreed potential equity and debt providers. The plan did its job by securing initial meetings with some of these. There were some notable success factors with our document:

- It came via a respected advisory firm.

- It was evidence based – Deloitte had worked with us tirelessly on almost every sentence, carefully avoiding needless assumptions or sensational claims.

- Coffee Nation had a complete management team, notably including an experienced chairman.

It was a 26-page document with pictures at the front of people using Coffee Nation at our Texaco Clerkenwell trial location. There was a separate document that comprised key appendices. Preparing the business plan was a valuable exercise in itself as it stimulated valuable discussion and brought together our knowledge of our category. The plan remained useful after fundraising and formed the basis of the first year's budget.

MEETING WITH POTENTIAL INVESTORS

First meetings with potential investors usually comprise a presentation of the business (a condensed version of the key sections of the business plan). You should present the latest results from market trials and recent developments that have happened since the business plan was printed.

These meetings should be enjoyable. Be confident. If you cannot give a definitive answer to a question, explain why without being defensive. Obviously it is impossible to know everything and investors won't expect you to. It's the maturity of your response that is important. Equally, if they raise a concern or are negative about an aspect of your business, it is important not to let this undermine your confidence for the remainder of the meeting. A concern voiced on their part does not mean they have ruled out investing.

Ask them some questions. It's as important they are right for you as it is that you are right for them. Many entrepreneurs mistakenly see all investors as the same. They are not – there are investors you would want alongside you and there are those you wouldn't. Terms offered may vary considerably. Find out about their fund, the decision-making process, what other companies they have invested in and how they work with management teams. Ask to speak with management teams of companies they have exited from, including those they would describe as unsuccessful. Find out what went wrong. These won't be showcased on their website.

Good early chemistry between the parties must not be mis-read as an offer will be forthcoming, while neither should a cooler initial reception be taken as evidence that one won't. Approach each investor in the same way. It is impossible and pointless attempting to second guess investor sentiment. With Coffee Nation, Deloitte followed up afterwards to gain an initial view.

The investors across the table will focus on four things:

1. *The first is you and your team.* Regardless of the business in question would they back you? Do you display passion, confidence and commitment? Do you show a deep understanding of the opportunity and the challenges? Are you level headed? How will you cope in a crisis, with setbacks and with disappointment? Will you always tell the truth? If they cannot be confident in the team as presented, that will either be the end of the process or investment will be conditional upon changes/additions to the team.

2. *What have you proven?* Is your plan underpinned by market trials with customers paying for your product? Are your customers as enthusiastic about your product as you are? Is there evidence of repeat and/or planned purchase?

3. *Is the market big enough to support your forecast growth?* Are powerful substitutes likely to undermine your proposition? Is it worth the effort? Do you have contracted growth already secured from major customers?

4. What might come along and derail this opportunity that is *beyond management control?*

Some investors rule out entire sectors as they are perceived to be too high risk, long term, speculative or potentially non-reputation enhancing (e.g. gambling). Do you have a long enough run up in order to get in and dominate your category before rivals start appearing or are there numerous players all at a similar stage vying for the same early lead with little to distinguish between rival offers?

We didn't attempt to set any price expectations for the deal. As an early-stage business this was probably appropriate. All funds raised were for investment in the business. Your cash flow forecast will show the funds required to launch and grow the business.

WORKING WITH INVESTORS

Once an offer was received and we agreed to enter an exclusivity period a process of due diligence started. Use the process of preparing the business plan to pull together all relevant documentation and identify any areas of the business that do need attention and address them before you get to this stage.

You can expect a long list of questions at due diligence, covering everything from customer contracts through to key man insurance, IT security and contracts of employment. We had numerous shirt-sleeve working sessions with our investor where we discussed the business model in more depth and agreed changes to how we would structure customer agreements in the future. These helped develop a sense of what it would be like to work together and allowed the relationship to grow even before completion.

Our investor stuck by the terms they had originally set out and we completed without drama. You should expect the same. If you have a serious concern during the due diligence process/exclusivity period then say so – you will be working with any investor for a long time into the future and you must have an atmosphere of openness and honesty from the start if it is to work. They see many opportunities, do few deals and accept not all will succeed. You may do this once or twice in your life. Don't forget that.

8. EARLY EXPANSION

FACING CHALLENGES

I had not bargained for just how challenging early expansion was to be. Once Coffee Nation had private equity investment it felt like the end of the beginning and I was keen to impress our new investors by over-achieving against our plan. I looked to multiply our business development efforts, confident that this would enable us to exceed the plan. The reality was quite different.

Thank God we had been able to test so much of the model down to the finest details ahead of fundraising. I cannot over emphasise how important this proved to be for us – it reduced the number of unexpected challenges that we had to face. We already knew our model really well – albeit in a micro-scale operation.

Some of the challenges of early expansion were identified in our business plan. Appendix 1 and our SWOT analysis pointed to hidden dangers of large markets that couldn't be addressed and "pilot sites that do not lead to roll-out contracts." We did indeed face these challenges.

The engine of a high-growth business is sales. For us that meant all machines achieving budgeted sales volumes and a strong pipeline of growth underpinning the next quarter, or ideally half year. I don't think the notion of over-achieving against plan was consciously dropped and it is a goal I would encourage and support any new management team to shoot for. The faster you can get ahead the better. What was patently apparent was that there could be no let up in the pace and intensity.

Maintaining the confidence of your board and shareholders is critical. If you absolutely know you and all of your team are doing all that can be done to grow the business then you will sleep at night. It is then about maintaining that energy and focus and eventually results will follow. Nothing can be taken for granted and there is little room for distraction.

Product extensions and brand tie-ups were rejected as non-core. We were often approached by other businesses looking to partner with us in some way on the basis that we could help each other. They were usually convenience food and snacking companies. Most talked a good story but were usually early stage businesses looking for growth opportunities or clutching at straws. Learn to spot these incoming *opportunities* that can take your eye off the ball.

Delivering the plan you sold to your investors and creating value for all shareholders is what you are there for. This requires ongoing discipline. Retain the ability to flex but don't get jumpy if growth is slow in coming initially. Don't grasp at quick wins or abandon the great business model that was the reason they backed you in the first place. Remember what got you here.

You need to be able to look yourself in the mirror and be sure someone else couldn't do a better job than you. You must ask the same question of all other members of the team. You must remain the best team that you can be in order to overcome the challenges ahead.

After five years Coffee Nation had delivered 50% of the growth we said it would in the first three years. Our investors maintained their confidence in us as a team because they could see we were genuinely doing everything we could – and then some – to build the business. Our vision was becoming real, but just more slowly than we had anticipated.

Early expansion is not the first year or two. Based on my experience I'd say it's the first five years. Expect some failures along the way and to travel down many blind alleys. Let the path you have successfully travelled reassure you for the journey ahead.

PITCH TO CUSTOMERS AT THE SENIOR LEVEL

Use your networks and personal contacts and those of your investors, advisers, chairman, etc., to gain an introduction at the highest levels in the organisations you seek to enter. We always pitched for senior level, if not directly at the CEO. If you try hard enough you'll get through to them.

Building and maintaining bridges at these levels, particularly in large companies, is a complex task. Part of the task is knowing who to field at what level and at what stage in the relationship. We underestimated how much time and energy we would need to invest in those key relationships in the first couple of years.

Afterwards, I was informed that had we been able to develop a genuine relationship with the CEO of one of our customer organisations we may have been able to do more and quicker with that company. I had met with him and he was highly supportive of us as part of their offer. We thought that was enough of an endorsement and those beneath him were therefore carrying our torch with the same enthusiasm. We should not have made that assumption and instead maintained our focus on a direct relationship between Coffee Nation and the CEO of the customer.

COMPETING WITH THE BIG FISH

Proving the test market and raising expansion capital is one thing. Once you start to grow and put your head above the wall you will put yourself in the full line of fire of incumbents or alternates. It was no good us opening the customer's eyes to the profit opportunity of self-serve gourmet coffee only to lose out to others. Being first to market only serves a purpose in so far as it gives us the opportunity to get in and secure the space ahead of anyone else and for as long as possible. It is also the time when you must become the company or brand name that the consumer associates with the category you created. You must own a space in their mind.

There was a book I read at the time which I would highly recommend to any high-growth, disruptive business or one creating a new market category. *Eating the Big Fish: How Challenger Brands can Compete against Brand Leaders* was a bible for us. It was the logical extension to how *The 22 Immutable Laws Of Marketing* had proved so defining and enlightening for me back in 1998.

Eating the Big Fish (ETBF) is all about engaging consumers with ideas, not trying to communicate with them. It is about an emotional identification and an intensity of desire with a brand. Challenger brands provoke a response rather than allowing consumer indifference to be maintained. We had created the category; we now had to behave as a true challenger to ensure we didn't have the opportunity to lead and own the category snatched from under us by a safe-bet, big corporate.

When Kenco lined up a brand new automatic bean-to-cup machine that was perfectly calibrated and filled with freshly roasted coffee beans they could produce a cappuccino just as good as Coffee Nation. If they could convince our marketplace that their coffee was as good as ours – and with the household name of Kenco over the door – their sales could be expected to exceed ours. The later market entrant could win the day.

We knew we couldn't argue with this rationale so we shifted the debate. We stopped talking about the coffee and talked about how our operating system enabled us to deliver terrific coffee 24/7, self-serve and in challenging environments. For big retailers like Tesco, managing espresso machines was not their business. We didn't win the battle by saying our coffee was better than Kenco's – we won it by reassuring Tesco (and other organisations) that only we had the infrastructure specifically designed to make this category manageable across their estate.

When we built our own technical and maintenance function we invited all our customers to come and experience it. Once we had a rudimentary system of real-time communication with each machine we sent statistical reports to Tesco showing how many hours of downtime each site experienced.

Our assertion was that you could rely only on Coffee Nation to deliver self-serve gourmet coffee reliably and to a consistently high standard. This was all we did. Kenco couldn't say that. We had to be about over performance and self-belief. Kenco and other competitors never went away but they never gained a foothold in our territory either.

ETBF puts forward the argument that brands and products that flourish are those that have a very clear sense of who they are – they stand out from the competition with their intensity and their confidence in themselves. They don't talk about the consumer, they invite the consumer to navigate by them. *ETBF* was published in 1999 but I think the principles are even stronger today. People go crazy to define themselves by the brands they buy. *ETBF* defines these challengers as *lighthouse brands* and sets out four defining characteristics of such a brand:

1. *Self-referential identity* – they tell us where they stand.
2. *Emotion* – they aim to create an emotional rather than rational relationship with consumers.
3. *Intensity* – they offer intense projections of who they are in everything they do.
4. *Salience* – they are highly intrusive – one cannot avoid noticing their activity.

As the years went by, more and more of our consumers told us they would go out of their way to find Coffee Nation. Everything mattered to us so deeply it was personal. That is why we won in the long run. It stands to reason really. Challengers have to over-perform because they do not have the luxury of being the brand leader. We were not a multi-billion revenue business we were less than 20 people operating from a studio in north London. Our biggest competitor had to be *ourselves.*

We applied the *ETBF* mentality to our culture and recruitment policies. We welcomed obsessive behaviour and even a degree of eccentricity. I am not sure we employed anyone who was unemployable, but none of our team would have looked at ease in a big, established company.

IMPATIENCE FOR PROFIT

Do not forget what got you to where you are today. Early expansion should be about an impatience for profit and patience for market share. Once you have proven the profitability of your model and category this reverses. Invest those profits in accelerating your progress to maximising market share and market dominance.

Stay true to your vision and focus on world-class implementation of all aspects of your business model. Vision without execution is just a dream. Execution without a vision is just a task.

Don't build your company to sell it. Build a great company, period. That way you'll get the great exit.

9. STAYING THE COURSE

DIFFERENCE BETWEEN PLAN AND REALITY

Our original business plan turned out to be nothing like the reality of how growth materialised. There were long periods of no new contract wins and no roll-outs, with the majority of activity focused on trials in new sectors. Cash was always tight and was the key consideration. We had a very slim marketing budget and drew criticism on occasion from customers who wanted to see more effort to grow sales once we had rolled out across their estate.

Our expertise in marketing was slow in building and we made a late decision to recruit dedicated resource to this area of the business in 2004, and even then that was only on an interim basis. A young and hungry marketer keen to prove themselves could have been part of the team much earlier and for less cost.

If you have a bold vision and are creating a new category look hard at your timelines. After five years we only had three major contracts. Four more arrived in the next two years but this was after Primary's original deadline for exit. There were many times along the way when we anticipated that a huge breakthrough in growth rate was just around the corner, but that never really came in one big convenient chunk.

In the eight years from Primary's investment to my departure from the board there was one constant and that was uncertainty. The job was never done. We had to remain our toughest judge – not any competitor or a customer's expectation. You must not lose focus on your vision. Don't mistake slower growth for a flawed model or vision. If you start indiscriminately grasping at opportunities you will rapidly diffuse your focus. Your team will start to question the loss of spirit and your loss of nerve. Momentum will rapidly fall away.

The gap between current reality and future vision propels ambitious management teams and growth companies forward. There has to be just enough tension to maintain a continued state of positive momentum. Robert Rosen's *Just Enough Anxiety: The Hidden Driver of Business Success* sets out that too much anxiety leads to cynicism, carelessness or chaos, whilst too little could lead to idealism or complacency. Either of these states would be ineffective.

Our aim was to remain optimistic and realistic, constructive and impatient, humble and confident. We and I did not always succeed at this. It was rare we were complacent but I can say for certain we never doubted the business we were in or if we would continue to grow. Doubt can destroy a great business from the inside. There was a constant state of constructive challenge across the board, executive team and down to the next level of leadership in the business.

We became so focused on the exit a year or two ahead and the need for growth in profits that we lost some opportunities that supported this aim. We lost sight of the bigger picture and were too rigid. We opted for profit maximisation – looking to get the best margin we could – when instead land grab was still where we were in reality. We could have relaxed the gross margin a little, won more customers and been happy with a slightly longer payback if it gave us new, profitable long-term contracts and locked down other major customers. We did learn this eventually.

Despite the pressure from ourselves for growth I can say with confidence we never felt under any pressure from our largest shareholder to compromise the principles or business model in order to achieve a dash for growth. You should look for similarly supportive investors in your business.

An inherent danger with the challenger business is that in an attempt to be flexible they fail to notice the fatal compromise they have just made. Too rigid the other way and you may appear monopolistic and arrogant in your category. Everyone loves to topple a monopoly. We had to make difficult judgement calls – you can have all or none of what we stand for but you can't have some.

LEADERS IN THE BUSINESS

You must adapt your style to becoming more of a strategist and leader as your business grows. Be careful that *strategic plans* are not merely documents that state what you hope will happen. I had learnt years before with my management consulting firm that all businesses, categories and markets grow at a natural rate. More push – beyond a certain level – will not make it happen faster.

Invest in developing others' talents at all levels. The more capable leaders there are across the organisation, the more built-in capacity there is for the business to withstand shocks. Supporting and helping others grow into great leaders of tomorrow takes patience and resources.

Built to Last talks of preserving the core and stimulating progress, momentum and consistency, particularly with reference to management development and succession planning. Manage and nurture carefully what you have built – strengthen the core. It is very rare for visionary companies to appoint successor CEOs from outside the business. It is not quality of leadership that most separates visionary companies from others, it is the continuity of quality leadership that matters – continuity that preserves the core.

Having a clear vision and a narrow focus will mean you know what has to be delivered in order to achieve success. This will aid management effectiveness. Without doubt, all members of the executive board should spend some time with other leaders, businesses and looking beyond their immediate environment.

When faced with difficult decisions take them. Don't be afraid to consult with others but stand in your own space and take the decision. Putting them off until immediate priorities are dealt with or calmer waters are reached is usually asking for trouble. I was faced with one such situation – my gut, heart and head all knew what I had to do and I knew the benefits it would bring across the business but I elected to wait. This was the wrong decision. Few are fatal but this did bite me years down the line.

Constant innovation and experimentation is crucial if you are to maintain your category killer status. We were bold to start trials in the Netherlands in 2003 and Germany in 2005. Neither of them developed into a European foothold in the way we hoped, but both were right to pursue – they aligned with our vision and shareholder aims. We had to be looking for ways to lengthen our time advantage, not over *any* competitor in particular, but over *all of them*. Don't wait to be threatened to respond.

AIM TWO FEET BELOW THE BRICK

Our vision was not so much a reality but a state of mind, an attitude and set of behaviours. Of course, we did create the self-serve gourmet coffee category and we expanded across forecourts, motorways, convenience stores, universities, hospitals and airports. But we did not literally achieve the goal of Coffee Nation stations being wherever people are, 24/7. This didn't matter. What mattered was that by setting sail to achieve the bold vision we came somewhere close. That was enough.

In *Eating the Big Fish*, Adam Morgan proposes that a challenger must aim "two feet below the brick" in order to put their hand through it. Aiming at the surface is not the over-commitment that is required to overcome the inertia and resistance that will be met along the way. Over-commitment translates challenger intention and strategy into behaviour and results. Coffee Nation stations never really became as easy to install and operate as an ATM, but that vision and comparison was a powerful image of the future that had just enough realism to propel us towards the ideal.

Strong financial management is required to support rapid growth. As momentum builds, future funding options should be more abundant as your growth record will attract offers. Use your growth to extract more favourable terms from banks, customers and suppliers. Banks love to be associated with high-growth success stories. Negotiate long-term deals that will still work for you when you encounter difficult times down the line.

Focus on budgets, cost control and cash flow. We did not consistently hit budgets until we were into our sixth year – rate of growth was beyond management control and so we could not accurately budget and achieve it. Once we became a mid-market growth company with multiple long-term contracts we were able to budget minimum growth levels accurately. Gross contribution, gross margin and overhead budgets were tightly controlled virtually from the start.

Don't expect an easy ride or people to be nice. I think I was shocked that one of our major customers, having recently signed a new multi-year contract, soon stuck a competitor offer under my nose and ran a trial with them alongside a Coffee Nation installation. Don't be naive – expect this as par for the course. He was in breach of contract but only displayed the same audacity that I had in getting there in the first place.

Watch for creeping bureaucracy. Internal control systems are there for one reason and that is to support rapid growth. We professionalised processes throughout the company that had previously been experimental, but this was always to underpin our credentials as category leader and enable rapid growth.

Be relentless and don't be stopped. There is a nineteenth century phrase – "the inevitability of gradualness." Make this true for your company's ascent.

INDEX

CPSIA information can be obtained at www.ICGtesting.com
Printed in the USA
BVOW05s1019120214

344732BV00012B/110/P

9 780857 192509